Across a Prayerful Planet

"This book is for you who need assurance that God is much bigger than your church, your holy book, your nation, and your certainties. Daniel Pawley is a wanderer and has understood that God is both local and global. It has to be so because the human heart—no matter where it's dwelling—longs to pour itself into the divine."

—JANET TROY,
Spiritual Director, Ruah Spirituality Center

"Daniel Pawley's *Across a Prayerful Planet* is an ideal combination of travel memoir and book of prayers. His compelling stories include a vivid sense of place, from Switzerland to New Zealand and many spots in between. It is also a remarkable collection of prayers, which are beautiful as literature and meaningful as appeals to the Almighty from people across the globe and across the centuries. The book inspires and enlightens. I wanted to linger over it and make some of these prayers my own."

—JOSEPH BENTZ,
author of *Nothing is Wasted* and *A Son Comes Home*

"This nonfiction narrative speaks to the unique experience of modern nomads, inserted by chance or by choice into unfamiliar places. Daniel captures the way mundane tasks and chance encounters in exotic and ordinary locations inspire profound moments of spiritual insight. Even though we only skim the surface of these places, we take something spiritually dynamic with us. The essence of that experience is captured here."

—MARILYN HOWE,
United States Air Force, retired

"*Across a Prayerful Planet* brings us to an intimate place and a desire for sincerity and sharing. Engaging, insightful, and arousing . . . this journey is one you will not want to miss."

—PATRICIA JOHNSON,
Career Librarian, Pasadena City College, Citrus College

"I have always been impressed by Daniel Pawley's sincere, seeking nature, and it comes across beautifully here. Dan's insight meshes with my own understanding of—and love for—travel. I often go to Berlin and stand at the remains of the shattered Wall to remember God has placed the craving for liberty in us all. Travel does that, as Dan reminds us, but he also shows how travel can inspire a prayerful and grateful heart for people of all faiths. As he says, 'Prayer might be the one form of human communication that cannot be critiqued by anything other than sincere intent.' This is a book that makes you stop, think, and bend a knee as you enjoy the stories this gifted writer has to tell."

—W. JAMES WILLIS,
author of *The Human Journalist* and *The 1960s on Film*

"With an open mind, inspired by family heritage and in the accommodating spirit of philosopher Iris Murdoch, Daniel Pawley has undertaken a wonderful journey exploring humanity in general, whose center is the sacred itself. This book is about the presence of the transcendent in human consciousness and the mysterious primordial touch that moves, and has always moved, life and society. It leads us to think of prayer not only as an instrument of the individual's relationship with this transcendent reality but also as a response to the nourishing, transforming presence of what stands beyond the human realm. It is both a memoir and an indisputable contribution to understanding the noble heritage of prayer."

—MARIA DE LURDES PONCE,
Integrated Researcher, Centre for the Study of Religious History,
Catholic University of Portugal

"The beauty and the peril of these travels leaves you with a mindful view of the world and compels you to contemplate your place in it. Dr. Pawley is the Anthony Bourdain of prayerful travel around the planet. Throughout this work, you will feel as if you have traveled to each place, learning the origins of carefully chosen public prayers as well as the lives of many compelling characters. Each chapter rests at the end with a prayer that soothes the soul and teaches us about the global language of meditation that we would all be wise to continue speaking."

—REGINA CHOW TRAMMEL,
coauthor of *A Counselor's Guide to Christian Mindfulness*

Across a Prayerful Planet

How the World Converses with God

Daniel Pawley

Foreword by Kate Klise

RESOURCE *Publications* · Eugene, Oregon

ACROSS A PRAYERFUL PLANET
How the World Converses with God

Copyright © 2022 Daniel Pawly. All rights reserved. Except for brief quotations in critical publications or reviews, no part of this book may be reproduced in any manner without prior written permission from the publisher. Write: Permissions, Wipf and Stock Publishers, 199 W. 8th Ave., Suite 3, Eugene, OR 97401.

Resource Publications
An Imprint of Wipf and Stock Publishers
199 W. 8th Ave., Suite 3
Eugene, OR 97401

www.wipfandstock.com

PAPERBACK ISBN: 978-1-6667-1610-8
HARDCOVER ISBN: 978-1-6667-1611-5
EBOOK ISBN: 978-1-6667-1612-2

JANUARY 13, 2022

Every effort has been made to contact copyright holders. However, the publishers will be glad to rectify in future editions any inadvertent omissions brought to their attention.

This book is dedicated to my parents, Walter and Ruth Pawley, who established the template for travel and prayer in my life; to my wife, Marisa Pires Marques, who shared many journeys herein and continues to be the source of my deepest affection, admiration, and marital joy; and to my daughter, Meg Amanda Pawley, who also shared journeys, located obscure books, and provided fresh conversational insights into travel and the world.

"The feeling remains that God is on the journey, too."
TERESA OF ÁVILA

Contents

Foreword | xv

Acknowledgments | xvii

Prologue | 1

Chapter 1   A Form of Love | 7

    "*O my God, teach my heart where and how to seek you.*"
        An Anselmian Prayer
        St. Anne's College, Oxford University,
        United Kingdom

Chapter 2   This Place Will Do | 10

    "*I have found you in all these places.*"
        A Reformed Minister's Prayer
        World Council of Churches, Geneva, Switzerland

Chapter 3   Angie in the Pouring Rain | 13

    "*Lord of peace, we come to you in our need.*"
        A Filipino Bishopric Prayer
        Subic Bay, Philippines

Chapter 4   Urgency from Anxiety | 17

    "*We cannot count on anything else but your promises.*"
        A Hong Kong Prayer
        Hong Kong

Chapter 5   The Best Parts | 22

    "*You alone watch over the interests of spiritual beings.*"
        A Pope's Ancient Prayer
        St. Peter's Square, Rome

Chapter 6   Muscles Flexed, Prayer Ready | 25

"*To fight for you and not to mind the wounds.*"
    A Jesuit Prayer
    Tomar, Portugal

Chapter 7   Immense Spirituality | 28

"*Living and self-loving Christ, you are our root.*"
    A Prayer from the LGBTQ+ Community
    Walt Whitman house, Camden, New Jersey, United States

Chapter 8   Karakia for Two | 35

"*Instill in us your sacred spirit.*"
    Two Maori Prayers
    Rotorua, New Zealand

Chapter 9   Listening to the Interior | 38

"*May you be blessed in the chase;*
    To where the life-giving road of your sun father comes out.*"
    Two Zuni Prayers
    Zuni Pueblo, New Mexico, United States

Chapter 10   Catharsis on Berber Soil | 41

"*Glory to you the Almighty, master of countless crowds.*"
    A Berber Prayer
    Marrakech, Morocco

Chapter 11   Prayerful Overlay | 45

"*We stand in awe and gratitude . . . Christian, Jew, Muslim, as well as those with other faiths.*"
    A Monotheistic Prayer
    Hagia Sophia Grand Mosque, Istanbul, Turkey

Chapter 12   Binaries, Balances, and Bali | 49

"*Grant us an understanding heart, equal vision, balanced mind . . . .*"
    A Hindu Prayer
    Denpasar, Bali

Chapter 13   ONE THUMB UP? | 54

   "*Lord, let us empty of all doctrines.*"
      A Taoist Prayer
      Sun Moon Lake, Taiwan

Chapter 14   VULNERABLE SOJOURNERS | 58

   "*A life has ended with the passing of a friend . . . .*"
      A Shinto Prayer
      Himeji Castle, Japan

Chapter 15   AROUND ALMODOVAR | 65

   "*Circle me, Lord.*"
      A Celtic Prayer
      Almodovar, Portugal

Chapter 16   TEMPLE OF FOREST AND STREAM | 69

   "*Through the open finger spaces of the hand that all things fashioned.*"
      A Finnish Prayer
      Helsinki, Finland

Chapter 17   NATURE'S MISSIONARY | 72

   "*Praise be to you, my Lord, though our sister, Mother Earth.*"
      A Franciscan Prayer
      Monteverde, Costa Rica

Chapter 18   A COMPLEX CHORD | 77

   "*This enticing, well-prepared food of a hundred flavors,
   I offer with faith to the Victors and their sons.*"
      Two Buddhist Prayers
      Blue Elephant Cooking School
      Bangkok, Thailand

Chapter 19   THE NECESSARY GODDESS | 82

   "*Aphrodite, I pray to you, goddess, grant me your gift of love.*"
      A Mediterranean Prayer
      Paphos, Cyprus

Chapter 20   TRUTH TRAVEL | 87

"Send us rose-bodied good government and her sisters on gleaming thrones."
    An Ancient Greek Prayer
    Delphi, Greece

Chapter 21   ROADS | 91

"My Lord God, I have no idea where I am going."
    A Mystic's Prayer
    Santiago de Compostela, Spain

Chapter 22   NUMINOUS | 97

"Oh Lord, we pray that you help us remember the legend that was John Lennon."
    Prayer for a Departed Beatle
    John Lennon Wall, Prague, Czech Republic

Chapter 23   TRIBAL COPING | 102

"We thank you for drama and sadness."
    An Otaku Prayer
    Akihabara, Tokyo, Japan

Chapter 24   MERMAIDISH | 106

"Teach me to love myself unconditionally and to practice self-care without reservation."
    A Folkloric Prayer
    Copenhagen, Denmark

Chapter 25   JAMIE FRASER UNCEASING | 110

"Be this soul on Thine arm, O Christ."
    An *Outlander* Prayer
    Linlithgow, Scotland

Chapter 26   OPPOSING FORCES | 114

"Prayers follow behind to heal the harm."
    A Homeric Prayer
    Ruins of Ancient Troy, Turkey

Chapter 27   GERTRUDE AND SYLVIA | 118

    "*Breathe peace into the horror chambers of the heart . . . .*"
        A War Prayer
        Shakespeare & Company, Paris, France

Chapter 28   GRACED | 123

    "*I will remain in the world no longer . . . and I am coming to you.*"
        Christ's Prayer
        Graceland, Memphis, United States

Chapter 29   FATHER-SON ROADMAP | 131

    "*Build me a son whose wishes will not take the place of deeds.*"
        A Father's Prayer
        Hans L'Orange Field, Honolulu, United States

Chapter 30   CANDLE POWER | 136

    "*Gods . . . you are near to my life, to my problems, my family . . . my future.*"
        An Icelandic Prayer
        Keflavik, Iceland

Chapter 31   CHANNELING LUCILLA | 141

    "*St. Jude, patron saint of lost causes, pray for me . . . my husband, my marriage.*"
        A Prayer of Regret
        The Colosseum, Rome, Italy

Chapter 32   SISTERS OF ECCE HOMO | 145

    "*I dare not ask for improved memory, but for growing humility . . . .*"
        A Nun's Prayer
        Ecce Homo Convent, Jerusalem, Israel

Chapter 33   GOOD HOPE | 150

    "*What misery it would be to suppose our friends . . . were annihilated at death.*"
        A Voyager's Prayer
        Macau, China

Chapter 34　　Foreseeing a Divided Nation | 155

"O powerful goodness . . . accept my kind offices to Thy other children as the only return in my power for Thy continued favors to me."
A Deist's Prayer
Philadelphia, United States

Chapter 35　　My Racial Timeline | 159

"Forgive me for hiding behind a façade of racial progressiveness . . . ."
A Personal Confession
Detroit, United States

Chapter 36　　Unprotected | 167

"I'm falling apart. My past no longer protects me."
A Prayer of Desperation
Chernobyl, Ukraine

Chapter 37　　Metered Migrants | 172

"But God of all, I am shaken in that faith, when I read of what is happening on the threshold of my country."
A Border-Watcher's Prayer
Tijuana, Mexico

Chapter 38　　Gaps Temporarily Unbridged | 177

". . . help us, God, to feel the suffering of every Bedouin parent."
A Rabbinical Prayer
Petra, Jordan

Chapter 39　　The Inevitable Response | 182

"Guide us to the straight path. The path of those on whom you have bestowed your grace, not of those who earned [your] wrath . . . ."
A Qur'anic Prayer
Jericho, Palestinian Territories

Chapter 40   AMID THE RESIDUE OF OCCUPATION | 187

"It is the Good Friday of sorrow and bitterness, of abandonment and powerlessness, of cruelty and meaninglessness that this . . . people experienced as a result of unrestrained ambition that hardens and blinds the heart."
   A Prayer from Pope Francis
   Museum of Occupations, Tallin, Estonia

Chapter 41   PICKING UP THE LIE TRAIL | 192

"May the Lord cut off insincere lips, every glib tongue that utters deceit."
   A Psalmist's Apocalyptic Prayer
   Museum of Communism, Prague, Czech Republic

Chapter 42   ETTY HILLESUM | 196

"At night, too, when I lie in bed and rest in you, O God,
   tears of gratitude run down my face."
   A Holocaust Victim's Prayer
   Auschwitz-Berkenau Extermination Camp, Poland

Chapter 43   FINGER PAINTING AND IMMORTALITY | 203

". . . all ye other Gods that dwell in this place, grant that I may become fair within."
   A Socratic Prayer
   The School of Athens, Apostolic Palace, Vatican City

Chapter 44   THE TOUCH OF A RAGGED HAT | 208

"Almighty God, of whose only gift cometh wisdom and understanding: We beseech thee with thy gracious favor to behold our universities, colleges, and schools, that the confines of knowledge may be ever enlarged . . . ."
   A Scottish Prayer

Edinburgh, Scotland, United Kingdom

Chapter 45   Denouement | 212

"O Educator, be gracious to your children . . . that we may be made tranquil . . . ."
A Second-Century Prayer
Hadrian's Wall, United Kingdom

Chapter 46   A Message of Tides | 216

"Prepare me to carry your presence to the busy world beyond, the world that rushes in on me, till the waters come again and fold me back to you."
A Monastic Prayer
Holy Island of Lindisfarne, United Kingdom

Chapter 47   "Where Were You When I?" | 220

"I shall soon lie down in the dust; you will search for me, but I shall be no more."
Job's Prayer
Tel Lachish, Israel

Chapter 48   The Omega Voice | 225

"Above all, trust in the slow work of God."
An Evolutionary Prayer
Drumheller, Canada

Chapter 49   Honor Thy | 230

"Then they cry unto the Lord in their trouble,
and he bringeth them out of their distresses."
A Renewable Blessing
Estero Bay, United States

Epilogue | 235

From the Author | 237

Selected Bibliography | 239

Index | 243

Foreword

I STILL CAN'T EXPLAIN WHY I tried to steal a bathrobe from a hotel in Casablanca, Morocco.

I was on spring break with two college friends, one of whom had been pickpocketed in Tangier within an hour of our arrival. This was back when everyone carried traveler's cheques, so it was just a matter of going to the American Express office and filing a claim for replacement cheques. Unfortunately, the office in Tangier couldn't process my friend's claim. Her loss exceeded their limit.

We ended up traveling to Rabat and later Casablanca, filing fraudulent police reports, claiming the crime happened there. When we finally found an American Express office that could issue replacement cheques, we celebrated with a nice meal. And the next morning, on my twenty-first birthday, I tried to smuggle a hotel bathrobe in my backpack.

I got caught, of course. When I handed over the stolen robe, I felt ashamed. But I felt something else, too. A quiet voice inside me whispered: *This is not who I am. Filing those bogus police reports isn't me, either. This lying and stealing business is exhausting. No more.*

Thou shalt not steal. Of course, I'd heard that plenty of times. But commandments aren't as convincing as intense experiences that lead us to respond in some kind of personal prayer.

Daniel Pawley's stories and prayers in this book are far better than my sorry tale. But like my Casablanca prayer, Daniel's all involve travel. Reading his wise collection makes me wonder why travel is the ultimate spiritual exercise. Is it because travel has a way of testing us? Is there something about being away from home that forces us to decide what kind of people we want to be? Maybe it's simpler than that. Maybe when we travel, we're fully present in a way that allows us to experience the prayerful world that is our rightful home.

Daniel and I discussed such things early on in our friendship, after we met in Lisbon. He had made the move to Portugal to be with his lovely wife, Rissy, several years before I bought a tiny apartment in Lisbon. We met at St. Andrews Church, a popular gathering place for expats and travelers, and where Daniel tells good stories from the lectern, beside the Celtic cross, on occasion.

We formed a casual writing group with two other friends from church. When Daniel asked what we thought of his plan to combine memorable prayers and travel stories in one volume, we all agreed it was a terrific idea. "You'll be the Paul Theroux of prayer," we told him.

I loved reading the tapestry Daniel weaves from a child road trip with his parents to his first trip abroad with a Christian rock band. From Walt Whitman's house in New Jersey to Zuni Pueblo in New Mexico. From Europe to Asia to North Africa to Central America. To the history conference in Athens where he met Rissy. Back to his former home in the United States. Then back to his new home in Portugal. Daniel chronicles it all with humor, heart, wonder, and the humility that asks, "What can I learn here?"

The night before a big trip, I often feel pangs of anticipatory regret. *Is this trip going to be worth it? Should I have spent the money on a home repair instead? Is it too late to cancel?* I sometimes feel the same way when I open a new book. *Is this author going to be worth my time? Maybe I should watch that new Netflix police drama instead. Is there any rice pudding left in the fridge?*

If you're feeling similarly antsy, relax. You're in good hands here. Daniel's words and wisdom are well worth your time. He's like the stranger you meet on the overnight train who's brought a baguette with *queijo* and is willing to share. And what could be better than breaking bread with a fellow pilgrim who has stories to tell? That, to my mind, is its own kind of prayer.

Kate Klise
Author of *Regarding the Fountain* and 43 *Old Cemetery Road*

Acknowledgments

ACKNOWLEDGMENTS FOR READING AND COMMENTING masterfully on the manuscript, or otherwise playing roles in the stories and backstories it tells, include the following: Adjeksenila Amado, Dr. Jon Balserak, Steven Ballantyne, Rabbi Rachel Barenblat, Dr. Gabriel Barkay, the late Dr. Abraham Bass, Dr. Joseph Bentz, Jim Bergquist, Emily Brook, Tiffany Yu Chia Chen, Junichi Chiba, Caroline Connolly, The Reverend Alex Douglas, Terry Eisele, Esther Fan, Joana Gomes Ferreira, the late Duncan Forrester, Anne Troth Foster, Anny Fong, Katie Gallof, Joyce Goodrich, the late Morley Halsmith, Dr. John Hamilton, Colonel Marilyn Howe, the late Paul Hoye, the Reverend Norman Hutcheson, Joao Silva Jesus, Josephine Jael Jimenez, Diana Johnson, Patty Johnson, the late Dr. Orville Jones, the girl at the hotel in Keflavik, Kate Klise, Alice Manso, John Maust, Jane Mckenzie, Dr. Ismael Lopez Medel, Aubrey Meyers, Neil Meyers, Dr. Jolyon Mitchell, Mohammad from Riad de la Belle Epoque, the guy on the train in Morocco, Dr. Teresa Mota, Nordeen of Nouralimo Tours, Dr. Ken and Irene Oakes, Iain and Nina O'Donnell, David Okum, Dr. Suzanne Owen, the Reverend Michael and Helen Parker, Nataly Pavlik, Paul and Ruth Pretiz, the late James Reapsome, Dr. Jaime Leote Do Rego, the late Angie Ricafrente, Maria Sanchez, Keith Schnell, Helena Marques da Silva, the late Dr. Amy Sparks, Dr. William Storrar, Janet Troy, Dr. David Ussishkin, Dr. James Willis.

Prologue

Dear Mom,

    Greetings from this side. I am confident that you're enjoying eternal peace and rest on your side, and greetings to Dad who is no doubt there with you. I miss hearing your voices.

    I am addressing this to you because I believe you would like the fact that I have thought enough about prayer over the years to write a book about it. Actually, it's a memoir about prayer and travel, in balanced proportions, but I would like to think that the travel story serves the prayer component rather than the other way around, and that prayer is the heart of the book.

    That being the case, however, I will first mention the travel part.

    Travel was the great gift bestowed upon me by Dad. Still fresh in my mind is the first road trip we made as a family, Michigan to Florida and back, when I was five years old. Like ageless Super-8 footage burned into memory, I can still see Dad unrolling the big map of the United States one evening on the kitchen table in Detroit, showing me the road we would be taking. First through Indiana, he said, then Kentucky, Tennessee, Georgia (which he pronounced "Jouja" to give it a southern flavor), and all the way to Fort Myers in Florida. So, what do you think about that? he asked me, noting that my eyes were wide open like he had never seen before. The ensuing conversation went something like this:

    Me: "But what comes after Florida?"
    Him: "Cuba, I guess."
    Me: "What comes after Cuba?"
    Him: "Oh, Central America," I suppose.
    Me: "What comes after Central America?"
    Him: "South America."
    Me: "What comes after South America?"
    Him: "Antarctica," with a visible sigh.

Me: "What comes after Antarctica?"
Him: "Go to bed."

And that is exactly how I remember the grand moment: the opening of eyes, and more importantly mind, to a spatial trajectory of roads, places, countries, people, the world. I've never lost it, and now I am writing about it. By the way, a big thanks also to Dad for the *Golden Book Encyclopedia* for children, which I kept next to my bed until I became a disengaged teen, and which further set an indelible template of curiosity and movement that has stayed with me all these years.

As thankful as I am for these things, Mom, what you gave me was something even greater: that sense of prayerfulness you embodied throughout your life. The image I have of you kneeling on a small carpet next to your bed has always stayed with me like a Warner Sallman painting, so full of authentic devotion it tends to relegate other memory images to the distant background. I used to feel your prayers, too, especially when I grew older and left home at nineteen. Or maybe that feeling was more of a psychological response to knowing that you were praying for me. Whatever the case, it was as real as hunger or thirst, and sometimes I still feel that you must be praying for me from beyond the divide.

So anyway, I have written this memoir on prayer and how it has tended to make all my journeys sacred.

More to the point, it's a collection of prayers from many different sources which have served to illuminate journeys and destinations with a kind of holiness they wouldn't otherwise possess. Prayers from many traditions, religions, orientations, and systems of belief and spirituality are included here. Already I can hear you saying, with your Wheaton College "For Christ and His Kingdom" educational background, that only Christian prayers uttered to our father in heaven truly matter. Perhaps I, too, carry that lingering sense of theological certainty with me, as many of the prayers are Christian. Yet I cannot or will not rule out any prayer that features a sense of authentic seeking, regardless of its origin. To me, sincere human seeking and a desire to converse with God are the only criteria from which to appreciate a prayer.

Come to think of it, Mom, prayer might be the one form of human communication that cannot be critiqued by anything other than sincere intent. Poetry can be analyzed through devices like metaphor and rhyme. Critics of prose fiction can evaluate plot, style, tone, and irony as they enrich or compromise a novel. Popular music can be critiqued by the interplay of lyrics and instrumentation. Public speaking, by quality of delivery and choice of spoken words. Even art and architecture can be critiqued by relationships between materials and execution, function and design. But no one, hopefully, is going to use any criteria other than felt sincerity to appreciate a prayer because any act of authentic seeking doesn't rely on tools or devices; they're attitudes nurtured by some kind of faith, and that is a different kind of perspective resting on the inward honesty of the person who prays.

I can also hear you question my inclusion of written prayers. Prayer should be a spontaneous conversation between an individual and God, I can hear you say, and not a polished, third-person form of writing like a poem. There is something to be said for that idea when you're talking about prayers said in private, I concede. But these are public prayers meant to edify and enlighten those who hear, or in this case, read them, and that changes the concept a bit. The question that occurs to me is this: Is a spontaneous prayer presented in public as meaningful as a thoughtfully composed prayer offered in the same conditions? Maybe, though I'll err on the side of putting a little thought into the construction of a prayer before it is sent out to the world and to the heavens. So, in that case, I guess prayer can be seen as a kind of thoughtfully constructed public poetry offered in conversation with God, and the kinds of prayers included in this book arise from that matrix.

In any case, here it is, Mom, and here they are: prayers and places integrated into a narrative whole that you on your side, and hopefully others on this side, find at least a little worth contemplating.

PART ONE

Chapter 1

A FORM OF LOVE

"O my God, teach my heart where and how to seek you."
- AN ANSELMIAN PRAYER -
ST. ANNE'S COLLEGE, OXFORD UNIVERSITY, UNITED KINGDOM

I BEGIN IN 1975, MY first time out of North America.

Traveling with four Canadian musicians playing what would eventually be called "contemporary Christian music," we had flown to London to begin a six-week tour of the United Kingdom.

Replete with my first taste of west-east jet lag, I remember drifting in and out of bad sleep as the band and our equipment traveled in a blue van from Gatwick Airport to our first lodging in Oxford. A very gray, very English, very April drizzle was falling, hampering any attempts to stay fully awake in the van, and after a seemingly endless drive we arrived in Oxford weary and looking for rest. After a curry lunch, we were escorted to a university dormitory where we were shown our rooms, and we didn't wake up until the next day.

The following afternoon, we played to a small auditorium of mostly women at St. Anne's College, Oxford. In a state of full jet lag, about the only thing I truly recall about the concert was a young woman in the audience who shouted, "Your accents are very becoming." These decades later I can look back with nostalgia on that tour that began in Oxford, though I eventually came to dislike contemporary Christian music for its lack of originality and its overly certain perspectives on life and faith. But that's not where this memory is taking me.

I didn't know it at the time, but St. Anne's College was where one of my favorite philosophers, the persuasively elegant Iris Murdoch, resided and taught. Many years later I began to use Murdoch in university courses I was teaching.

She was refined silver in the classroom, and I still have my original lecture notes from that time. They included the following statements: *We must develop a mystical openness to the world. We must die to self. We must reject worldly attachments in favor of spiritual seeking. We must appreciate points of truth in other religions. We must accept the reality of the spiritual void existing at the heart of Western consciousness. We must engage in communication that counteracts verbal inadequacy and imprecision. And above all, we must know that our rhetorical habits are killing us.*

She wrote much about loose language and the need to escape it through the precise rhetorical content of authentic art, literature, and yes, prayer. In fact, I always wished she had said more about prayer being a superior form of communication that works against human obstacles to true spirituality we experience in our earthly state: selfishness, greed, closed mindedness, addiction, hate, and the me-first mentality which tries to strangle living faith. She did leave the door open in her book, *The Sovereignty of Good*, when she wrote, "But, whatever one thinks of its theological context, it does seem that prayer can actually induce a better quality of consciousness and provide an energy for good action which would not otherwise be available."

"We are anxiety-ridden animals," she said, in the same breath, possessed of fabrications, fantasies, reveries, trivialities, and other prisons that we could never pray ourselves out of if we saw prayer only as, what she called, "petition."

"Prayer is properly not petition," she added, "but simply an attention to God which is a form of love. With it goes the idea of grace, of a supernatural assistance to human endeavor which overcomes empirical limitations of personality."

Sadly, I was never able to find any actual prayers Murdoch herself might have published or delivered orally in public. However, an article from Fall 2005 published in *The Saint Anselm Journal* argued that Anselm, the Archbishop of Canterbury from 1093 to 1109, could serve as "a neglected source for recovering what Murdoch thinks" on a range of subjects from ethics to human goodness to moral transformation to the nature and power of prayer, and the seeking of God. Thus, the following prayer, the first offered in this book, comes from Saint Anselm of

Canterbury, and could reasonably be the prayer Murdoch herself might have given.

> O my God, teach my heart where and how to seek you,
> Where and how to find you.
> You are my God and you are my all and I have never seen you.
> You have made me and remade me,
> You have bestowed on me all the good things I possess,
> Still, I do not know you.
> I have not yet done that for which I was made.
> Teach me to seek you.
> I cannot seek you unless you teach me or find you unless you show
>   yourself to me.
> Let me seek you in my desire,
> Let me desire you in my seeking.
> Let me find you by loving you.
> Let me love you when I find you.

Chapter 2

This Place Will Do

"I have found you in all these places."
- A REFORMED MINISTER'S PRAYER -
WORLD COUNCIL OF CHURCHES, GENEVA, SWITZERLAND

Fast forward twenty-one years, to 1996.

It was February in Geneva, Switzerland, and no one wants to be in Geneva, Switzerland in February.

Even under the best conditions, Geneva has little to offer as a travel destination. In the middle of winter, especially, its gray skies and perfectly efficient infrastructure of buses that run on time, banks that run on commerce, and international agencies that run on the goodwill of diplomatic intent, tend to leave one wondering if the city has a soul and, if it does, where that soul might be found?

"People really like to get out of here at this time of year," said Maria, my former Filipino student who was working at the United Nations High Commissioner for Refugees (UNHCR). "They work here, but they live across the border in France where it's not so crazy expensive and there is at least a little culture." At a communal dinner with a number of her Asian friends employed by the local relief agencies, the conversations were about getting out. One woman wanted to go home permanently to Malaysia. Another wanted to see if there was anything he could do professionally in Paris. Another wanted to go anywhere else. Maria herself was planning a diplomatic mission to Somalia. "Not exactly Shangri La," she said, but it would get her out of town for the foreseeable future.

Geneva's winter dullness, however, wasn't really a problem for me as I spent most of the week hunkered down in the basement archives of The World Council of Churches (WCC). I had been given a sabbatical by my small college in Minnesota to study the history of women contributors to *The International Review of Mission*, a journal I had long admired for its theological openness. It had grown out of a 1910 ecumenical missionary conference in Edinburgh, Scotland and within two years had begun a noble calling of publishing articles outside the mainstream of doctrinaire Christianity. I was immediately hooked, as it were, by a 1914 article, "God's Ways in the Bantu Soul," an acknowledgment of godly qualities within sub-Saharan individuals and communities in Africa, albeit in the context of the anthropology of its time which accommodated the idea that some races were further ahead than others in their evolution. There was hope, though, lots of hope, and love, and kindness, and intelligence in the journal, and much of the best work was done by forward thinking women, which I also needed to see at that time in my life.

So, there I was in the nondescript Geneva archives, collecting old photographs and documents that told the story. At the end of the week, I showed my collection to Christopher, the Indian clergyman who was editor at the time, and he said, "My goodness, I had no idea." Old, authentic, archival material has a quality that goes beyond the backstory it tells, a physicality like old fingerprints that make you realize real people had their hands on great and ordinary things you should have known about and now see before you. Research performed digitally has lost that quality. Something old you encounter through a screen isn't the same as holding the real thing that has been filed away in some kind of place. Real people exist physically and spiritually but not digitally, in my opinion, and past or present you find them in real places.

The last thing I remember before leaving the WCC that day was a farewell from Francesca, Christopher's secretary, who recommended I visit a fondue restaurant before leaving town. "Make sure you drink plenty of white wine," she said. "Your stomach will thank you."

Outside the WCC complex was cold, gray Geneva.

And it was perfect.

"I have found you in all these places," says the Reverend Martin Hoegger, who contributed a prayer to the WCC. He writes,

> The pearl of great price, the hidden treasure,
> where should I seek them Lord?
> Do I seek them in the depths of my soul,

where you pour out your Spirit?
Or in Scripture where your word speaks to me?

Do I seek them in prayer or hymns,
where you unite us with the angels?
In the bread and the wine,
where you gather us to yourself?
In your church,
where you teach your wisdom?

I have found you in all these places.
But the pearl and the treasure,
for which I would give all I have,
is love, reciprocal and without end:
it enlightens my soul,
grants me understanding of Scripture,
and makes my heart sing,
it gathers us in unity,
it offers us true wisdom.

And this love has a name, Jesus.

Chapter 3

ANGIE IN THE POURING RAIN

"Lord of peace, we come to you in our need."
- A FILIPINO BISHOPRIC PRAYER -
SUBIC BAY, PHILIPPINES

"I'LL BE THINKING OF ALL those war stories you used to tell us as kids," I said to my father as I prepared to spend a month in the Philippines. It was early December 2008, and we were speaking by phone, he in Florida, me in California.

"Like the time you were offloading artillery in Subic Bay under sniper fire and were afraid someone was going to hit the ammo dump, blowing everyone to who knows where," I said, recalling a story I had known since childhood.

"Another time a group of us were standing around talking when a mortar shell exploded, and a piece of it carved out the back of the guy standing next to me," Dad said. "I still remember the gurgling sound of his exposed lungs as the medics carried him away. I never saw him again."

"I'm planning to take some pictures for you when I'm there," I told him. "Any places other than Subic Bay you want me to go?"

He was having a hard time, at eighty-eight, recalling specific World War II locations and said everyone and everything were under great stress in the Philippines then. Things got a lot better when after many months the army moved his unit to Japan to assist in the post-war reconstruction there under General Douglas MacArthur. That was actually fun, he said, especially getting acquainted with the Japanese women. They were a breath of fresh air.

"But, in the Philippines we were always wet, for one thing," he said. "So much rain every day and for months. We just could never dry out. And what the war did to that country was tragic." Starting to recall a few other places, he talked about seeing beautiful buildings in Manila, constructed by the Spanish during their occupation of the country, "and now they were reduced to rubble," he said. "So, I don't have particularly good memories."

"Did you ever think you had PTSD?" I asked.

"We didn't talk much about those things," he said. "We did our job, and that was it. Hopefully, we made it back home in one piece. I don't know, maybe Hank had some problems. Or maybe Bill. But not me, at least not that I was aware of." Hank, his brother-in-law and my uncle, had actually killed men point-blank on the battlefield. And Bill, another brother-in-law-uncle and a B-17 bomber pilot, suffered physically after parachuting from his burning plane into Germany under heavy fire and then being placed in a prison camp. I knew both of them well, though, as a nephew, and never noticed anything out of the ordinary. But with men of that World War II generation, you never knew, perhaps, what was going on below the surface. They didn't talk a lot.

So anyway, I traveled to the Philippines that year, taking in as many places as my limited budget allowed. There was Manila, of course, a cacophony of civic defilements under skies so polluted you couldn't walk fifty steps without a handkerchief over your mouth. And tiny children playing on city curbs with vehicles roaring past, literally inches from their filth-covered hands and feet. Endless barrios of shacks and cubicles, peopled by millions in abject poverty, completed the picture, as if it had been extracted from *The Year of Living Dangerously*, CJ Koch's novel about 1960s Jakarta under the disastrous Sukarno regime in Indonesia. "What then must we do?" Koch had written, about the masses of people crushed by poverty, quoting Luke 3:10 from the New Testament.

But then there was Tagaytay, a lovely mountain village two hours by car out of Manila, and Boracay, a pristine island to the south. Both locations provided an escape for Manilenos who could afford to get away.

I headed north to Olongapo City and Subic Bay.

In Olongapo I visited the Ricafrente family, whom I had gotten to know through their daughter, Angie, who had provided so much help organizing a previous trip through her work as an Expedia call-center agent that I committed to looking her up if I ever made it to her country. Traveling by bus across a scrubby tropical landscape, which included sections of the Bataan Death March in which sixty-thousand-plus American and Filipino soldiers were forced at gunpoint to endure a torturous relocation during the war, I again thought about Dad. His generation possessed a sense of honor and duty my own baby boom generation could only dream about. They knew how to work together, suffer together, and to put political preferences aside for the good of everyone. I frankly don't know if we'll ever get back to that way of life.

When I arrived at the tiny house where the Ricafrente family lived, that tropical nonstop rain Dad had mentioned was falling. After a lunch of chicken adobo and pancit with Father and Mother Ricafrente, their daughters Angie and Joann, their sons Andy and Joven, a daughter-in-law Jenny and her three children, Angie and I hired a pedicab to carry us out to Subic Bay.

The rain kept falling.

At the Bay, we walked for a long time amid deserted, decaying barracks with faded symbols and markings of war on them. We looked out at the remains of military ships, including a large one still anchored next to a long, weathered dock. I wondered if anything I was photographing would be remembered by Dad when I showed him the pictures after returning to the United States. He was vague about it when I got back. Angie told me about her job, which allowed her to move out of the house and acquire bed-space in a public rooming house. She loved her family, but everyone needs their own space, she said. She attended an Iglesia ni Cristo church on weekends and wanted to go to Boracay with her friends from the call center. She prayed a lot for one of her brothers who had been in poor health since birth. And when her family couldn't afford specialist medical care, Angie died from tuberculosis. The family wrote to tell me.

"Lord of peace, we come to you in our need," says the first line of a prayer from Zenit.org by a group of Catholic bishops from the Philippines. Here is the complete prayer:

> Lord of peace, we come to you in our need.
> Create in us an awareness
> of the massive forces of violence and terrorism
> that threaten our world today.
> Grant us a sense of urgency
> to activate the forces of goodness, of justice,
> of love and peace in our communities.

Where there is armed conflict,
let us stretch out our arms to our brothers and sisters.
Where there is abundance and luxury,
let there be simple lifestyle and sharing.
Where there is poverty and misery,
let there be dignified living and constant striving for just structures.

Where there is selfish ambition, let there be humble service.
Where there is injustice, let there be humble atonement.
Where there is despair, let there be hope in the Good News.
Where there is wound and division, let there be unity and wholeness.
Where there are lies and deceit, let your truth set all of us free.
Where there are thoughts of vengeance, let there be healing and
　　　forgiveness.

Help us to be committed to the Gospel of Peace,
in spite of our differences in faith traditions and ethnic roots.
Teach us your spirit of mercy and compassion.
For it is only in loving imitation of you, Lord of Peace,
that we can discover the healing springs of life
that will bring about a new birth to our earth,
a new era of peace,
and a new harmony among all,
forever and ever.
Amen.

Chapter 4

Urgency from Anxiety

"We cannot count on anything else but your promises."
- A HONG KONG PRAYER -
HONG KONG

ON A SUNNY THURSDAY MORNING in November, I am sitting at my home in Portugal reading Adeline Yen Mah's memoir, *Falling Leaves: The True Story of an Unwanted Chinese Daughter*. I'm only about seventy-five pages into it, and thus far most of the story and its foreboding mood has taken place in Shanghai. It began, however, on May 19, 1988 in Hong Kong with the reading of a will left by the author's father whom everyone in the family believed was extremely wealthy.

"Your father died penniless," says Niang, stepmother to the author, who added that there was no reason to read the will because the estate was empty. Yen Mah, her sister Lydia, and her brothers Gregory, Edgar, and James, acquiesced to Niang without a peep, like "mindless robots," according to the author. But to understand that acquiescence, she says, we needed to go back to the beginning in her story of regret, disappointment, and excessive cruelty.

Hong Kong itself seems to be in an especially cruel state these days, at least as of this writing. Daily, deadly riots protesting mainland China's suffocating domination of law and commerce make international headline news, and beneath the headlines even more disturbing problems occur. And as with Adeline Yen Mah, Hong Kongese have found there's not much they can count on anymore.

Ten years ago, when I traveled there for an academic conference, things appeared quite different, at least to a casual visitor. You could sense some stress below the surface of ordinary conversations, but externally the city was lively and peaceful.

The conference, *Brain, Behavior, and Mind* (2010), brought psychologists, neurologists, and interdisciplinary researchers together to share insights from the latest findings in neuroscience. My small contribution was a poster, *Fandom and the Brain*, which visually articulated areas of study that might be useful to researchers seeking to understand psychological implications of being a fan. Which areas of the brain might be activated by sports fans seeking cathartic release by following a sports team or celebrity, for instance? This was the perfect conference for such a poster as all insights into common, contemporary mental functioning were welcome.

The conference venue was easily accessible by Hong Kong's inexpensive taxi system, and all the drivers spoke fluent English. On the final day of the event, one driver offered to give a group of us a private tour of the city, assisted by a Hong Kong guide who could explain what we would be seeing. So, the following morning about a dozen of us met the driver and the guide, a friendly but highly stressed woman, outside the hotel, and we were off. Victoria Peak high above the city, the Tian Tan Buddha, Lantau Island, and an interesting outdoor market were visited, accompanied by informative comments by the guide. "Yes, Hong Kong is beautiful," she said at one point, "but we are in a state of transition causing much anxiety." Then, after lunch when some of the group members returned a few minutes late to the bus, she exploded. "We said two-fifteen, and look what time it is!" she shouted. "Did you hear me? Do you even care?" We were all a little stunned by the outburst and didn't say much on the way back to the hotel. Was she simply having a bad day? No one knew. Rightly or wrongly, we attributed it to a detectible undercurrent of stress.

Today, that stress has become unbearable for many Hong Kongese.

I know this from my regular correspondence with Anny, a young woman who used to attend my church in Lisbon but has returned with her family to Hong Kong during the current crisis with mainland China. She has written often to me as I am an elder in the Church of Scotland, and with her permission, I offer some of her recent comments, which speak for themselves about the mood in Hong Kong:

"The HK police are insane. They shot those peaceful young people in the head. They beat people who are picking through the rubbish. They are all brainwashed. They love revenge.

"My family is feeling unsafe here. There is proof that the HK police are a gang with the Triad Society, a mafia-type group. They organized an attack on a train. My son saw it happen.

"The police shot a journalist and a social worker. They circled people at the shopping mall and train station. They attacked old people, kids, and a pregnant woman.

"We only want to withdraw the Fugitive Offender's Ordinance, which would allow extradition to mainland China. They will be able to arrest anyone they don't like, for any reason. That is the firewall for us.

"My mom went to Taiwan to live. That is where I will go if the situation gets worse. We seek help from the international community. China is penetrating everywhere here."

In some traditions of contemporary Christianity, social and political tensions like those terrorizing Hong Kong produce authentic soul-searching which expresses itself through forays into biblical prophecy. Warnings and predictions of what will occur prior to Christ's return are a common response to terrible events and oppression inflicted on real people in real time. This has been a strain of thinking throughout Christian history, and at least in the context of sincere prayer, it should be respected. My own faith tradition tends to take me down a different path, which sees oppression more as the byproduct of evil regimes motivated by power and order, which must be met with as much real-world resistance as can be mustered. But then I do not reside in the heat and terror of such oppression.

In this context, I offer "An Urgent Prayer for Hong Kong" from the organization, *His Kingdom Prophecy*. Fervent and comprehensive, this prayer presents a response that is at once complete, sane, balanced, and biblical:

> Lord God we acknowledge that you are the King of kings and Lord of lords,
> and you alone are in control of history.
> Father, we pray for Hong Kong and for those you have put in authority.
> May you give them wisdom, discernment, compassion, and humility
> to rule your city.
> May they be filled with love for the people they serve.
> May they seek to follow the example of Jesus to be servant leaders

and not to seek personal gains and favors.
May they be motivated by a desire to please you alone
and not to please other powers/authorities
at the expense of doing good for the people of Hong Kong.

Father, we pray also for the people of Hong Kong.
We pray for those who are disillusioned, those who feel there is no hope.
May this be the time when they see that only you alone are unchanging
and only your love is faithful.
We acknowledge that our ultimate hope is in you alone.
Help us to see that we cannot count on anything else
but your promises through your Word;
that we cannot count on anyone else in our lives, but you alone
who faithfully seeks us and loves us, unconditionally.

We pray for our young people, especially.
Thank you for their love for Hong Kong and their courage to step up.
We pray for their safety as they protest and gather.
May you grant them patience and humility.
Grant them wisdom to make good judgment.
Help them to seek the good of the city
and seek self-controlled, law-abiding and loving ways
to stand up for what they believe.

We pray for the security bureau officials, our law enforcement agency,
our police force, and other security personnel.
We pray for the decision-makers,
that they are able to assess the situations wisely,
balancing the need for maintaining law and order
and respecting the protesters' freedom of expression.
May they give orders which are practical and effective to achieve this
    end.

Father, we especially pray for our front-line police officers.
Father, we thank them for their service
and we acknowledge the importance of the work they do.
We [realize] they are not the ones who push forward the controversial
    bill
and they are simply doing their jobs, following instructions.
May you keep them safe, help them to have self-control
and not be easily provoked;
and help them to act in a professional way even under immense
    pressure.

Father, we trust that the Holy Spirit intercedes for us (Romans 8: 26–27),
Just as you could use nations and kings who didn't acknowledge your reign,
you can do the same now.
Help us to keep trusting that you are in control
and may your righteousness and justice be brought into the world you created,
at your perfect timing.
In Jesus we pray, Amen.

Chapter 5

THE BEST PARTS

"You alone watch over the interests of spiritual beings."
- A POPE'S ANCIENT PRAYER -
ST. PETER'S SQUARE, ROME

ON A BRUTALLY SUFFOCATING DAY in Rome, my wife Rissy and I wandered jet lagged from somewhere in Vatican City to St. Peter's Square.

Vaguely, we wanted to see in person what we had seen all our lives on television: the place where the Pope steps out of his papal apartment to give his annual address to faithful hearers packed into the square below, like overcrowded U2 fans, ready to receive their blessing.

It was August 2013, and we had spent the day visiting Vatican museums, gardens, a necropolis, and other obligatory locations, all in the intense heat of late summer. Inside was better than outside that day as a high-pressure dome had trapped sizzling Saharan air from North Africa that was now settling over Italy and all of southern Europe. The only relief came in the cool Apostolic Palace where Raphael's famous fresco, *The School of Athens*, spreads out gloriously on its surface of dry lime plaster. Temperature-wise, I could have stayed there all day in refuge from the heat. Content-wise, I could also have stayed there in refuge from over-exposure to Vatican history. Contemplating what Socrates, Plato, and Aristotle might have been thinking in Raphael's painting seemed as refreshing as rereading Linda Johnsen's book, *Lost Masters: Rediscovering the Mysticism of the Ancient Greek Philosophers*.

Sometimes you can get too much of a good thing. Roman Catholicism is lovely, but occasionally you can identify with the old Crosby Stills and Nash song, "Cathedral," about a man wishing to escape a church collapsing under so many stories of saints, sinners, and ecclesial history that faith gets lost in the trappings. Any place and anything different are where you want to go when that happens.

I was from a Protestant family who grew up between two Catholic families in the United States, and from the beginning there was always a sense of moderate suspicion directed toward Catholics. They wore blue and white uniforms to school, couldn't eat meat on Fridays, attended the big scary gothic church in downtown Detroit, and talked about the Pope. I still remember some of the jokes circulating at the time, too. One went something like this: A Protestant minister died, went to heaven, and was given a shiny new Rolls Royce by a welcoming Saint Peter. A Catholic priest died next, went to heaven, but was given a beat-up old Ford. The priest complains to Saint Peter about his inferior gift, and Peter says, "Don't feel bad, the Pope's going around on roller skates."

It was all silly and somewhat cruel, these conceited theological and ecclesial remnants of a bygone era. But they were powerful conditioning agents, and many years later I'm not completely sure I'm free of them. It has always been easy, for instance, to join in the skepticism directed toward the Church for the Crusades, the Inquisition, the Templars, the cult surrounding Mary, the over-focus on suffering, Jesus un-ascended from the Cross, the forced celibacy of priests, and the now-ubiquitous tales of sexual abuse, to name just a few troubling issues. But then one day I'm sitting in some magnificent cathedral here in Portugal, or in Spain, or in France, or in the Vatican away from the pressurized heat outside, and I'm thinking how incredibly beautiful is this millennia-surviving institution. This is the same one that gave us the mystical Thomas a' Kempis with his timeless work, *The Imitation of Christ,* and Saint Teresa of Avila, Saint John of the Cross, Thomas Merton, Henri Nouwen, Flannery O'Conner, G.K. Chesterton, not to mention Saint Augustine of Hippo and Saint Thomas Aquinas. It's very hard for me to imagine life without having received the literary baptism facilitated by these and other Catholics who have fashioned the best parts of my mind and consciousness. So, I'll be taking the strange with the good, applied in moderation, for at least a while longer.

Possibly the oldest Christian prayer outside of the Bible itself is attributed to Saint Clement of Rome, the Church's fourth pope. Presented in the first century CE, "A Prayer for All Needs" offers a rhetoric which acknowledges human imperfection and begs for healing.

> You alone watch over the interests of spiritual beings,
> you are the God of all flesh.
> You gaze into the depths,
> you watch what men are doing.
> You are our help in danger,
> you save the despairing,
> Creator and Keeper of all that is spiritual.
> You give increase to the peoples of the earth,
> and from them all you chose us out to love you,
> through Jesus Christ, your dear Child,
> who brought us instruction, holiness, and honor.
>
> We beg You, Lord, to help and defend us.
> Deliver the oppressed,
> pity the insignificant,
> raise the fallen,
> show yourself to the needy,
> heal the sick,
> bring back those of your people who have gone astray,
> feed the hungry,
> lift up the weak,
> take off the prisoner's chains.
>
> May every nation come to know
> that you alone are God,
> that Jesus Christ is your child,
> that we are your people, the sheep that you pasture.
> You have shown by what you have made and done,
> how the world has been planned from eternity.
> The earth is your creation, Lord,
> Yours that are true to every generation.

Chapter 6

Muscles Flexed, Prayer Ready

"To fight for you and not to mind the wounds."
- A JESUIT PRAYER -
TOMAR, PORTUGAL

Taken in moderation, all good travel is a pilgrimage of sorts, which is to say there is meaning beyond the naturally occurring dopamine spike one receives in anticipation of some life-relevant location, and more meaning when one arrives. Any student of Christian history, moreover, experiences this slow rush, especially in Europe where remnants of stone and metal often tell a story the curious mind wishes to hear. Yes, as previously mentioned, one can get too much of the story, but when it is accompanied by other means of interpreting and enjoying life, one is better for it, as balance and a measured pace, prayer and reflection, take center stage.

In this regard, Rissy and I often take day trips out of Lisbon to historical micro-locations around Portugal and sometimes Spain. It is less about historical wanderlust than it is about ferreting out what is important to us on the levels of soul and spirit. What are the things in life we want to remember or to forget? What do we want to enjoy? What do we want to fight for or against? What do we want to go in our obituaries, or on our gravestones, when the time comes? It's all about the essence of what stands beyond the travel and life and ranges into the spiritual.

The prayer.

In this instance, the prayer, "Just Because You Are My God," is one attributed to Saint Ignatius of Loyola, co-founder of The Society of Jesus, otherwise known as The Jesuits. But before we get to it, we need to consider the much older Christian order, The Knights Templar.

The stories of both the Jesuits and the Templars, different as they may be, are written indelibly into the soil and consciousness of Portugal, and the best place to contemplate the Templars is the city of Tomar. It lies gleaming in the Portuguese sun on beautiful rolling countryside about two hours out of Lisbon, along highway A-13 north. Leaving Lisbon in the morning, and stopping in the town of Almeirim for the slow-cooked broth of beans, sausage, potatoes, carrots, and cabbage known locally as *sopa de pedra*, stone soup, one arrives in Tomar ready to experience a Templar world. The Convento de Cristo is the biggest draw as it was where the Templars operated during the 1100s before it transformed into the Knights of the Order of Christ roughly two centuries later. A main church with its pinnacles, nave, stone staircases, cloister, and medieval mood all work together to smile with indifference at the passing of time. One feels small and insignificant there, both physically and in the context of our few years of life on earth.

One also feels as though he or she must know a lot about the Templars from having been exposed to their constant interpretation and reinterpretation existing in culture, especially popular culture. Books such as *The Da Vinci Code*, and movies such as *Kingdom of Heaven*, as well as numerous television shows, Templar rock songs, and even Templar video games such as *Medieval Total War* and *Assassin's Creed*, have blanketed contemporary media culture with a confusing mesh of fiction based on fact. Yet, somehow the core essence of Templar history survives. They were founded on Christmas Day 1119 at the Church of the Holy Sepulchre in Jerusalem, twenty-four years after Pope Urban II had called for the first Crusade and the liberation of the holy city from the Seljuk Turks. They occupied Jerusalem's al-Aqsa Mosque shortly thereafter and commenced their mission of protecting holy land pilgrims and launching military operations when needed. They became wealthy and powerful from tax breaks and banking throughout Europe, to the extent of being granted land and authority over castles in Portugal during the 1130s, always accompanied by their role to drive out Muslims from the Iberian Peninsula. Here, they morphed into the Knights of Christ, taking in Portuguese luminaries Henry the Navigator and later Vasco da Gama before diminishing in power and prestige both in Portugal and across Europe.

It was a real-life tale of *muscular* Christianity and a *fight for Christ* ethic extending from the beginning of Christendom throughout Medieval Europe and beyond, which brings us to another muscular order of faith, the Jesuits, and to our prayer.

Different as they were from the Templars, the Jesuits, whose mission was a combination of evangelization and martyrdom, were linked to the older order by their intense devotion to Christ and their fearless, selfless obedience. They lived to proclaim salvation through Jesus Christ alone everywhere in the world, no matter how dangerous, and they welcomed death in the service of their Lord. Two remarkable portraits of the Jesuits include Shusaku Endo's novel *Silence*, the story of Christianity's original entry into Japan through the efforts Portuguese Jesuit priests, and the movie, *The Mission*, about Jesuit priests confronting slave traders in South America. Though their methods were peaceful, they nevertheless *fought* for God through the power of intellect, advanced learning, and rock-solid biblical theology. Co-founded in 1540 by Ignatius of Loyola and Francis Xavier, a prayer articulating a theology and mission that knew exactly what it was about, survives.

According to Ignatius,

> Oh, my God, I want to love you,
> Not that I might gain eternal heaven,
> Nor escape eternal hell,
> But Lord, to love you just because you are my God.
> Grant me to give to you,
> And not to count the cost,
> To fight for you,
> And not to mind the wounds,
> To labor and ask for no reward,
> Except the knowledge that I serve God.

Chapter 7

Immense Spirituality

"Living and self-loving Christ, you are our root."
- A PRAYER FROM THE LGBTQ+ COMMUNITY -
WALT WHITMAN HOUSE, CAMDEN, NEW JERSEY, UNITED STATES

REWIND TO SUMMER 1989 AND to the Walt Whitman house, which I had visited on a personal journey to places relevant to the traditional, and mostly male, canon of American literature. That *canon* no longer exists, having been replaced by a broader and more rewarding race- and gender-inclusive body of books and authors we celebrate today. Yet, I still retain a few earlier voices such as those of William Faulkner, Nathaniel Hawthorne, and "Uncle Walt," as Whitman was known in the classic film, *Dead Poets Society*.

I vividly remember arriving at Whitman's Mickle Street house after making strange little circles around Camden, New Jersey, across the Delaware River from Philadelphia. Lost as though in a *Twilight Zone* episode, I suddenly came upon the poet's small white house as it popped up from a red brick sidewalk behind inoperable parking meters. It was a nondescript urban dwelling. I walked from the car to the front door of the house, which opened before I had a chance to knock. Seemingly waiting for me was an ebullient African American woman who introduced herself as Eleanor. She was one of the guides in charge of the house, had something to do with the nearby Camden campus of Rutgers University, and she seemed delighted to have a visitor.

We stood in a dreary hallway, then walked into a living room full of Whitman memorabilia: his favorite rocking chair, his leather shoes and famous Quaker hat, letters he had written, nine editions of *Leaves of Grass*, photographs of the woman from England who first recognized Whitman's genius, and a portrait of his idol, Abraham Lincoln. In the shadow of his own portrait, where he looked like Santa Claus in a gray flannel suit, Eleanor spoke of her love for Whitman's verse. She had been the product of a Baptist church somewhere until she discovered his poetry which "liberated her spirit," she said. She immersed herself in Whitman, and escorting literary pilgrims through the house was her mission and her calling.

Whitman had purchased the house in 1884 for two thousand dollars, Eleanor said, and it was the only home he ever owned. His seventh edition of *Leaves of Grass*, the Philadelphia edition as it was known, had surprised everyone by selling enough copies to make money, and with furnishings provided by the widow of a ship captain, he took residence. The widow, one Mary Davis, became his housekeeper, and he lived there until his death in 1892. I remember scaling a stairway to Whitman's bedroom where there were stone busts of him resting on a bureau, more photographs, and his narrow, high-backed death bed. You'll definitely want to see his tomb in the local cemetery, Eleanor had said, which also included the resting places of his parents, sister, and two brothers. He had been the most congenial person on earth, she added, welcoming all and rejecting no one, and longing to be near his loved ones even in death.

Moving through the rest of the house, Eleanor said that curious literary pilgrims always ask her if Whitman was gay. Personally, she had doubts about it, she said, as he seemed attracted to some women, too, so maybe he was bi-sexual. Who on earth cares? The homoerotic images in a lot of his work may have been an expression of deeper human longings that could be expressed only through male joining, she added. At any rate, when you read Whitman, you acquire something much larger than sexuality, something immense and overwhelmingly spiritual, she said. Reading his poetry had driven her back to the Bible, in fact, which she said she had been reading with new zeal. And he was so purifying and Christlike, as his work comforting wounded, dying soldiers during the Civil War demonstrated. "He did what Jesus would have done," Eleanor said, "visiting the wounded in hospitals, and tending to each soldier's spirit in unwavering compassion." Even after the war ended, he consoled those who had lost loved ones, quoting Scripture as he went. He wrote a letter to the mother of a fallen soldier, saying, "Such things are gloomy, yet there is a text, 'God doeth all things well,' the meaning of which, after due time, appears to the soul."

"The poetry is special, like prayer," Eleanor said, a statement I committed to memory, repeating it now, thirty years later.

Also, three decades later, it's possible to see that Whitman may have viewed himself as a Christlike representative of God to his generation, with more than a hundred references to Christ in his poetry. His broad, welcoming verse draws everyone in, regardless of gender, race, background, or sexual preference. "There is neither Jew nor Greek, there is neither bond nor free, there is neither male nor female: for ye are all one in Christ Jesus," would likely have been his mantra, from Galatians 3:28 (KJV). He tended to the sick and wounded as his nonfiction account of hospital searching, *Specimen Days*, persuasively showed. And he combined an apparent sense of mission and ministry to a superficial and increasingly corrupt America during the final decades of a century diminished by civil war.

The prayer I have chosen to close this part of the book is taken from *The Huffington Post*, December 6, 2017. Offered by Kittredge Cherry and Patrick Cheng, it seems consistent with the spirit of Walt Whitman in its borderless, inclusive rhetoric within the LGBTQ+ community, employing rainbow colors to symbolize connectivity, life, sexuality, self-esteem, love, self-expression, and vision. Ultimately, what lies beneath its words is grace and hope that we might honor each other despite our differences.

> Rainbow Christ, you embody all the colors of the world. Rainbows serve as bridges between different realms: Heaven and Earth, east and west, queer and non-queer. Inspire us to remember the values expressed in the rainbow flag of the lesbian, gay, bisexual, transgender, and queer community.
>
> Red is for life, the root of spirit. Living and self-loving Christ, you are our root. Free us from shame, and grant us the grace of healthy pride so that we can follow our own inner light. With the red stripe in the rainbow, we give thanks that God created us just the way we are.
>
> Orange is for sexuality, the fire of spirit. Erotic Christ, you are our fire, the Word made flesh. Free us from exploitation, and grant us the grace of mutual relationships. With the orange stripe in the rainbow, kindle a fire of passion in us.

Yellow is for self-esteem, the core of spirit. Out Christ, you are our core. Free us from closets of secrecy, and give us the guts and grace to come out. With the yellow stripe in the rainbow, build our confidence.

Green is for love, the heart of spirit. Transgressive Outlaw Christ, you are our heart, breaking the rules of love. In a world obsessed with purity, you touch the sick and eat with outcasts. Free us from conformity, and grant us the grace of deviance. With the green stripe in the rainbow, fill our hearts with untamed compassion for all beings.

Blue is for self-expression, the voice of spirit. Liberator Christ, you are our voice, speaking out against all forms of oppression. Free us from apathy, and grant us the grace of activism. With the blue stripe in the rainbow, motivate us to call for justice.

Violet is for vision, the wisdom of spirit. Interconnected Christ, you are our wisdom, creating and sustaining the universe. Free us from isolation, and grant us the grace of interdependence. With the violet stripe in the rainbow, connect us with others and with the whole creation.

Rainbow colors come together to make one light, crown of universal consciousness. Hybrid and All-Encompassing Christ, you are our crown, both human and divine. Free us from rigid categories, and grant us the grace of interwoven identities. With the rainbow, lead us beyond black-and-white thinking to experience the whole spectrum of life.

Rainbow Christ, you light up the world. You make rainbows as a promise to support all life on earth. In the rainbow space we can see all the hidden connections between sexualities, genders, and races. Like the rainbow, may we embody all the colors of the world!

Amen.

PART TWO

Chapter 8

KARAKIA FOR TWO

"Instill in us your sacred spirit."
- TWO MAORI PRAYERS -
ROTORUA, NEW ZEALAND

MOST UNIVERSITY STUDENTS, EVEN FROM Christian universities, would rather experience popular culture than reverent prayer. Indeed, popular culture is a sort of religion itself, and a better one in the minds of such people, case closed. I had known this anecdotally since researching and writing a PhD thesis on fandom at the University of Edinburgh, and data extracted from nearly three hundred fans of various cultural products seemed to confirm it.

But one doesn't need to have advanced degrees to know that this is true. Ask any parent, school teacher, youth pastor, club leader, or guidance counselor, and you will hear stories of young people (and not only young people, frankly) coming spiritually alive when consuming objects of their fandom, and falling spiritually dead when exposed to non-popular, non-entertaining things.

Or, you can ask me. I can talk for quite a while about it.

I might even start in New Zealand, where the last thing I ever did as a professor was to lead a group of students through a program combining media studies with various subtopics including religion and culture. My hope was that media students might learn to appreciate spiritual elements of New Zealand's indigenous Maori community even as they were traveling to movie sets and television stations across the country. I was mostly wrong.

When, for instance, I invited all twelve students to a *karakia* time in a beautiful Auckland park, only one student showed up, possibly so I wouldn't feel alone and humiliated. Karakia is a spiritually uplifting form of Maori prayer incanted to achieve positive outcomes in daily life. A few of the students knew about karakia from having read three required books: *The Whale Rider* by Witi Ihimaera, *Maori Tattooing* by H.G. Robley, and *Maori Religion and Mythology* by Edward Shortland. But these reads seemed to have minimal discernible impact, especially in comparison with all the fun travel experiences New Zealand has to offer.

On the way south from Auckland, for instance, study and reflection had little chance of survival when we arrived at Hobbiton, the movie set where scenes from Peter Jackson's *The Lord of the Rings* were filmed. Suddenly, excitement filled the misty air as we crouched into hobbit houses, taking hundreds of selfies designated for Facebook and Instagram. It was what it was, and you might as well enjoy it, I thought to myself, while mildly lamenting the fact that not much education was happening. Most professors are numb and unable to be humiliated anyway these days, desensitized by Rate My Professor and ego-climbing university administrators enforcing the latest layer of performance reviews. You celebrate genuine learning when and where it occurs, but you can go a long time between fleeting moments of fulfillment.

When we arrived in Rotorua things seemed to change but only slightly. This town of thermal springs, bubbling mud pools, a sulfuric odor, and its thirty-five percent Maori population sent students to the course syllabus and its requirement to gather data as an ethnographer does in field ethnography. "Is it okay to do my data collection on my phone?" one student asked. "I write all my papers straight from my iphone." The student was planning to start collecting at the touristy Tamaki Maori Village later that day, though the eventual interactive fun of choreographed villagers tended to compromise any serious intent. And the *foodgasmic* meal, the *hangi*, with its whole-foods paleo items cooked in a pit on heated rocks, stopped it altogether. We ended up singing old chart-topping songs on the bus back to the hotel.

You had to love *study abroad*.

In the days ahead, we actually did have isolated moments of meaningful introspection, as after a discussion of *moko*, Maori tattooing, commenced. "Drawing from the Maori notion that *moko* is worth the pain of being inked, pierced, and scraped, what would you say about pain in general, and what things in life are worth getting pained over?" the syllabus asked. Surprising responses ranging from a story of kidney donation for a relative in dialysis, to having painful blood platelet extraction and transfusion in another family context, were shared. But still not much on *karakia* and how styles and habits of prayer might be instructive for people who care about such things.

"Fascinating discussion of karakia, which seems most potent in addressing and removing curses," the syllabus added, after a required book chapter. "What gets branded as a curse is mostly the result of ignorance and superstition toward sleep disorders and diseases of mind and body. Fast-forward to today, and ask yourself how you address superstition and true, living faith in your life or in the life of others. Should we look at true faith as belief and service removed from all elements of superstition, or does superstition get a bad name as a part of genuine faith experience?"

Silence.

In higher education it's good not to let moments of silence hang on too long, bringing resulting, palpable discomfort. And there is a precise moment when you need to move on, as I did then in Rotorua with two actual karakias: a traditional one and a more contemporary karakia, both taken with permission from the archives of the University of Otago:

> Cease the winds from the west,
> Cease the winds from the south,
> Let the breeze blow over the land,
> Let the breeze blow over the ocean,
> Let the red-tipped dawn come with a sharpened air,
> A touch of frost, a promise of a glorious day.

***

> Honor and glory to God,
> Peace on Earth,
> Goodwill to all people.
> Lord, develop a new heart
> Inside all of us.
> Instill in us your sacred spirit.
> Help us, guide us,
> In all the things we need to learn today.
> Amen.

Chapter 9

Listening to the Interior

"May you be blessed in the chase;
To where the life-giving road of your sun father comes out."
- TWO ZUNI PRAYERS -
ZUNI PUEBLO, NEW MEXICO, UNITED STATES

HIGHWAY 53, WEST OF ALBUQUERQUE, New Mexico, is a deserted two-lane road that curves south and west through the Cibola National Forest to Zuni Pueblo. It travels through the heart of Navaho country, then Zuni country, and is a good time to listen to a Zuni-language news broadcast on your car radio. You don't need to understand Zuni to appreciate it. The soft, unforced intonation of voices sounds a little like Japanese, when people in or from Japan speak quietly, and it is an enjoyable, peaceful experience.

Perhaps this linguistic sound had something to do with inspiring anthropologist Nancy Yaw Davis to spend years of painstaking research for her book, *The Zuni Enigma*, which theorizes a connection between Japanese and Zuni. Knowing of my interest in all things Native American, and most things Asian, my daughter found the book for me in Santa Fe when we were spending a week there on holiday in 2013. I read it with fascination while hanging out in Zuni Pueblo later that summer, only to discover through scholarly reviews that the book had been heavily criticized by anthropologists. Davis had built her theory partially on the fact that the Zuni language is an *isolate* with no known connections to any other Native American tongue, yet it contained many words similar to those in Japanese. Then, through comparing likenesses of blood type, skull shape, tooth similarities, and visual patterns of folk art, she theorized that fourteenth-century Buddhist monks had departed a Japan in turmoil and made their way across the ocean to the West Coast before settling in now-Zuni for possible religious reasons.

The book was seldom taken seriously by those holding to the documented theory that all Native Americans trace their ancestry to waves of paleo immigrants who crossed the Beringia land bridge from Siberia to Alaska approximately seventeen thousand years ago. Yet it's an engaging speculative read, and one tends to admire risk-takers like Davis who follow their deepest inner voice.

A more accepted source on the Zuni is the anthropologist Ruth Bunzel, a disciple of the revered author of *Patterns in Culture*, Ruth Benedict, who was a mainstay of anthropological education throughout the twentieth and into the twenty-first century. The two Ruths visited Zuni Pueblo in the early 1930s, and Benedict encouraged Bunzel to get to know firsthand all she could about the Zuni. Bunzel's interests were said to have originated in her appreciation of skilled women potters who were held in high esteem throughout the Zuni nation. Later, she said it was not the pottery she was after but the human behavior surrounding the pottery. What is it that forms the basis for how we value human beings according to gender, race, performance, achievement, personality, and spirituality, for instance, and how will we come to know this basis? Through the stories we tell? Through our rituals and ceremonies? Through the songs we sing and the poems we write? Through our prayers?

Likely through all of these sources, according to Bunzel. Her writings, *Zuni Origin Myths, Introduction to Zuni Ceremonialism,* and *Zuni Ritual Poetry,* all published in 1932 and updated since, present a readable narrative of Zuni life. They were and are certainly a spiritual people and, in fact, had felt wrongly represented by the first anthropologist who traveled to the pueblo, fifty years prior to Bunzel, to document their way of life. No one likes to be observed, studied, photographed, or to have their sacred moments exposed visually, without proper context, for the consumptive appetites of curious onlookers. Yet, in the early 1880s a Smithsonian associate, Frank Hamilton Cushing, brought his camera to Zuni and was accused of violating sacred privacies in his exploitative method of field anthropology. It didn't sit well with Zuni nation, as it doesn't sit well in ethnographic research today.

Bunzel, on the other hand, chose an approach characterized by listening, and to treat Zuni interior life with reverence. "According to Zuni belief, man has a spiritual substance, a soul," she wrote in *Introduction to Zuni Ceremonialism*, which will only be appreciated by respectfully accommodating the authenticity of native rituals. Prayer was accompanied by deep breathing, especially at the end of a prayer when everyone present moved their folded hands to just beneath their nostrils and joined in a deep collective inhalation. Pray, breathe, and thrive. This was about "the essence" of something deeply felt, said Bunzel. In *Zuni Ritual Poetry* she added that prayer was a kind of "magic formulae," combining the inhaling of memory, hope, nature, strength of spirit, life-affirming conversation, traveling peaceful roads to purifying lakes, respecting family, respecting age, respecting life. "To this end, my children, may you be blessed with life," she quoted from a Zuni prayer numbered 671.

Prayer 721, from the same source, added the blessing of an illuminated existence:

> May you be blessed with light;
> May your roads be fulfilled;
> May you grow old;
> May you be blessed in the chase;
> To where the life-giving road of your sun father comes out.
> May your roads reach;
> May your roads all be fulfilled.

And Prayer 777 said be blessed, and do not forget all that is good:

> The thoughts of your fathers
> You have fulfilled.
> Do not forget your house.
> Here in your own house
> You will go about happily.
> Always talking together kindly,
> We shall pass our days.
> Our child,
> Your road will be fulfilled;
> Your road will reach all the way to Dawn Lake.
> May your road be fulfilled;
> May you grow old;
> May you be blessed with life.

Chapter 10

CATHARSIS ON BERBER SOIL

"Glory to you the Almighty, master of countless crowds."
- A BERBER PRAYER -
MARRAKECH, MOROCCO

"WE WERE HERE FIRST. PLEASE do not forget that we were the first ones."

Those were the words of Nordeen, night manager of the small *riad* Rissy and I checked into one May evening in the noisy center of Marrakech. He was of Berber ancestry and enjoyed telling us that the Berbers had been living in northwest Africa long before the Arabs; for at least twelve thousand years, he said, their indigenous origins documented by ancient cave paintings and rock art in the region.

And not only Morocco, he added. "From Egypt in the east, all the way through Libya, Tunisia, and Algeria, you're going to find Berbers still celebrating our culture and speaking our language." By day, Nordeen operated a tent-and-camel tourism company out in the desert somewhere east of Marrakech and wondered if we might be interested in joining a caravan sometime. We're still considering it.

Earlier in the week we had done what visitors to Marrakech often do: people-watch. Jostling through the swelling crowds in the central square, we worked our way daily to the broad veranda of a restaurant, sipped mint tea, and just observed. The art of watching was better here than on our previous trips to Tangier and Fez, we agreed, though all of Morocco is a spectacular traveler's playground. Less than two hours by air from Lisbon, one jets away from the modern world and into an ancient medina soukscape of twisting passages and mercantile cells that never seem to change, thankfully. Moreover, in a world of technology accelerating at the speed of cybergnostic light, one appreciates a place where old men still charm cobras in a public square and goats still climb trees. Back in a moment to that thought.

Occasionally as an ordained church elder, I am asked to lead the Sunday morning service at my church in Lisbon. This is a glorious task of choosing hymns for the congregation to sing, selecting prayers of approach, thanksgiving, and intercession, and offering a public address. I enjoy it. As someone who was raised in the church, but left it completely for extended periods of time when I became convinced it was a silly relic in an age of science and postmodern thinking, I have returned to enjoy everything a church is and should be. It's an imperfect, peculiar, and sometimes embarrassingly backward assembly of people who crave connection and hope, and I choose not to be without it. Theological arguments, however, and even the articulated certainty of faith no longer are the main part of the picture for me personally, even as discipline to participate and minister with genuine love, where possible, are central. I doubt I will leave again, so long as the ecclesial end game of virtual religion doesn't kill it.

The most recent public address I had the pleasure to present bore the title, *The Holiness of Travel*. I had found more than fifty verses in the Holy Bible that offered insight into travel and then suggested five biblically-supported insights: 1) that travel is never about mere tourism, 2) that travel ought to be attached to some kind of purpose, 3) that travel should possess an element of spontaneity, as in the parable of the Good Samaritan, who had interrupted his travel plans to aid a distressed person, 4) that travel with others is preferred to traveling alone, and 5) that God goes with us on our journeys. Each suggestion was borne up adequately by passages and contexts, but as with most public addresses the speaker needs to tell a story.

This was the story.

Rissy and I were traveling in our car south of the river Tagus in Portugal one day when, for no reason in particular, I said I never needed to travel anywhere but straight north or straight south from Lisbon to be a happy traveler. And there were only three points on my straight north-south angle: Scotland, and particularly Edinburgh, on the north; Morocco, and primarily Marrakech on the south; and Portugal in the middle. Rissy thought that was interesting, so I gave the idea more thought in the weeks leading up to my public address. I like to return to Scotland and Edinburgh, I told the congregation, because those places are about the past for me, mostly my educational past. I love to go back to my university and soak up the academic atmosphere still prevalent there. And the past is important, I added, quoting Isaiah 46:9 (NIV) which states, "Remember the former things long past."

Then, for the Portugal midpoint I said that I identify with the Portuguese on the basis of their overall curiosity about the world. Centuries ago, Portugal was the first European nation to travel long distances on the high seas to learn about the world and to bring that world back home. Today, that former empire might no longer exist, but the sense of curiosity has never diminished. For this thought I quoted Proverbs 25:2 (NIV): "It is the glory of God to conceal things but the glory of kings to search things out." Next, I shared that I am empowered by Portugal on the basis of its tranquility. It's a peaceful place, I said, number three in the world according to the latest Global Peace Index, and we all benefit by living in this peaceful land. Here, I quoted Hebrews 12:14 (NIV): "Make every effort to live in peace with everyone and to be holy," adding that Portugal, more than most nations, has fulfilled that wise command from the Bible.

Now, to Morocco and Marrakech. In my address I stated that Marrakech is an especially crazy place. And from time to time, I need a crazy place. Why? For reasons of emotional release and what Aristotle once called *katharsis*. Having cathartic experiences is about periodically releasing the build-up of emotional pressure within our lives for the purpose of maintaining a healthy mental state. It's a controversial theory because some researchers say it doesn't work, and it might even make hostilities of mind and mood worse when initial cathartic releases wear off. Yet, there are certain cathartic experiences, I contend, that we need to drive away fear and the potential explosiveness we need to let go of, just as Aristotle said. So, I need to see those snake charmers and tree-climbing goats, not to mention finding ways to get through swelling crowds of noise and omnidirectional movement, which the dusty Moroccan environment provides. I laugh. I shout. I am joyful. I release. Save the seriousness of life for another day, and enjoy the cathartic truth of Psalm 42:4 (NIV) which states, "I pour out my soul . . . with shouts of joy and praise among the festive throng."

We had many long conversations with Nordeen that week at his riad, and shared a long goodbye as we left its sanctuary for the noisy streets of Marrakech yet again. We'll always be going back, too, for that Berber essence that gives the place its real, unfiltered magnificence.

And I will remember that the Berbers were the first ones there.

Appropriately, here is a poetic prayer from the Berber poet, Si Mohand ou-Mhand, translated into English by Abdenour Bouich for *Xanthos: A Journal of Foreign Literatures and Languages*. Si Mohand lived mostly in the 19th Century (1845–1906) and offered timeless praises to a compassionate God, as well as thoughts of despair during times of trouble and confusion:

> Compassionate, you are the most merciful,
> Glory to you the Almighty,
> Master of countless crowds.
>
> You provide for those who have no money,
> Your power is unmatched,
> You keep watch over us.
>
> Since even those who do nothing live,
> without debts or worries,
> I swear to you, hunger, I do not fear you anymore.
>
> Distributor, come down and talk to us.
> May God convince you
> to have pity on us, the helpless.
>
> For some you have given the zest of life,
> far from the miseries,
> in cozy beds.
>
> For me, you have given endless nights in the barn,
> Sleeping beside junkyards,
> Braving cold, sickness, and stench.

Chapter 11

PRAYERFUL OVERLAY

"We stand in awe and gratitude . . . Christian, Jew, Muslim,
as well as those with other faiths."

- A MONOTHEISTIC PRAYER -
HAGIA SOPHIA GRAND MOSQUE, ISTANBUL, TURKEY

BEFORE DEPARTING MOROCCO FOR ANOTHER season of adventures in Turkey, I recount the following experience.

On a train from Tangier to Fez, Rissy and I were seated in a compartment with a conversational Muslim man who was on his way to Fez for Ramadan. He had interrupted his intensely focused reading of a pocket Qur'an to chat with us, sharing stories of life as a civil engineer in Tangier. Rissy and I spoke of meeting friendly people in Morocco, enjoying the mood, and how we loved dropping down from Portugal to step into its welcoming embrace. "So, you are Muslim," he said. "We're Christians," we answered, and suddenly the energy of our positive dialogue was sucked out of the compartment like air from a deflating balloon. "Oh," said the youngish man, in a lowering, less exuberant voice, effectively ending the conversation. Clearly, he was disillusioned that otherwise inquisitive people like ourselves were not Muslim. Or perhaps it was because we were Christians, we never knew. In any case, he smiled in resignation and returned to reading his Qur'an.

It seemed odd to us that disappointment would be the emotion of choice exhibited by an interesting and devout man toward us because of our faiths. It's hard to feel as though you're an object of pity. Maybe we'd rather feel scorn because then the borders between us are more clearly drawn, giving us the feeling that we know who you are, and we're certainly not going to change who we are. Perhaps, also, that's what is occurring between faiths in the world at large, Rissy and I agreed as we checked into our hotel next to the train station in Fez. We don't dislike each other, we're just disappointed that we don't share what is most important to us. Years earlier I had served for three years on the steering committee of *Muslims and Christians*, an annual conference at Luther Seminary in Saint Paul, Minnesota, and we were always concerned with de-radicalizing the past before we could build a future together through constructive dialogue. In truth, I think that except for the minority of caliphate-seeking terrorists in the world, and the forces of anti-Muslim rhetoric and violence in the West, we have de-radicalized the past, in both faiths, and what remains is a kind of peaceful sadness that our relationships go only so far before they terminate for lack of effort to find common ground.

We should pray together more.

In Istanbul, during the holiday season of another year, Rissy and I found ourselves enjoying the energy of a remarkable city, historically placed at the cultural crossroad which is Turkey. After a conference on the meaning of public space at Bilgi University, we ventured back and forth from our hotel near the Galata Bridge. The beautiful regularity of the Muslim call to prayer each day echoed in the background as we made numerous visits to Muslim, Christian, and Jewish places of interest. Back at the hotel, we conversed often with Sevgi, the girl at the front desk, who was getting married soon in her rural hometown, and during evenings we enjoyed the underrated food culture of Istanbul.

Turkey in general and Istanbul in particular seem fairly secular, given the hybrid nature of their cultural life and politics, which contrasts with the authoritarian states of other majority-Muslim countries and cities. Not quite as free as the Indonesias and Malaysias of the world, at least according to annual *Democracy Index* ratings, they certainly are in the mix of places anyone can enjoy for any reason and despite any cultural background.

Our personal highlight was an afternoon spent wandering through Hagia Sophia, the ancient church which became a mosque, a living museum, and now another mosque in the heart of Istanbul. From outside in the milky sunshine, the enormous structure had a peach-pink glow that was both radiant and inviting. Inside, we walked eyes-upward beneath the soaring dome revealing its passage of time by means of small anachronistic windows and fading pigmentation on stone. And then, of course, there were the many examples of Islamic symbolism competing visually with original church structures, such as a mihrab pointing toward Mecca where the church's main altar once stood and a faded cross behind a Muslim ceiling decoration. A plastered-over Virgin-with-child mosaic and ones depicting Christ and also the fourth century Archbishop of Constantinople, Saint John Chrysostom, completed this kaleidoscope of Islamic triumphalism in a way similar to the visual supremacy of the Dome of the Rock in Jerusalem rising above the Western Wall of the long-gone Jewish Temple.

It's a vivid chapter in an illustrated textbook of Christian-Muslim history.

It's also a survivor of destructive forces: three ruinous fires, five calamitous earthquakes ranging from the sixth to the fourteenth centuries, and more than a millennium of competing faiths.

In his book *Sea of Faith*, Stephen O'Shea describes Hagia Sophia as "an echo chamber of indistinct murmur" and a structure "rich in the strata of overlaid faiths and cultures." O'shea adds that converting the place into a museum was "an act of secularization."

Secularization was certainly the intent in 1935 when under Turkish President Mustafa Kemal Ataturk the complex became a place to see but emphatically not a place to worship, whether by Christians or Muslims. Eighty-five years later that prohibition is gone. Muslim prayers were offered there in 2016, and a well-publicized event of the Anatolia Youth Association rallied to reconvert the museum into a mosque. Since that time, moreover, the current President Recep Tayyip Erdogan has reconverted Hagia Sophia to a Grand Mosque in order to rectify the "very big mistake" of ever having it become a museum. Erdogan has also paid lip service to the city's conqueror, Mehmed II, who had taken the city for Islam in the 1450s. Many have seen Erdogan's action as retaliation for Pope Francis's 2015 acknowledgment of the Armenian genocide by Turkey's Ottoman Empire one hundred years earlier.

Politics and religion make strange bedfellows. Throw in weaponized prayers that serve to promote exclusion and the belief that only our approach to holiness is *the* approach, and we have old world problems resurfacing on a modern stage, which causes many to throw out faith altogether. However, prayers that acknowledge God, which begin in thankfulness, seek God's will and purposes, ask for forgiveness, and plea for mutual respect, restraint, and a healing rhetoric to carry our thoughts, emerge as valid points of hope in a spiritually diminished world. The following prayer from the website of The World Council of Churches, is an example. "Prayer for Peace by Christian, Jewish, and Muslim Clergy," offered in 1991 during the Persian Gulf War, can lead us to the peace of coexistence many people of faith seek:

> Eternal God, Creator of the universe, there is no God but you.
> Great and wonderful are your works, wondrous are your ways.
> Thank you for the many splendored variety of your creation.
> Thank you for the many ways we affirm your presence and purpose,
> and the freedom to do so.
> Forgive our violation of your creation.
> Forgive our violence toward each other.
> We stand in awe and gratitude for your persistent love
> for each and all of your children:
> Christian, Jew, Muslim,
> as well as those with other faiths.
> Grant to all and our leaders attributes of the strong,
> mutual respect in words and deed,
> restraint in the exercise of power,
> and the will for peace with justice for all.
> Eternal God, Creator of the universe, there is no God but you.
> Amen.

Chapter 12

BINARIES, BALANCES, AND BALI

"Grant us an understanding heart, equal vision, balanced mind . . . ."

- A HINDU PRAYER -
DENPASAR, BALI

AS THIS MEMOIR IS A book about prayer and travel, now might be a good time to mention prayer *during* travel.

I don't have a lot to say about it other than the fact that prayer, or specifically prayerful meditation, is the only way I have ever found to make long plane flights bearable. Sleep, of course, can also be a solution, though the interruptions of flight meals, bathroom breaks, air turbulence, cockpit announcements, crying children, and working flight attendants can make sleep difficult. Even more problematic is when I impose distractions on the flight experience through reading, writing, playing games, or watching movies on my tablet. If anything, such distractions make things worse because they have a way of calling attention to themselves, as activities to occupy the mind, rather than accepting the situation you're in and in the process freeing your mind to experience the consciousness of the moment.

Deep prayerful meditation, if and when you can get to it (and I'm not always successful), weds your conscious mind to what is happening externally. It takes you to a place of greater awareness, where nothing is to be feared or avoided, and it causes the passage of time to recede in the mystical warmth of acceptance and peacefulness. I start by closing my eyes and emptying my mind of distracting thoughts, which can be hard to do. If I succeed, I then allow myself to be distraction-free for as long as possible. No thinking, no feeling, no dreaming, no seeking, no anything. Then, at some point I try to begin visualizing where I am at this moment, in this case speeding through earth's atmosphere in an airframe, moving through high clouds, and heading straight into a kind of pleasurable infinity without fixed points of reference or any kind of end point. This is when prayer begins. I try to see my life as a fluid timeline recalling events, experiences, and people whose lives I floated through, saying a word to God for each one as my trance-like state continues, and as the plane continues its trajectory. Temporal time seems to disappear completely, and before I know it the pilot is telling the crew to prepare for landing.

That's it.

And when it happens, even a transpacific flight into a stiff headwind offers no threat of anxiety or boredom. Upon arrival, I have even wished that the flight had been longer, as prayerful meditation has removed all constricting pressures, leaving my mind refreshed and ready for new adventures.

The flight to Bali, this chapter's focus, involved fifteen hours from Los Angeles to Shanghai, three hours in Shanghai's Pudong International Airport, and another six hours to Bali's capital city, Denpasar.

Retrieving my baggage and going through security at Ngurah Rai International Airport occurred without incident, and I was wide-eyed with curiosity in the taxi from the airport to my rural Indonesian villa. The ride was chaotic, though, as the scrum of motorcyclists and competing taxis merged onto a road too small to serve everyone. Each time the taxi stopped in traffic panhandlers tapped on the closed windows of the car seeking handouts. This sudden first-world-meets-third-world engagement again reminded me of scenes from CJ Koch's novel *The Year of Living Dangerously*, and its movie version starring Mel Gibson and Linda Hunt, which was set in poverty-ridden Jakarta of the 1960s. Most memorable was a conversation between Gibson's character, an Australian journalist, and Hunt, a dwarf cameraman played by Hunt, who amid inner city squalor asked the question, what then must we do? Hunt then paraphrased Luke 3:10 and 11 (ESV): "'What then must we do? the crowd asked. 'John the Baptist answered, anyone who has two shirts should share with the one who has none, and anyone who has food should do the same.'" I wonder how far removed we twenty-first-century first-worlders are from such moments of empathic reflection? Does prayer restore compassion, or do spoken words of devotion give us something to hide behind while we're avoiding concrete acts of reaching out? Sometimes I think the latter is true, though I still pray. Often, well-intentioned words are all you have to give.

At my villa, placed across an unpaved side street from a sprawling rice paddy, a friendly Balinese hostess showed me to my bungalow. A light tropical rain was falling, followed by a strong rain, followed by a humidity-tinged sunset which I snapped with my phone camera and posted on Instagram. My daughter in the United States immediately saw it and gave me a like. As I set my luggage down in a corner, suddenly there was a loud sound. I thought I had activated a smoke alarm, though it turned out to be a giant gecko, bellowing after entering the bungalow through an open area in the bathroom. Later, when I mentioned this to the hostess, she said, "He think he own the place, sorry." Well, I guess he has as much right to be there as I have, I thought. Then, each day when I returned from my conference in Denpasar, I noticed a single pellet in the middle of the bed, so apparently the gecko felt the same way.

The conference was held a few miles away at Udayana University. Well-attended and enjoying the positive Balinese vibe, keynote presentations were made in an auditorium before the large audience dispersed into smaller classrooms for short papers and discussions. By the time my moment arrived, my paper printout had soaked up so much humidity the paper itself felt like damp cloth. I could have used it as a rag to wipe off windows dripping with moisture. The conference itself had brought together researchers from emerging fields of cultural and indigenous psychology, so my thoughts on psychological processes within fan communities seemed a reasonable fit. There were many engaging papers exploring the unusual ways human beings understand themselves according to the unique cultures they inhabit. If one overarching theme emerged, it was a recognition that psychological theories of belonging, participating, socializing, consuming, and living were not universal, and each culture had to be appreciated on its own terms and by its own dictates.

Years later, I'm thinking that prayer, too, cannot be appreciated through universal theories, themes, or contexts. It may be that *prayer* is too broad a concept and that *prayers*, plural, emanating from whichever situated platforms they are offered, is the only reasonable mode of appreciation. Praise the plurality, suspect the singularity.

Conference evenings were equally illuminating as participants enjoyed exotic Indonesian delicacies, and activities such as the *wayang* shadow puppets, with their visual depictions of balance between right and left, east and west, male and female, and perhaps a host of other symbolic binaries.

The rest of the week was spent traveling around the island, visiting art galleries, admiring sunsets, hiking through the Sacred Monkey Forest Sanctuary in the town of Ubud, and learning about Balinese Hinduism from new friends with whom I still keep in touch through social networking. No one knows exactly how and when the Hindu religion arrived from India, or why Bali is Hindu while the rest of Indonesia is Muslim, or even why Balinese Hindus retain some Indian beliefs but have evolved their own localized theology. They respect traditional Hindu gods such as Vishnu, Siva, Shakti, and Brahma, for instance, but they are also monotheistic, worshipping one supreme being who has many manifestations, including gods associated with nature, the cultivation of rice, and the sea. As with the wayang shadow puppets, they seem predisposed toward achieving balance in faith and living.

When Elizabeth Gilbert emphasized her need for balance in her best-selling book, *Eat Pray Love*, she chose the perfect place, Bali, through which to see this elusive concept play out in her own life. "To lose balance sometimes for love is part of living a balanced life," she wrote, emphasizing the risk-reward nature of giving yourself to another person and receiving the reward of healthy life balance in return. Perhaps William James, a favorite of mine, had something similar in mind when he separated healthy-minded religion from sick-soul religion in his classic, *The Varieties of Religious Experience*. Balance produces health of mind, grows out of it, or likely acts as both giver and receiver of healthy mind attributes, even as it encompasses spiritual strength and the equality of internal and external realities in our lives. The following prayer from the archives of Xavier University, attributed to the Hindu spiritual teacher, Sivananda Saraswati, may help to illustrate these virtues:

> O Adorable Lord of Mercy and Love!
> Salutations and prostrations unto Thee.
> Thou art Omnipresent, Omnipotent and Omniscient.
> Thou art Satchidananda (Existence-Consciousness-Bliss Absolute).
> Thou art the Indweller of all beings.
>
> Grant us an understanding heart,
> Equal vision, balanced mind,
> Faith, devotion and wisdom.

Grant us inner spiritual strength
To resist temptations and to control the mind.
Free us from egoism, lust, greed, hatred, anger and jealousy.
Fill our hearts with divine virtues.

Let us behold Thee in all those names and forms.
Let us serve Thee in all these names and forms.
Let us ever remember Thee.
Let us ever sing Thy glories.
Let Thy Name be ever on our lips.
Let us abide in Thee for ever and ever.

Chapter 13

One Thumb Up?

"Lord, let us empty of all doctrines."
- A TAOIST PRAYER -
SUN MOON LAKE, TAIWAN

BALI HAD BEEN A CHRISTMAS recess trip funded by my university in California for the purpose of presenting a paper. Two years earlier, a grant from the National University of Taiwan allowed me to participate in its annual Global Initiatives Forum, exploring innovations in business around the world. My topic, "Raving Fans Revisited," looked into the validity of visualizing consumers as fans in order to provide goods and services to changing product audiences in every stratum of society.

After the week of meetings had ended, two friends and I hopped into a rented van and headed south toward Sun Moon Lake in the heart of central Taiwan. Under a blazing July sun, we stopped in villages along the way, stepping into Buddhist temples for relief from the heat.

People were always praying.

On their knees, hands and fingers together chest-high, and amid the aroma of incense, they prayed long, meditative prayers. The quietness of the temples provided welcome relief from noisy marketplaces, even as the incense blunted the stinky tofu smells from vendors outside.

We canoed near the shoreline of Sun Moon Lake and walked through a settlement peopled by the Thao, one of Taiwan's indigenous nations. A pagoda built by Taiwan's Buddhist-turned-Methodist leader, Chiang Kai-shek, in memory of his mother, was also on our itinerary, as were more temples, reliefs, sculptures, and landmarks. The large blue-green lake itself had once been named Lake Candidius after a Dutch missionary, Georgius Candidius, back when the nations of western Europe were each trying to carve out pieces of Asia for themselves. First came trade, followed shortly after by politics and faith. And western names imposed on local places were often dropped in favor of traditional designations, or in the case of Sun Moon Lake, a descriptive moniker owing to the fact that the east side of the lake bears some resemblance to a sun while the west side, some say, looks like a moon.

In one of the temples near the lake, a green and gold image presumed to depict the ancient Chinese sage, Confucius, and the even more ancient founder of Taoism, Lao Tzu, exists. Both figures occupy a special place in my Asia-influenced mind.

For twenty years, 1996–2016, I opened a course on communication ethics with insights from these wise sages. They were easy to teach, easy to make relevant to the lives of students seeking some kind of ethical structure for their future careers. Confucius emphasized seeing ourselves as members of a group, rather than focusing on ourselves as individuals. The *we* of life is more important than the *me* of life. Free to recognize the nobility of persons in a group context, looking at all sides of any issue, using precise language to articulate thoughts, and mixing with others as often as one recedes to his or her own private world, were touchstones for lively discussions of balance and moderation. Doing anything for shameful self-promotion or attacking the character of others was another. When our Confucian unit ended, students always gave him two thumbs up, as they did when we studied Aristotle.

Lao Tzu was another story, usually evoking only one slow thumb up, similar to the way students responded to Plato. This was better, however, than the two-thumbs down responses given to Niccolo Machiavelli, Ayn Rand, and others in our course, for the perception of self-centered thought and action, though I always hoped Lao Tzu would receive greater affirmation. Students had difficulty with his extreme mysticism which emphasized achievement through inaction and the emptying of all personal desires. "That's just weird," I remember one student saying, "and how am I supposed to do anything by sitting back and doing nothing, and living without wanting anything. It's illogical and makes no sense."

But perhaps Lao Tzu was getting at something larger with which to frame our thinking, I often said. I then told the story of a meeting that took place between Lao Tzu and Confucius, as mentioned in the book,

Three Ways of Thought in Ancient China, which had been published by Arthur Waley in the 1930s. Confucius, full of theories and ideas he believed were air-tight, wanted very much to have his material accepted for publication by the Royal House of Chou Library. In his work, he spoke of being a good person, being noble, showing acts of kindness and respect to others, and abiding by discipline and duty to be a person of action at all times. He had acquired many followers by that time, and one of them urged him to contact Lao Tzu before presenting his work for publication.

So, Confucius did as his follower suggested. He went to the older, wiser Lao Tzu, who was as much as 50-plus years his senior. Lao Tzu listened carefully, and after a significant amount of time had passed, he admonished Confucius for emphasizing codes of conduct and dutiful moral acts, saying those were the very things that would destroy the hearer's sense of tranquility. He called them *perpetual pinpricks* that served only to irritate people who heard them as superficial rights and wrongs, detached from inner spirituality which was the real source of power. "'If you indeed want the men of the world not to lose the qualities that are natural to them,'" said Lao Tzu, by way of Arthur Waley, "'you had best study how it is that Heaven and Earth maintain their eternal course, that the sun and moon maintain their light, the stars their serried ranks, the birds and beasts their flock, the trees and shrubs their station. Thus, you too shall learn to guide your steps by Inward Power.'"

You don't improve yourself or anyone else by studying codes of ethics, I often said to the class. Jesus said, "You must be born again" (John 3:7, NIV) before you can even approach authentic resolutions on how to live. Change starts from within. Perhaps, we don't really know these truths until we are older, I concluded, at least for many people. This was probably not the best way to end a discussion with university students, as a second vote usually produced the same results: two thumbs up for Confucius, one for Lao Tzu. But maybe an impression had been made.

At Sun Moon Lake, while canoeing on clear water under the sun's glare with my conference cohorts, I told this story to Esther, a judge from San Francisco traveling with her daughter. She related to it, she said, and wouldn't it be fun to meet up in the Holy Land at some future time for more conversations on the teachings of Christ. Yes, I look forward to it, I said, though right at this moment I'd like to think a little more about Taoism's path to knowledge and truth.

A prayer from Lao Tzu:

Lord, let us empty of all doctrines,
The Tao is wisdom eternally inexhaustible.
Fathomless is the mere intellect,
The Tao is the law wherewith all things come into being.

It blunts the edges of the intellect,
Untangles the knots of the mind,
Softens the glare of thinking,
And settles the dust of thought.

Transparent yet invisible,
The Tao exists like deep pellucid water.
Its origin is unknown,
For it existed before Heaven and Earth.

Chapter 14

Vulnerable Sojourners

"A life has ended with the passing of a friend. . . ."
- A SHINTO PRAYER -
HIMEJI CASTLE, JAPAN

The final prayer in this part of the book is a Shinto meditation on a friend who has died, leaving those left behind with memories, images, silence, and the recognition of a loved one's journey well-traveled. The place is Himeji, Japan, which I visited with a Japanese friend in May 2005 while in the throes of divorce from my first wife. Divorce is itself a kind of death. The day it becomes final is the one day of your life that has *best* and *worst* written all over it. Your sudden freedom from pain, and the joy of getting your life back, is also a recognition of finality and failure, and when it happens you don't really know how to make sense of it, much less wanting to talk about it.

Thus, in a fog of vulnerability and silence, I met Akiko while walking along a main street in Edinburgh. I was looking for a wine-tasting put on by friends from the university. Akiko was on her way home. As she passed by, I asked her if she knew where a certain side street was located. She couldn't tell me, but we had a short conversation before parting ways, and I watched her walk away under a waning spring sun. Days later, I saw her again from a distance in a shopping mall south of the city, and still one more time on a bus headed toward the university. We both exited the rickety double-decker in front of Edinburgh's Old College, had another conversation, and that is when we decided to become friends.

At a Mongolian restaurant later that week, we talked about almost everything over a four-hour meal, which would have gone longer if the restaurant hadn't closed for the night. A deeply interesting woman of humble mannerisms and quiet intelligence, Akiko talked about her life as a student of languages. She taught Japanese part-time in Edinburgh and had purchased a small flat in the city. As one topic blended into another, she spoke a little about her own divorce years earlier, then a lot about her mother who had passed away recently in Japan. Her eyes grew heavy with tears as she recalled times with her as a child, and also with her father who had died many years before. The three of them had a favorite holiday cottage near the sea in Japan. I determined to find a painting of a similar scene for her, which I did in the days ahead.

After spring and summer in Edinburgh, I returned first to Minnesota, then to California for a teaching job, and we began to exchange visits, culminating in the 2005 trip to Japan. We met at an airport in Tokyo, then fanned out across the country by rail and road, visiting Kyoto, Kobe, Nara, and Akiko's hometown, Himeji, before returning to Tokyo for a few weeks. We pet deer in a park, hiked a path through a bamboo forest, attended a baseball game, had drinks in a hotel lounge above Tokyo—the same lounge from *Lost in Translation,* starring Bill Murray and Scarlett Johansson—and enjoyed many noodle dishes, bowls of miso soup, and okonomiyaki, the savory Japanese pancake, accompanied by periodic green tea and red bean ice cream flights.

Spirited Away was Akiko's favorite animated Japanese film, so we rented a copy and watched it one evening. It seemed to me a combination of *The Wizard of Oz* and *Alice in Wonderland* with a bit of Disney's Magic Kingdom thrown in, I said, respectfully. Akiko responded by saying that it was purely Japanese as anything with its Shinto-Buddhist themes incorporated into an animated narrative. Truthfully, I knew nothing about Shinto, and not all that much about Buddhism, I said, but that I would like to learn more about each faith at some point. Then, I might better understand places like the Heian Shrine, I said, a Shinto palace with a big red entrance gate we had visited in Kyoto. Crowds of school children in uniform had been a delightful sight there, though they kept us from learning much about what we were seeing that day.

My knowledge of Japan up to that point in 2005 had been conditioned mostly by the novels of Shusaku Endo, the Japanese-Catholic writer whose stories were primarily Christian in their theology. Endo's books, especially *The Samurai, Deep River,* and his universally-acclaimed masterpiece, *Silence,* while brilliant, had left me with an indelible sense of my own Christian faith entering and leaving Japan without ever understanding the country itself. I have tried to rectify that situation through reading, though my knowledge is still that of a beginner. My faith, however, continually pushes me to investigate other places and faiths when possible.

Shinto, it can be said, is Japan's indigenous religion, though some scholars say its calculus of beliefs and ritual practices makes it too complex to be understood so simplistically. Nevertheless, it seems to have four key emphases: family, love of nature, bathing and purity, and worship. A polytheistic faith predating Christianity by at least a few centuries, Shintoists worship *kami,* the many gods and spirits believed to inhabit all things living and inanimate. Dead people, in fact, are sometimes worshipped as kami. Somewhere in Japan's history, Shinto merged with Buddhist influences, though the two faiths did not necessarily create a perfect marriage, as Buddhism teaches transcendence from the earthly state through suffering while Shinto is more concerned with practical aspects of daily life. Creativity is also built into Shinto through its operative principle known as *mitsubi.*

Shinto prayers, my main interest here, are said to be based on practical requests such as seeking rain for crops, purification for good health, and protection from things that might cause physical harm. Death may be seen as dark and negative by Shintoists, though it is perhaps the Buddhist influences on Shinto that cause it to take death seriously and not to avoid it as a topic for reflection and meditation. *Ema* prayers are best described as wishes written on small plaques of wood and hung at the many Shinto shrines throughout Japan. They are similar to Buddhist notes on paper hung on prayer walls of Buddhist temples, and not unlike the tiny prayer scraps of Jewish worshippers tossed into crevices of the Wailing Wall in Jerusalem. Akiko said that sometimes the *ema* are burned in a ceremony, and the smoke that rises is seen symbolically as wishes set free into the world.

We spent an afternoon at Himeji Castle, wandering through its rooms of smooth wood and stone. Built in 1333 and expanded in later centuries, its bright terraced construction is said to be the best example of castle architecture in Japan. When much of the country was firebombed by the United States in World War II, the castle, which would have gone up like a bonfire, was miraculously spared. Some Himeji residents say that was proof of the castle being divinely protected. Akiko's aged Aunt

Myoko said as much when we visited her after leaving the castle. She opened an album of black and white photographs that showed the city in ashes but the castle standing untouched. She also remembered running under small bridges with her friends for protection from the bombing raids. No one can know what it was like then, she said.

The exact point Akiko and I decided we weren't right for each other, I cannot say. We'd had a few years of friendship, romance, travel, and the sort of camaraderie two bruised sojourners needed at vulnerable times in our lives. To this day, she remains the passing friend I hold in prayerful remembrance.

The following Shinto prayer, from the prayer data base at Prayers.co.uk, is about someone who has died and yet lives on in the memories of a survivor left behind. But it is relevant here because people don't have to die to be remembered favorably. They only have to have lived and known you before passing out of your life to some other place.

> A life has ended with the passing of a friend,
> the memories of times have come to an end,
> their threads were the fabric of an earlier day.
>
> A life has ended with the passing of a friend,
> sunrises and sunsets, bright days and dark nights,
> circled again and again, and gave context to this life,
> moment after moment, their life was lived each day.
>
> A life has ended with the passing of a friend,
> lives have been touched by the dear one's journey,
> laughter, tears, hopes, fears, a life has come to an end,
> memories hold their spirit alive, in my own life.
>
> A life has ended with the passing of a friend,
> the loss of future moments, that will not be,
> grateful for moments shared, that nourished me,
> moments lived, in casual belief, they would never end.
>
> A part of me has ended, with the passing of a friend,
> be they gone from the earthly plane, their spirit soars,
> to renew again, in summer land, heaven or another life,
> I know not where, but their love remains with me,
> for in this life, we friends, did share.

I miss my friend, but they will always be near,
inside of me, inside you, and all who took time to hear,
the music of this life so dear, a life now silent,
living only in the memory, of those who survive.

PART THREE

Chapter 15

Around Almodovar

"Circle me, Lord."
- A CELTIC PRAYER -
ALMODOVAR, PORTUGAL

WE'RE GETTING ON TOWARD CHRISTMAS in Portugal. A cold, early morning haze blankets the city of Lisbon. Outside, one of our eleven cats is ready for breakfast, her feeble meowing distinguishable only between the sounds of a crowing rooster from a neighbor's yard. I drop some food in a dish outside the back door and reenter the house to escape the morning chill.

Downstairs, Rissy is still asleep. I quietly tiptoe upstairs and put on *A Celtic Christmas* in CD format, which I have played since acquiring it more than twenty years ago. It still spins well. The music itself is not very Christmassy, but it is very Celtic, inasmuch as I know anything about Celtic music. I imagine that I'm hearing flutes made from bone, a *carnyx* horn, some *crwths* (Celtic lyres, like u-shaped harps), and possibly some *crotales* (Celtic hand bells), but I can't be sure.

Track 5 is a lovely tune, *Ciara*, by the Irish folk musician Luka Bloom. Track 9, *Galician Carol* by Carlos Nunez brings a spirited, *ceilidh*-like instrumental into the mix, reflective of music native to Galicia, the square of land just north of Portugal's Douro River, in what is now northwestern Spain. Both sides of the Douro are historically Celtic as is much of the Iberian Peninsula, though we associate the Celts more with lands farther north, in France and mostly in England, Scotland, Wales, and the Irelands.

Last year, Rissy and I headed down to the village of Almodovar in south central Portugal. Almodovar comes from *al-Mudawwar*, Arabic for "place in the round," and traces its existence to Muslim Portugal. There isn't much to see or do there. It's not ugly, but with hundreds of other places to visit in the country, no one is going to spend much destination time there. A few houses, a pastelaria, some commercial buildings, and at least one restaurant can be visited, though you'd be better off taking the hilly drive down to Loule in the Algarve for a good meal. We recommend the African-Portuguese restaurant, Angolana.

Almodovar, however, has one important reason for traveling there, especially if you like history and most especially if you're interested in the Celts: the *Museu da Escrita do Sudoeste* (Museum of Southwest Writing).

I learned about the museum from reading *The Celts: Search for a Civilization* by Alice Roberts. In her readable popular history, Roberts spends a good forty pages speculating on where the Celts originated, suggesting against decades of accepted scholarship that they may have been a people of the Atlantic Oceanic fringe rather than a tribe from central Europe who eventually moved west. Her evidence includes *stelae*, upright stone slabs housed at the museum, which feature Tartessian script, possibly the oldest Celtic or pre-Celtic language. We've always thought of the Celts as a collection of ethnic groups spread between Turkey in the east, Spain and Portugal in the south and west, the British Isles in the north, and Germany, France, and northern Italy in between. This newer Atlantic seaboard theory, supported at least in part by Oxford archaeologist Barry Cunliffe, theorizes an origin point during the Atlantic Bronze Age and possibly somewhere around present-day Almodovar.

In any case, the Celts are always fun to read about and rewarding to integrate into how one thinks about their own faith experience. One Celtic prayer inscribed on Gaelic runes flows like an eternal, elemental current: "Deep peace of the running wave to you. Deep peace of the flowing air to you. Deep peace of the quiet earth to you. Deep peace of the shining stars to you. Deep peace of the infinite peace to you."

Their well-documented polytheistic religion tells an engaging narrative of gods and goddesses, druids who were part priest and part intellect, shrines built on hills near lakes and within lush groves of trees, and a kind of gender equality not present in patriarchal societies. Purist Celt enthusiasts lament their Christianization under Roman-Christian rule and the theological compromises they had to make when forced by the fifth-century missionary, St. Patrick, to become monotheistic. Patrick becomes the muscular evangelist fighting with druids, overthrowing pagan idols, and cursing Celtic royalty on the way toward the emergence of Celtic Christianity.

But the revised calculus of faith elements growing out of centuries-old Celtic Christian revivalism is, in its own way, tonic to the soul. A less-authoritarian church, kinder to women, more connected to nature, comfortable with pre-Christian history, and fused with ancient spirituality, raise the experience of faith to a freer, non-orthodox plane. Even within my generously accommodating Church of Scotland, one can feel suffocated by doctrines and structures that inhibit free breathing space. As an old friend from India once said to me, "I'm always okay with the teachings of Jesus, but when things turn doctrinaire I lose interest fast."

My wife, Rissy, and I chose Celtic wedding bands, which we found in Edinburgh after an exhaustive search, to symbolize our eternal commitment to each other in Christ. The bands are of simple silver, decorated with an interlocking mesh of Celtic braiding over a deep green enamel, pressure-treated into the base of the rings. They are beautiful, and we both feel incomplete without them. They're as spiritually romantic as the famous Celtic cross: the cross of Christ with a nimbus circling the four intersecting points, an image said to symbolize the celestial sphere, thereby universalizing the central image of Christianity.

As we left the "place in the round," Almodovar, that day, we drove back to Lisbon musing over the circle we form around the communion table at our church when we celebrate the Eucharist. The locum minister breaks a loaf of bread and sends it out into the circle where we all take a small piece into ourselves in remembrance of Christ's body. A large goblet of wine then circles the group of parishioners, each person taking a small sip in remembrance of Christ's blood shed for the human race. Where would we be without circles, rings, bread, wine, and all things that ground our faith in ritual practice, we wondered. It's a kind of poetry we live by, not unlike the following Celtic Christian prayer from the *Carmina Gadelica*, the Gaelic collection of prayers and hymns from the 19th Century:

> Circle me, Lord.
> Keep protection near
> And danger afar.
> Circle me, Lord.

Keep hope within.
Keep doubt without.
Circle me, Lord.
Keep light near
And darkness afar.
Circle me, Lord.
Keep peace within.
Keep evil out.

Chapter 16

Temple of Forest and Stream

"Through the open finger spaces of the hand that all things fashioned."

- A FINNISH PRAYER -
HELSINKI, FINLAND

SIMILAR TO HOW CHRISTIANITY'S ONE-GOD concept infiltrated Celtic polytheism, so the ancient mythical concept of Ukko in Finland became conflated with the God of the Bible, probably during the 11th Century CE. Until that time, Ukko was likely considered to be the most highly regarded god of many, like Zeus in Greece, Jupiter in Rome, Indra in ancient India, and Thor, the god of ancient Norse mythology.

Natural phenomena occurred in ancient Finland "by the grace of Ukko mighty," as this chapter's prayer offers. Sky, clouds, weather, wind, lightning, and thunder, were all cause-and-effect experiences relevant to Ukko's existence beyond the realm of human activity. Indeed, thunderstorms were believed to occur when Ukko was having sex with his wife, or possibly when he drove his chariot across the skies. There was an annual festival, too, the Vakkajuhlat, celebrating Ukko each May during the season of planting, though it faded away sometime in the early twentieth century.

There were mentions of Ukko at the conference, *Imagined Worlds - Worldmaking in Arts and Literature*, which I attended in Helsinki in late summer, 2013. Presentations such as *Love in a World of Dreams*, *Doorways as Conduits to the Divine Realm*, or my own, *A Fan Culture's*

Make-Believe World During a Time of Public Crisis, explored various aspects of what sometimes is called *cognitive narratology,* the science of understanding what happens in the mind when storytelling impacts how we think, feel, and live. I enjoyed it immensely, though I have to confess that what I most remember about these events is the food. Our conference dinner of lime-marinated shrimp, thyme potato cakes, beetroot steak, creamy smashed spinach, and fresh herb couscous, still evokes tastebud memories.

Our time in pre-autumnal Helsinki, under slate gray skies, also included a rector's reception at the University of Helsinki, a Helsinki city government reception, and a visit to the Uspenski Orthodox Cathedral perched on smooth gray rock supporting its red exterior beneath seagreen roofs and gleaming white crosses. Best of all were the misty walks through sheep pastures and local forests, which effectively offset the sterile hallways and classrooms at the university. Finns have shown that they are among the best in the world at education and lifestyle simplicity based on living enveloped within the natural world.

My favorite statement from Katja Pantzar's common-sense memoir, *Finding Sisu: In Search of Courage, Strength and Happiness the Finnish Way,* is this: "For Finns, the forest is akin to a church or temple."

Pantzar, who now lives in Helsinki, was a Canadian journalist who returned to her Finnish roots out of desperation. She had material prosperity and some degree of career satisfaction, but those things weren't enough to counter the depression caused by living without greater purpose, enveloped within the emptiness of city life deprived of nature and wholeness. "I lacked little," Pantzar writes. "Yet, I often felt utterly empty inside." It's a familiar story of opposing envelopments: urban sterility versus pastoral fertility, civic lostness versus agrarian foundness, and so forth. Pantzar, moreover, took control of her life and watched her serotonin rise, not through antidepressants but through ritual practices in the temple of forest and stream. Her new rituals included cold-water swimming, healthful meals and eating times, anti-dieting, sleeping long and well, and *greencare,* which she defines as "forest therapy or nature therapy . . . the power of nature to provide an antidote to the stresses of modern life."

A similar story is that of Jennifer Furner, a self-described atheist and guest writer for the *Huffington Post* newspaper. In her story, "I'm Not 'Blessed,' I'm an Atheist and I Don't Need God to Give Thanks or Show Gratitude," Furner writes about ritualizing nature apart from any traditional concepts of God or faith. She no longer values the symbols of accepted belief systems and doesn't use the word "blessed." But she is still grateful, and she contends that eliminating God from her life has given her more space for other people and, more importantly for her, a way of seeing how her actions impact the world around her. When she walks through nature across her Michigan landscape, she is reverent, writing, "I do fall to my knees, but instead of folding my hands, I plant them on the earth, then allow my forehead to follow. I hug the ground, and instead of sending my prayers up to heaven, I whisper them into the grass."

Nature ritualists like Furner and Pantzar have much of value to say, though sometimes one wonders why belief in the natural world has to mean cancelling out all traditional faith approaches. On his deathbed, Henry David Thoreau was said to have been asked what Christ meant to him, to which he replied that a snowstorm had more meaning.

Nevertheless, whispers into the grass, or into a cold-water stream, or into a snowstorm, are beautiful, like the following Finnish *Prayer to the Sower*:

> Blessing to the seed I scatter,
> Where it falls upon the meadow,
> By the grace of Ukko mighty,
> Through the open finger spaces
> Of the hand that all things fashioned.
> Queen of meadowland and pasture!
> Bid the earth unlock her treasures,
> Bid the soil the young seed nourish,
> Never shall their teeming forces,
> Never shall their strength prolific
> Fail to nourish and sustain us
> If the Daughters of Creation,
> They, the free and bounteous givers,
> Still extend their gracious favor,
> Offer still their strong protection.
> Rise, O Earth! From out their slumbers,
> Bid the soil unlock her treasures!

Chapter 17

Nature's Missionary

"Praise be to you, my Lord, though our sister, Mother Earth."
- A FRANCISCAN PRAYER -
MONTEVERDE, COSTA RICA

I DIDN'T THINK THE WIND would ever stop.
Even though it was the tropical cloud forest of Costa Rica, the wind, especially at night, rattled the windows and roof of the hostel so violently, it sounded like a fierce blizzard outside. Everyone was inside on painted benches at plywood tables, drinking coffee.

The weeks before traveling up the muddy road to the town of Monteverde had been spent mostly in and around San Jose. A winter chillax at the Don Carlos Hotel was the hub for some academic work at the University of Costa Rica and The University for Peace. It was February, I was on sabbatical, and this was my second trip to the compact country placed geographically between Panama on the south, Nicaragua to the north.

When work was finished there was plenty of time to visit coffee plantations, the town of Sarchi where painted oxcarts had caught my fancy, and to take a road trip with Paul, a missionary from the Latin America Mission in Miami.

Traveling north out of San Jose, we had noticed street people, many of them, a realistic counterweight to Costa Rica's otherwise image as Latin America's model nation. "You see these people and wonder how they became homeless," said Paul. "My wife, Ruth, and I have people we are giving to—people in ministry to the poor and people who are just poor. There are so many who need help."

Under a partly cloudy sky, we were on our way to Paul's house, twelve miles north of San Jose, where we would have breakfast with Ruth, then head east to the Atlantic port town of Limon. The three-hour trip would be good for conversation.

The sky had clouded over by the time we reached the house. A mist was falling, and Paul mentioned that the dry season hadn't yet visited the Central Valley. Rainfall was up everywhere. And wind, lots of wind.

The house sat several yards up the road, resting on a small hill overlooking a village. Ruth greeted us at the door. With the smell of brewing coffee permeating the house, my eyes scanned a colorful Amerindian interior. Paul's upright piano stood against one wall, the other walls featuring gallery-quality paintings by two of their four children: the porch of a country home by a daughter, a rainforest waterfall by a son. Another son, also an artist, had picked up an ornate stained-glass lamp in Mexico that now hung over the dining room table. Paquita, the family dog, wagged her tail.

"Do you drink coffee?" Ruth asked, remarking that years before in Mexico City young women she was mentoring would ask her to mix chocolate and cinnamon into the coffee before they would drink it. Over coffee and baked goods, I found myself jotting down some of Ruth's thoughts for a magazine article I had been working on: "We're not here to make evangelicals." "We're here to help people become genuine believers in God." "It's a beautiful experience as a Christian just to be a good neighbor."

She spoke of growing up in New England where she had been raised Episcopalian but later found herself in a rigidly conservative church that became a source of financial support in the early days of her missionary work. Then one day the church withdrew its assistance because of Ruth's "broad-minded outlook" and her habit of associating with "all kinds of people." Questioned rigorously by a male church board before being cut off, Ruth said, "We want you to understand that we're not here to turn people into clones, and we will follow God's leading wherever and to whomever that leading takes us. That means any group of people that wants to know about God's love. Anyone. Two weeks later a letter arrived saying, 'We're sorry that we can no longer support you.' Funny, but we never had money problems again," Ruth laughed.

After breakfast Paul and I said goodbye to Ruth and Paquita and were on the road again. While heading toward an ominous eastern sky, I listened to Paul describe missionaries he had known. One was a completely unstructured young man, highly educated, "free as the wind," whose peculiar form of genius was that he sojourned not by his own will but by forces of nature that moved him about. "He'd wind up at a bus station in some remote corner of the world, sit around talking to people, until someone would say that they'd heard of a church that needed a minister," Paul said. "He'd end up being that minister. Not exactly my style, but you need people like that."

A lot of missionaries burn out, Paul added. Some become corrupt, manipulative, psychologically unstable, and linked to political movements that do more harm than good. "A whole generation of university young people was lost here in Latin America due to missionaries preaching all kinds of foolishness," he said. "Be political, be a liberator, adopt Marxist theology, be this and be that and be the other thing, without ever just being a simple follower of Christ who reads the Bible and prays. And the result was atheism on a grand scale. Kids were left without anything to hold onto. When you saw these things affecting friends and family, it was tough."

Rain.

Water gushed out of steep cliffs that rose above the highway, and the rain striking the roof of our car was deafening.

"We're getting into banana country," Paul said, as we came into a clearing. Under the slanting rain he told me what he knew about Costa Rica's Caribbean coast: that the first missionaries to the country had come to Limon with African-Caribbean settlers; that the big regional employer, the United Fruit Company, had one day pulled out of Limon leaving the people without a security net; and that despite being one of Costa Rica's main ports, Limon Province received the least amount of help from the Costa Rican government. "A big problem here has been the use of herbicides and insecticides that have been banned in other places," Paul said. "There's been no control over how much gets sprayed on the banana plants. Now a whole generation of workers has become sterile because of these chemicals."

We arrived in Limon, passing through a depressed corridor of decaying houses built on stilts. To our left was a sprawling cemetery on hills with mossy monuments marking the graves of banana merchants from Limon's former prosperity. We passed storefront after storefront where young and old men sat in idleness. The blankness of their faces made them seem hopeless and adrift. North of town we got out of the car and walked among the shipping docks with the choppy, brown Caribbean Sea churning beyond. We ended up back in the center of town, dodging potholes and eventually stopping at a Chinese restaurant for lunch.

"Missionary work isn't what it used to be," said Paul.

"How so?" I asked.

"It's the world, probably. The world has changed. It's a world of megachurch entertainment, small churches that are closing from lack of interest, designer churches that do whatever, diffuse message currents everywhere, and everyone just kind of blowing in the wind, like the song."

"Ah, that's the beauty of it," I said half-jokingly. "Blame the wind."

After lunch we drove away from Limon and passed through the last of the rain on the way back to Paul's house. Shadows fell and we could see lights of the central valley coming into view. I dropped Paul off and drove back to San Jose, spending another night at the Don Carlos.

The following day I headed west in my rental car to Monteverde. Turning onto a potholed dirt road off the main highway, I drove through a muddy landscape and stopped at a small *soda* for gallo pinto and a coke. While sitting at my picnic table, reading about Monteverde in my overused *Lonely Planet,* I watched a family of toucans fly one-by-one from a tree to another tree. Monteverde itself was beautiful with its moss-cushioned hiking paths, sprawling ficus trees, frequent wildlife sightings, and intermittent showers followed by blankets of silvery sunshine, all gifts from the cloud forest bestowed upon anyone who goes there.

And in the years since that sabbatical, the prayer that comes most readily to mind is one commonly known as the *Canticle of the Creatures* by the Franciscan father, St. Francis of Assisi. Written toward the end of his life in the 1220s CE, Francis ritualized nature's beauty as few others before or since. He had been a persistent traveler through many corners in the world of his day, and I like to think he would have savored Monteverde had he been born in a different time. The natural world provided his constant companionship in God, from the celestial bodies all the way to the smallest created plants and animals ordained to accompany him through life.

He was never alone.

> Most High, all powerful, good Lord,
> yours are the praises, the glory, the honor and all blessing.
> To you alone, Most High, do they belong,

and no human is worthy to mention your name.
Praised be you, my Lord, with all your creatures,
especially Sir Brother Sun, who is the day and through whom you give us light.
And he is beautiful and radiant with great splendor;
and bears a likeness of you, Most High One.
Praised be you, my Lord, through Sister Moon and the Stars:
in heaven you formed them clear and precious and beautiful.

Praised be to you, my Lord, through Brother Wind;
and through the air, cloudy and serene, and every kind of weather,
through which you give sustenance to your creatures.

Praised be you, my Lord, through Sister Water,
who is very useful and humble and precise and chaste.

Praised be you, my Lord, through Brother Fire,
through whom you light the night:
and he is beautiful and playful and robust and strong.

Praised be you, my Lord, through our Sister, Mother Earth,
who sustains and governs us,
and who produces various fruit,
with colored flowers and herbs.

Praised be you, my Lord,
through those who give pardon for your love,
and bear infirmity and tribulation.

Blessed are those who endure in peace:
for by you, Most High, shall they be crowned.

Praised be you, my Lord, for our sister, Bodily Death,
from whom no one living can escape:
woe to those who die in mortal sin.

Blessed are those whom death will find in your most holy will,
for the second death will do them no harm.
Praise and bless, my Lord, and give him thanks,
and serve him with great humility.

Chapter 18

A COMPLEX CHORD

"This enticing, well-prepared food of a hundred flavors,
I offer with faith to the Victors and their sons."
- TWO BUDDHIST PRAYERS -
BLUE ELEPHANT COOKING SCHOOL
BANGKOK, THAILAND

THE FOLLOWING TIBETAN BUDDHIST PRAYER, and a Buddhist prayer of unknown origin from the archives of Xavier University, celebrate the preparation and partaking of good food. The place is the Blue Elephant Cooking School in Bangkok, Thailand, where I was taught how to cook good Thai: specifically crispy sea bass with red curry, young coconut soup, southern yellow beef curry, shrimp fried rice with carmelized chicken, and a few other delicacies. Regrettably, I have forgotten most of what I learned.

I had been sent to Bangkok by my university for the 5th International Conference on Language and Communication, a gathering that featured seminars on such topics as *IM/politeness in Japanese Twitter, Movie Mobile Branding in Malaysia, Language Variation in Bangladesh Media,* and *Data Journalism in Thailand.* Heads were spinning by the end of it, and one would rather have been in the hotel pool than swimming in information from more than a hundred presenters.

Thus, on the last day of the conference, I decided to de-word by heading off for some authentic Thai food. I had many choices. Scrolling through them ended when I tumbled on an ad posted by the Blue Elephant, which said you could dine and also take a culinary course on the same day. As Thai had been my forever favorite, the choice was easy, and I hailed a tuk-tuk to carry me through heavy traffic to the restaurant. Bangkok is a delightfully chaotic city of more than eight million, with another six million in the metro area, and even during the Christmas holidays it is a heat island floating within Thailand's tropical savanna climate. It is also the hub of southeast Asia's sex tourism industry, something one can hardly avoid when strolling through the central Phra Nakhan district where my hotel was located. Sex for sale, however, has to compete with culture even for the most debauched tourists, I was guessing, and many promising alternatives exist, such as sprawling night markets, street choirs, political rallies, religious gatherings, and of course, food. Much of the pre-cooked food comes from the many canal-networked floating markets where fresh produce is purchased from sellers on boats.

At the multilevel, yellow, veranda-adorned Blue Elephant, I arrived just as a new course was commencing, so I decided to defer my lunchtime appetite. If I was a quick learner, I would be able to eat my own creations, said the lady who collected tuition fees. I wondered about this, but maybe it was worth a try.

The instructing chef seemed thirty-something or younger and stood in white under two large video screens which allowed students to see his activities both at eye level and from overhead. Before falling to work, his comprehensive lecture included mentions of Thai cuisine as intricate, detailed, full of taste and texture, and with many colors. Musically, some people liken it to a complex chord, like a thirteenth or a flattened tenth on guitar with some suspended chords to offset the main one. The influences of other national cuisines, mainly Chinese but also Japanese, Indonesian, Indian, and Portuguese, were also present in the methods of cooking and in the ingredients. A long list given to each student included ginger, turmeric, basil, garlic, coriander (which I imagined came from the 16th Century Portuguese expansion into Asia), spearmint, lemongrass, shallots, bamboo shoots, bok choy, mustard greens, coconut, cucumbers, and bean sprouts; plus, innumerable oils, starches, herbs, spices, pastes, sauces, roots, fungi, algae, and of course, popular meats, fish, fruits, nuts, and vegetables.

Many Thai dishes are included among the world's greatest foods, the chef continued, and today we're going to focus mainly on *gaeng* (curry) dishes and *yam* (spiciness). He cooked all the day's dishes, explaining each step carefully, and next we were led into a large kitchen, where each student was given a wok, an attendant, and a large rectangular pan of ingredients contained in small glass bowls. Slowly, each dish was created through trial and error, and the attendants made sure we didn't screw things up too badly. A couple of hours later when all cooking was finished, we were told we could dine on our own creations in the restaurant or have them packaged up for takeaway. I chose takeaway.

Back at the hotel and by now ravenous, I placed my dishes on a table and began to eat. Sometimes we surprise ourselves. Sometimes we get lucky. It was good. It was better than good, as flavorful as anything from President Thai, my go-to Thai restaurant in Pasadena, California. I was in foodie heaven.

There is a holiness in savoring a good meal, and when you have one to enjoy, solitarily or with company, it is natural to express thankfulness through prayer or at least a prayerful attitude. Mark Twain once wrote that we naturally look upward in thankfulness when romantic love finds us. The same can be said for a satisfying dining experience and the simple enjoyment of good food. Perhaps the saying of grace, as the prayer that accompanies a meal is known, emerged as much from the experience of eating as from the desire to thank a higher power.

In any case, every religion has its own tradition of saying grace, and usually there is a sacred text to support doing it. In Christianity we read in Luke 24:30 (NIV), "When [Jesus] was at the table with them, he took bread, gave thanks, broke it, and began to give it to them." Or in Acts 27: 35 (NIV) we see Paul, Christ's apostle, doing the same thing: "After he said this, he took some bread and gave thanks to God in front of them all. Then he broke it and began to eat."

When we look at grace-saying among the many Christian denominations, we see multitudinous variations on the same root theme, and prayers can be offered before the meal or after it. Incorporating either archaic or modern terminology into graces, Catholics pray about "gifts we are about to receive" before a meal and then thank God "for all thy benefits" afterwards. Eastern Orthodox Christians ask God to "bless the food and drink of thy servants" before eating and then thank God because, "Thou hast satisfied us with thine earthly gifts," after eating. Wesleyan Methodists speak of feasting "in fellowship with thee" before and asking God to apply "manna to our souls" after.

My mother, an educated woman of faith, had our family combining Anglican and Lutheran traditions. We prayed the Lutheran prayer, "Come

Lord Jesus be our guest, let these gifts to us be blessed," and then spliced in the Anglican moment of thanks for receiving "gifts for our use and us to thy service." Other traditions offer a grace-saying experience which intentionally avoids any set formula, in favor of an in-the-moment, conversational prayer linked to the day's happenings. The formulaic grace experience, however, applies a nice structure and meaningful repetition to daily life, even though some seem a little exclusive. The ancient *Selkirk Grace* I came across during my years in Scotland says, "Some hae meat and canna eat . . . but we hae meat and we can eat. Sae let the Lord be thankit."

In Judaism sometimes the meal blessing includes food categories such as fruits, grains, and most importantly, bread. It's not a formal meal unless bread is on the table, my paternal grandfather used to say, a comment likely conditioned by east European Jewry. He grew up on the shifting border between Poland and Ukraine. In Islam, this prayer is offered before a meal: "*Allahumma batik lana fima razaqtana waqina athaban-nar,*" which translated into English means, "O Allah, bless the food you have provided us, and save us from the punishment of hellfire." After the meal another prayer is offered: "*Alhamdulillah il-lathi at'amana wasaqana waja'a lana Muslimeen,*" meaning "Praise be to Allah who has fed us and given us drink, and made us Muslims."

The Bahai grace-saying tradition speaks of "heavenly food" sent from God along with a blessing," and in Hindu tradition grace-saying is often based on verses from the *Bhagavad Gita*. Chapter 15:14 says, "Becoming the life-fire in the bodies of living beings, mingling with the upward and downward breaths, I digest the four kinds of food." Another Hindu grace says, "Take the name of the Lord when putting a morsel into your mouth."

All of this brings us to Buddhist graces, as Thailand and its splendid food arise from within the cultural amalgam of Theravada Buddhism. At first glance the idea of this easily-savored cuisine would seem to contradict the teachings of all forms of Buddhism, which focus on being detached from worldly pleasures. The purpose is to find a balance between mind and body so as to eliminate the causes of personal suffering, and not feeding one's desires is key. Thus, many Buddhist monks, as the preservers of Buddhist teachings, for instance, do not cook but rather rely mainly on donated food from their local community. This food may well be enjoyed by them while not being sought, but its larger purpose is to facilitate communication with the community at large. It is, moreover, an object of non-attachment while at the same time accommodating the tastes and preferences of others. Enjoyment, flavors, satisfaction, fulfillment, gratefulness, and the recognition of all beings and their needs, are part of this picture.

A Buddhist prayer from Tibet acknowledges faith first, food second, as it appeals to the "unsurpassable teacher" before speaking of its "food of a hundred flavors":

> The unsurpassable Teacher is the precious Buddha,
> The unsurpassable protector is the precious holy Dharma,
> The unsurpassable guide is the precious Sangha,
> To the unsurpassable Three Jewels I make this offering.
>
> This enticing, well-prepared food of a hundred flavors,
> I offer with faith to the Victors and their sons,
> So that all wanderers may enjoy,
> The richness of the food of Samadhi.

And a Buddhist prayer of unknown authorship and origin is one I have come to associate lovingly with Thailand, its delicately prepared and balanced cuisine, and the free associations of mind and spirit as it is enjoyed:

> This food is the gift of the whole universe,
> Each morsel is a sacrifice of life,
> May I be worthy to receive it.
> May the energy in this food,
> Give me strength,
> To transform my unwholesome qualities
> into wholesome ones.
> I am grateful for this food,
> May I realize the Path of Awakening,
> For the sake of all beings.
>
> The joys and pains of all beings
> are present in the gift of this food.
> Let us receive it in love
> and gratitude.
> And in mindfulness of our sisters and brothers,
> among living beings of every kind,
> who are hungry or homeless,
> sick or injured,
> or suffering in any way.

Chapter 19

THE NECESSARY GODDESS

"Aphrodite, I pray to you, goddess, grant me your gift of love."
- A MEDITERRANEAN PRAYER -
PAPHOS, CYPRUS

BEFORE WORKING MY WAY TO the lovely "Prayer to Aphrodite to Bring Love into One's Life," and its accompanying location, the Mediterranean island of Cyprus, I want to revisit the mention of Mark Twain and his experience of romantic love alluded to in the previous chapter. Whether or not Twain is still relevant nearly two centuries after writing his way through the latter half of the 1800s is another discussion, as is the one about many of the male authors enshrined in the classic American literary canon. Nevertheless, here is a piece of Twain's life that seems worth recalling.

By most accounts Twain was a religious skeptic who leaned toward atheism in his writing and life. You don't have to look far in his books, journals, and personal letters to see the evidence. Free thinking and science were his heroes while selected biblical passages, church practices (such as its approval of slavery), and occasionally individual Christians evoked his scorn. He mostly stopped short of attacking Jesus, but Christ's followers received no such exemption. "If Christ were here," he once scribbled into a notebook, "there is one thing he would not be — a Christian." And in *The Mysterious Stranger*, he empathized with Satan, a misunderstood being, in his mind, who questioned God's wisdom and very existence for allowing human suffering on such a grand scale.

Twain, however, had a long career, and there were times when he softened suddenly into the mindset of a hopeful seeker. Occasionally, he had almost become a believer, he said, until that belief slowly drifted away. Toward the end of his travel narrative *The Innocents Abroad*, moreover, he wandered the streets of Jerusalem in a way that persuasively revealed a below-the-surface pilgrim moved by the history of faith in God and spiritual searching. And even more persuasive were his gushes of thankfulness and belief when romantic love touched him at age 35. The deeply religious Olivia Langdon, whom he referred to as his "incomparable wife" for the rest of his life, had agreed to marry him in 1870, and he would "turn" toward Christ as she had done before him.

But enough about Twain.

Probably for most people, the most tangible evidence for the existence of a higher power who cares about us occurs when we fall in love. Objectively, even the most logical, skeptical, and disbelieving individuals recognize glimpses of supernatural influence occurring behind the veil of temporal existence, calculated to place us together with "the right one." This is the work of a romantic God who loves us, cares for us, wants us to live safely and effectively, and delights in seeing us experience the warmth and sexual pleasure of a loving partnership; the same God of Psalm 18:19 (NIV) who leads "me to a place of safety and delights in me."

We're all characters in our own personal *When Harry Met Sally* movie, with each script varying only in the details of externally orchestrated events. My own script wasn't written until I was in my fifties and was placed together with my wife, Rissy. Both of us had gone through painful divorces, and broken rebound relationships, before we found ourselves in Greece, speaking at an Athens history conference. I noticed her immediately in a crowded lecture hall during the first few minutes of the conference and thought what a lovely woman I would give anything to meet. She was sitting a few rows in front of me, dressed in a copper-colored coat which brought out the copper highlights of her shoulder-length hair.

After it was my turn to speak, I saw her again, sitting alone at a large round table and realized this was my chance. But I hesitated. She won't want to meet me, I thought, and won't want to be hit on at a scholastic event which participants were supposed to take seriously, keeping it from turning into an academic meat market. Furthermore, she had to be either married or in a serious relationship, being as attractive as she is. So, I backed away and didn't see her for the duration of the conference, which

I left early to explore the historical sites of Athens. Days later, and with the conference now a memory, I boarded a passenger ferry destined for three islands off the Greek coast. And, of course, who was on the same boat? You guessed right. She was, though I still would never have seen her among the passengers unless Helena, her fellow conference participant, had approached me, mistakenly thinking I was someone she knew. Something, someone, a personal, verifiable force, had opened a door of fulfilled desire to the rest of my life, and Rissy and I now live happily, romantically, married in Portugal.

We spent that first day hopping on and off the boat, strolling through the ancient streets of villages on Aegina, Kythnos, and Poros, sampling cuisine, sipping Retsina, sharing stories, telling jokes, dodging memories, getting to know each other, and suddenly realizing we had a future ordained specifically for us.

In a timeless, effortless way, that first day has never ended, as we were ourselves two islands in an ocean of strangers, who had found our destiny together, alive and vibrant to this day.

Now, on to Aphrodite.

Much earlier, in 1983, I had boarded another boat, this time from Haifa, Israel to Limassol, Cyprus. Traveling with four companions from a summer archeological dig in Israel, we disembarked in Limassol on an early August morning.

We rented a car and sojourned through the Greek portion of Cyprus, which had been separated from the Turkish side since the 1974 war. Along sandy shores and through quaint villages; sleeping in mountain monasteries; eating one-course-at-a-time Cypriot dinners of quail, fried potatoes, and cucumber salads, in restaurants adorned with grapevines; drinking wine; visiting churches; and indulging in archeological sites with recently excavated mosaic floors; we ended up in Paphos, the Aegean center of Aphrodite worship. Paphos was also where Barnabas and Saul of Tarsus proclaimed the Word of God to Cypriot Jews living on the southern coast, leading to the conversion of the Roman proconsul, Sergius Paulus. And according to Acts 13:9, Paphos is where Saul changed his name to Paul in a likely symbolic gesture calculated to document his transformation from a Jewish zealot to a Gentile follower of Jesus Christ.

But the land and seascape surrounding Paphos really belong to Aphrodite. The sunshine and wind-caressed coast speak of her beauty.

As the Greek goddess of love, pleasure, and procreation, and a parallel to the Roman goddess, Venus, she stays alive across time through many generations of her pagan cult, also surfacing occasionally in art and literature. One such addition to her myth is Woody Allen's 1995 film, *Mighty Aphrodite*, about a gifted male child born to a prostitute, then adopted by an infertile couple. Inspired by *Pygmalian*, the George Bernard Shaw play about a mythic sculptor who falls in love with one of his sculptures which subsequently comes alive, Allen's film explores the life of a beautiful living symbol of sexual gratification who eventually becomes mother to the narrator's son even as he becomes father to her own child. As Greek chanting encapsulates the drama, many critical themes emerge: emotional versus physical love, women as property, the timeless search for mother, and, of course, the meanings of adultery.

While one might be tempted to criticize Aphrodite on modern Puritanical grounds, focusing on her endless affairs with both men and gods, the greater story of love and sexual pleasure being necessary for a happy life is what emerges triumphant and unconfined by time and superficial moral enquiry. She is about companionship, passion, the soul and spirit, innocence, experience, healing, casting away fear, seeing life romantically, and other themes echoing within the *Prayer to Aphrodite to Bring Love into One's Life*. From author Hester Butler-Ehle writing for greekpagan.com, we read,

> Tender-hearted Aphrodite, friend of the lonely,
> friend of those who seek a lover, a companion for life,
> a mate to share their sorrows and delights;
> Aphrodite, you touch the center of the soul,
> you light the flame of passion in men and women,
> you hold our hearts in your gentle hands.
> Goddess, fair one, kind one, giver of the most precious gifts,
> open my spirit to joy and gladness,
> open my mind to possibility,
> open my mind to love.
>
> Heal me of hurt, release me from fear;
> grant me the innocence of first love,
> that I may see the world in all its promise and beauty;
> grant me the wisdom of experience,
> that I may choose with sense and judgment.
>
> May my eyes be keen,
> may my vision be true,
> may I see more clearly than what may be.

Aphrodite, I pray to you, goddess,
grant me your gift of love.

Chapter 20

Truth Travel

"Send us rose-bodied good government and her sisters on gleaming thrones."

- AN ANCIENT GREEK PRAYER -
DELPHI, GREECE

WHILE STILL GLOWING IN GREECE from the first encounter with the woman who would become my wife, I wandered about Athens in a state of elevated dopamine. A steady rise in serotonin was sure to follow, I imagined. Rissy had returned to Portugal, where even in those first days of our relationship I determined I would join her as time and circumstance allowed, or even if they didn't. Screw the decades-long career as a professor, I thought, and I was equally ready to let my country of birth, the United States of America, slip away in favor of a new life of love in an old place of unfiltered existence. That life became reality as I was transformed into we, and we live day-to-day where the stones don't roll and every ruin tells a story.

Having a few remaining days in Athens after Rissy's departure, I decided to head north to Delphi and soak up some more history. My travel bible, *Lonely Planet*, had stated, "Of all the archaeological sites in Greece, ancient Delphi is the one with the most potent 'spirit of place.'" That phrase "spirit of place" drew out my inner pilgrim, and I followed the ever-rising highway, stopping periodically to gaze at the Valley of Phosis from the heights of Mount Parnassus. Blue mountains amid lots of winter green trees colored the view. Piercing December cold provided the sensory backdrop. Soon I was in the central part of the peninsula, not far from Corinth, Thebes, and Thermopylae, with all their church-school textbook lore, and with the Agaean Sea distantly off to the east, the Adriatic Sea to the west.

In Delphi itself the mood was one of silence.

I was told that same mood doesn't exist in summer, when the tour buses line up at the sites, and you're lucky to take a selfie without the pictorial background noise of tourists taking their own selfies.

So, essentially, I had the place to myself, including an airy stroll past the Temple of Apollo's peach-colored columns, the Theatre of Delphi in gray stone, the Athenian treasury on a hillside of deep green cedars beneath a powder-blue sky, the Athena Pronaia Sanctuary overgrown with thick grass, the Gymnasium, and the Stadium where up to sixty-five hundred spectators could live and die at the Pythian games. The Stadium held special interest for me as the previous week my role at the Athens conference had been to compare ancient spectators with modern sports fans. Linked by cathartic behaviors, I had suggested that it was possible to see modern fans as more capable of violence than ancient spectators because of unlimited opportunities for cathartic aggression via media. They just take out their explosive tendencies in different ways. A history scholar sitting in the front row was ready to clear me off the stage for the assertion.

Silence. Wind whistling through cedars. Inhaling the timeless spirituality of Zeus, Apollo, Plato, Homer, and perhaps most of all, Gaia, the mythical mother of all life, the Greek version of the mother earth goddess. Alone in the winter quietude of ancient Delphi, I thought, one could believe almost anything: any numinous in any form. Places such as Delphi and Jerusalem, Stratford on Avon and Walden Pond, Wrigley Field and Graceland, can do exactly that: make you believe.

Thomas F. Gieryn's book, *Truth Spots: How Places Make People Believe*, is the latest substantive contribution to this theme. His story begins in Delphi before moving on to an interesting personal canon consisting of America's Walden Pond, Sweden's Lapland, Spain's Santiago de Compostela, and other *truth* locations. Every truth spot has three ingredients, he argues: location, materiality in the form of natural or human-made objects, and narrative that inspires imagination. No constant pattern exists for how these components are employed, or for whom they produce a spiritual effect, but they are present in all universal sojourning. In Delphi, Gieryn confesses, he might not believe the god Apollo ever existed, but the Apollo narrative, combined with Delphi's material objects and the ancient city itself, is so strong as to remove his agnostic mindset. He believes.

"See how places make people believe?" Gieryn writes. "There sits Delphi, given meaning through stories connecting this sublime spot to Zeus and Gaia, with a location that separates its sacred activities from compromising politics, and consisting of human edifices that serve as a heartening scorecard of successful prophecies past."

Delphi has a high scorecard, indeed.

While meandering through the city's excellent museum I attempted to piece together a lay person's understanding of its history, which is a bad way to construct history but sometimes it's all you have. Dating back as far as 1700 BCE, Delphi may have been an early sanctuary of worship to the deity Gaia until it was destroyed by falling rocks from Mount Parnassus. By 1100 BCE, Apollo is enshrined. The next few centuries see Delphi grow in immense fame and spiritual authority throughout Greece, leading to a challenge by neighboring communities and what is known to historians as The First Sacred War in 595 BCE. As if to give religion a forty-year breather, 590–550 BCE, a construction boom commences, capped by the raising of a dozen treasuries plus the marvelous stadium suitable for holding games. The Temple to Apollo is then destroyed by fire in 548 BCE, and the next few hundred years, going all the way to 398 CE, sees a succession of catastrophes: two more sacred wars, an earthquake, a violent takeover by the Romans, a brief renaissance under the Roman emperor Hadrian, a public ban on pagan worship, and the destruction of the great city itself. Lost in antiquity, Delphi wasn't rediscovered for over a thousand more years, until 1676, and archaeological excavations didn't commence until 1892.

The biography of an ancient place is an exercise in human suffering and a recognition that nothing is permanent. It's a biography that calls for prayer in the form of divine petition and is probably best entrusted to poets and playwrights. One such playwright would have to be Aeschylus, who in 467 BCE produced the play *Seven Against Thebes*, which tells the story of a city terrorized by an invading army camped outside its gates. But instead of reducing the narrative to violence and gore, the play is mostly dialogue between the residents of Thebes and their ruler, Eteocles, with divine petitions to the gods for deliverance uttered by a chorus of women. It's about prayer being the only source of hope in a world of impending tragedy.

Another divine petition comes from *The Illiad* by Homer, which portrays an anxiety-ridden Achilles who prays to Zeus for courage in the face of battle. "Pelasgian Lord Zeus," Homer writes, "who live far off, ruler of wintry Dodona, surrounded there by your . . . priests and interpreters with unwashed feet, who sleep on the ground, you who have heard me before when I prayed, who have honored me by striking hard at the Greek army, fulfill my prayer now."

Still another prayer, attributed to the Greek poet Simonides of Ceos (556 BCE), is addressed to the fates (the Moirai), and cries into his world's endless night of fear and disaster. Simonides is said to have had a moral worldview focused on human imperfection and the unstable nature of accomplishments and achievements; in short, a pragmatic doubter who, apparently, included prayer as a form of survival speech worth uttering regardless of what is believed or in whom one believes.

Here is his prayer:

> Listen, Moirai, who of gods sit closest beside the throne of Zeus,
> and weave with adamantine shuttles countless, inescapable plans
> for all manner of designs.
>
> Aisa, Klotho, and Lachesis, fair-armed daughters of Night,
> listen to our prayer, heavenly and chthonic,
> fear-inducing divinities,
> Send us rose-bodied
> good government and her sisters on gleaming thrones,
> Justice and crown-bearing Peace,
> and rid this our town of down-heartening disasters

Chapter 21

Roads

"My Lord God, I have no idea where I am going."
- A MYSTIC'S PRAYER -
SANTIAGO DE COMPOSTELA, SPAIN

ANOTHER "TRUTH SPOT" INFUSED WITH transcendent location, materiality, and narrative for Thomas Gieryn is Santiago de Compostela in northwestern Spain, which he approached from the air on a flight from Barcelona. Not a big problem as his purpose was scholarly commentary on an idea rather than travelogue, though he may have benefitted from walking the Camino de Santiago ("Way of Saint James") as a pilgrim like thousands of others. I'm not one to talk, however, as I have walked only the last few miles of it after approaching the city by car, and I recall it now before offering a relevant prayer by the Catholic mystic, Thomas Merton.

Gieryn refers to this truth spot as "a trap door to the transcendent." The image is taken from the film, *Being John Malkovich*, in which a trap door behind a file cabinet in a random New York City office opens a passage to another place and time. Pilgrims on the Camino are looking for something like that, Gieryn suggests, "some kind of purpose," as they walk mile after mile "with floppy hats, heavy packs, walking sticks, sturdy boots, blisters on blisters, [and] scallop shells," the main Camino symbol, which competes with the Cross, the gourd, the stick, the yellow arrow, and the pilgrim's credential.

A scholar's skepticism is present in Gieryn as he recounts the myth of Santiago de Compostela: that it was the mission field of Saint James the

Greater, that he was executed by Herod Agrippa on his return to Jerusalem, that his remains were mysteriously returned to Galicia and buried, discovered nine centuries later by an Iberian shepherd, and finally that the city took on its role as a pilgrimage destination equal to that of Rome and Jerusalem. "It only seems like every single pilgrim who has walked the Camino since the ninth century has written a book about it," Gieryn quips, not to mention the blogs, Instagram pictures, how-to manuals, personal testimonies, architectural commentaries, and religious epiphanies. Both pre- and post-Rick Steves and Shirley MacLaine, a voluminous canon has indeed emerged, and I will add here the rather obvious title war waged by publishers in their enduring battle to say something new. *Therapy* (David Lodge, 1995), *Two Steps Forward* (Graeme Simpson and Anne Buist, 2017), *Travels with a Stick* (Richard Frazer, 2019) and my personal favorite, *I'm Off Then: Losing and Finding Myself on the Camino de Santiago* (Hape Kerkeling, 2006), illustrate. I guess I can be a little skeptical, too.

Perhaps it's best just to enjoy the Camino for no set reason, as was the case with my longtime Canadian friend, David, who walked it last year. Sending me an email while I was visiting a Knights Templar church in Jerez de los Caballeros, Spain, he invited me to join him on his hike. But it wasn't going to be a pilgrimage, he said. A few weeks later he was there with his camera and tablet in a backpack, walking 320 kilometers/198 miles in the Galician spring. "I enjoyed the hiking and photography," he told me later. "And while I usually hike alone," he added, "I decided I wanted to meet as many people as I could. I knew that some would be on a pilgrimage. I was not a seeker myself but felt I could add to other people's experiences. I met a lot of interesting folks from all walks of life, all ages, and from around the world. We wanted to help and encourage each other along the way. Everyone seemed open and receptive to spiritual things."

From here in Lisbon, some Camino hikers walk the entire 616 kilometers/382 miles to Santiago de Compostela, or even a little farther by including the city of Fatima to experience some *Our Lady of Fatima* culture. Most, however, approach the Camino from Porto or Braga in the north, where the distance is less than half along the coastal route. Some praise May and September, April and October, as the best times to go, with high summer being hot and crowded and winter, rainy and empty. Once on the Camino itself, most hikers and pilgrims stay in the many affordable albuguerias, which in turn place a required stamp on the passport-like credential which allows them to proceed to the common goal: the Cathedral of Santiago de Compostela, the destination.

Rissy and I got there, but mostly by car.

It was a December of mists and cold wind as we made our way with lingering coughs across sprawling green fields past Vigo and Pontevedra, Spain. In Braga we had stopped at a coffee shop to meet up with our friend, Salome, a history of science scholar who said jokingly that she seeks truth in science, we seek it in religion, and our smart friend Joao, who usually joins us, seeks it in video games. We laughed, caffeinated. By the time we reached the outskirts of Santiago de Compostela, a hard rain was falling. Unable to find our hotel, we hired a taxi to lead us there through a mesh of ancient passages and checked in. The following morning, gray and lifeless, we hiked to the cathedral, joining a few winter pilgrims taking their final Camino steps. The cathedral's Gothic-Romanesque-Baroque facade seemed, in some sense, liberated from a somewhat suffocating interior of incense, sculptured reliefs, and final-judgment overkill. Historically rumored to have been built over the grave of Saint James the Greater, we were happy to let him continue his long rest as we made our exit.

"It must be about the road," I whispered to Rissy. It must always have been about the road, I thought: the way here, the hike, the anticipation, the experience of being alive, the feeling of progress, the liminality, the sociality, or something. Because all the fuss can't be about this place. Some places look large from a distance but small and insignificant up close, and it was exactly its far-away quality that had made Santiago de Compostela so potent across the centuries, Gieryn stated; a remoteness which made sure pilgrims would experience "the energy of the path," and where they would have the time and conditions necessary for releasing pain, de-structuring lifeless routines, and becoming a revived person. Those are things for which one needs a road, a very long road.

Published road stories are a mythology all their own, according to Brendan Leonard, a contributor to *Adventure Journal*. They're about the need for adventure, romance, and clarity, he adds, and what storytellers from *The Odyssey* by Homer to *Travels with Charley* by John Steinbeck have in common is the expression of their own unique hungers and circumstances. "'A journey is a person in itself,'" he quotes Steinbeck; "'no two are alike. And all plans, safeguards, policing, and coercion are fruitless. We find after years of struggle that we do not take a trip; a trip takes us.'" I would add to Leonard's list of road classics the spiritual journey narrated by the wandering author of *The Way of a Pilgrim*, a timeless account of a ruble-less Russian sojourner whose sole purpose in walking great distances along solitary roads through nineteenth century Russia and Ukraine was to learn how to pray. Prayer was about the road, and the road was about prayer.

Thomas Merton understood this as perceptively as anyone. In "The Pilgrim Prayer" he acknowledges the road as the symbol of his directionless existence, where he realizes he has no idea who he is or where he is going, but that his desire to please God is the one thing that will place him on "the right road" where he will never travel alone. His prayer closes this part of the book:

> My Lord God, I have no idea where I am going.
> I do not see the road ahead of me.
> I cannot know for certain where it will end.
> Nor do I really know myself, and the fact that I think I am following
>   your will
> does not mean that I am actually doing so.
> But I believe that the desire to please you does in fact please you.
> And I hope I have that desire in all that I am doing.
> I hope that I will never do anything apart from that desire.
> And I know that if I do this, you will lead me by the right road,
> though I may know nothing about it.
> Therefore, will I trust you always, though I may seem lost in the shadow
>   of death.
> I will not fear, for you are ever with me,
> and you will never leave me to face my perils alone.

PART FOUR

Chapter 22

NUMINOUS

"Oh Lord, we pray that you help us remember the legend that was John Lennon."

- PRAYER FOR A DEPARTED BEATLE -
JOHN LENNON WALL, PRAGUE, CZECH REPUBLIC

EACH OF THE FOLLOWING PLACES and prayers have some relationship, however marginal, with popular culture. This doesn't mean that either the places or the prayers are trivial. To the contrary, each place is authentic and overflowing with meaning for its devotees, whether super-contemporary such as the Otaku center of Akihabara, Japan or the setting of ancient Troy in western Turkey. The prayers, too, must be seen as equally authentic expressions of the pray-er's truth, passion, conscience, and intent. To quote Matthew 7:1's timeless warning about the opinionated assessment of people and things, "Judge not, lest ye be judged" (KJV). May we extend this biblical courtesy to all who pray and all who dwell in places of subjective meaning.

In March 2012 I joined a dozen other media people for a weeklong conference in Prague, Czech Republic. Put on by an interdisciplinary group out of Oxford University, we sat at a large rectangular table to exchange ideas on diverse topics relating to fetishistic communities, binary motives in fandom, and the evolution of playlist patterns among street musicians. Prague is an appropriate setting for any of these topics, not the least being the discussion of street music as the city's civic recesses teem with players of every musical genre. The Charles Bridge, connecting the

Prague Castle area with Old Town, stretches beautifully over the Vltava River, and even in late winter features bundled instrumentalists of talent.

After each day's presentations and cocktails, participants fanned out across the city to sample Prague's underrated cultural treasures. I headed straight for the Lennon Wall, a fan site celebrating John Lennon for the past forty years. Imagine a quiet area near the French Embassy where layer upon layer of paint blankets a vertical stone structure dedicated to the late Beatle. Song lyrics make up the dominant scrawl content, and when I was there a huge yellow heart with green borders enclosed the final lines of "In My Life," a Lennon masterpiece about places and people tenderly remembered, from the *Rubber Soul* album. Even a few words joined to a song-memory inspires pause and a sigh.

The wall had been there since the 1960s as a public setting for love-inspired graffiti. Then, immediately following Lennon's murder in 1980, it morphed into a forum for Lennon alone. Common Beatle and solo-career themes of peaceful revolution, imagination, free expression, and visionary storytelling occupied the space. The country's communist leader, Gustav Husak, was said to have been annoyed by the wall, and when students, many of whom were Lennon fans, protested his leadership during the *Prague Spring* of 1988 they were branded as drugged up, deranged agents of the capitalistic West. This produced new layers of *Lennonism* on the wall plus periodic clashes with police on the Charles Bridge, not far from the wall. Vandalism has occasionally visited the structure, too, though the wall is reclaimed by fans within a day or two.

Prague's Lennon Wall isn't the only place where John Lennon is commemorated in public space, as other walls in Hong Kong, Tokyo, Taipei, Berlin, Auckland, and Sydney attest. He even exists in stone and mortar within the communist world, at the John Lennon Park in Havana and the Tsoi Wall in Moscow. And on West 72nd Street, New York City, a piece of Central Park within eyesight of The Dakota, where he was shot by Mark David Chapman, combines nature with Portuguese pavement spread out over an acre as the Strawberry Fields Memorial, recalling Lennon and "Strawberry Fields Forever," perhaps his most distinctive song rival to his post-Beatles classic, "Imagine."

In Prague, one visit to the wall was not enough, I thought, so I returned all ten days of my stay. It was a short walk from my hotel, and I wanted to witness the daily alterations made by fans, of which there were many. Scribbles on top of scribbles on top of scribbles is often what fandom's poaching, revisionist culture is about, and so many years of overpainting have repeatedly called for monitoring by locals. The result is that television cameras have been placed at the wall along with restrictions to the onslaught of graffiti during pub crawls, and some prefer to have the wall shut down permanently.

"Prague's Famous John Lennon Wall: Is it Over, or Reborn?" was the question asked by Smithsonian Magazine in 2014. I will answer by saying that the wall may end at some point, but not the fandom.

The enormous reach of John Lennon fandom around the world can be understood from several perspectives: the power of the lyrical text, the motivations of fans, and how the violent and untimely death of Lennon catapulted the collective memory of him into the religious stratosphere, to name three. The textual power is self-evident as we consider song masterpieces ("I Am the Walrus," "A Day in the Life," "Tomorrow Never Knows," "Come Together," "Strawberry Fields") which are primarily Lennon (not Lennon and McCartney) and are arguably The Beatles' most original and artistic classics. Then, there is the solo work which produced "Imagine" and its "brotherhood-of-man" theme, which seemed to spawn a memorabilia industry of its own. The basic human desire of *saving* causes fans to collect and display everything from t-shirts to shot glasses, and who hasn't seen something in their lifetime featuring the *imagine* theme in its specific John Lennon context?

The motivations of fans are more difficult to assess, though they can be approached by considering four contexts: attachment, catharsis, identification, and empowerment; a motivational quadrilateral. When young fans begin to follow Lennon, for instance, it is quite possible they are doing so for reasons relevant to attachment theory, the idea that what we do across the life course emanates from our past, the people who nurtured us, and the socio-cultural conditions in which we were raised. These fans likely heard, and heard about, Lennon from their parents or grandparents, and now their fandom exists in an attachment context of nostalgia and idealized memory. The prayer that closes this chapter was written by a British middle school student from Derbyshire, England and may illustrate this context.

The catharsis context in fandom is based on the common need many fans have for cathartic release from emotional pressure looking for an escape valve. It is common in sports fandom and in the consumption and socialization of cultural products that facilitate aggressive forms of release. Certainly, some of Lennon's music and forceful emotional content can be cathartic, though less so than, say, aggressive hip-hop or heavy metal. And as recent research has shown, cathartic release is an overrated means of acquiring more than temporary emotional release; as a permanent form of release, it fails badly, and cathartic fans are often angrier and more frustrated in the long run. It is nevertheless a factor.

The identification context in fandom is about consubstantiality: literally the joining of the fan's substance with the substance of someone or something else because she or he believes they are mystically joined in the reciprocal understanding of self. I witnessed it in my interviews with many fans of Harry Potter who experienced deep reciprocity with book characters. And among interviewed music fans, I once had a fan of Mary J. Blige tell me, quite seriously, that she knew the two would meet someday because they shared the totality of existential pain, and that was their destiny. I have little doubt, moreover, that John Lennon fans experience something similar. He is very easy to identify with on the level of personal suffering.

Beyond these three contexts, fans are also empowered by the object of their fandom, the empowerment context being by far the largest factor. The possibilities are endless here, as they say, and I have employed the 16 Basic Desires theory of *normal* personality espoused by psychologist Steven Reiss in my understanding of fans. All 16 basic desires (power, order, curiosity, independence, acceptance, romance, honor, vengeance, social contact, physical exercise, status, family, eating, idealism, saving, and tranquility) are at play in fandom. Taken together as a whole, and fused into other fan contexts, it's easy to see how powerful fandom can be, even to the point of serving as a kind of cultural, all-encompassing religion for fans. Indeed, one controversial contemporary religion, Scientology, began with the fans of science fiction author, L. Ron Hubbard.

Is John Lennon a *true-believer* object of religion today, or over time is he becoming one? That is difficult to say. Because like Elvis Presley, Jim Morrison, Curt Cobain, and others (Michael Jackson might be the best candidate of all, clothed in transfiguration white), one would have to prove the existence of a numinous: the authentic believed existence of a divine being for fans. That may well be true, but it seems quite a challenge to prove.

Nevertheless, the power of Lennon's life and legacy on fans of all ages cannot be underestimated, as the following "Prayer About John Lennon" illustrates:

Oh Lord, we pray that you help us remember the legend that was
    John Lennon,
We hope to remember his songs and that his music will inspire others,
We thank you for providing him with the talent
that helped him create great songs,
We hope the remaining Beatles stay safe,
and our respects go out to them and their families,
We carry on the ideas of John Lennon
by spreading peace, love and harmony across the world,
We hope that his music will continue to be bounced around the globe
to inspire others,
We hope everybody stays safe and begins to show respect to each other,
We hope that his family remains happy, in spite of their dreadful loss,
We still hope that everyone still believes in John Lennon
and that his memory lives on,
In loving memory of John Lennon,
Amen. Thank you.

Chapter 23

TRIBAL COPING

"We thank you for drama and sadness."
- AN OTAKU PRAYER -
AKIHABARA, TOKYO, JAPAN

EXPERIENCING TOKYO FOR A MONTH in 2005, I spent only an evening in Akihabara, Japan's and the World's center of Otaku culture. It was an eye-assaulting visit. Seven years earlier, I had read *the rise of the image the fall of the word* by Mitchell Stephens, which argued that our world's all-visual future was coming faster than expected, and we'd be communicating through a language of images, like musical hieroglyphics, in a world of surplus pictorial forms. That world has yet to arrive as we continue to appreciate words as the primary carriers of thought, though the iconography of certain places staggers us when we try to take them in. Case in point: Akihabara.

One seems prepped for this Japanese image world, even before stepping out of the local metro station, by the tangled, udon-noodle-like subway route maps posted everywhere. Then, suddenly you're in it: more lights, more flashing signs, and more young people in costume than you ever imagined. Words fail you in this ultra-baroque, byzantine, convoluted, labyrinthine environment as you walk around, mouth open and eyes transfixed in multi-directional gazing.

Through swelling, noisy night crowds you might stop at any of the following places: Three Maids Cafe, where subservient young women greet their male guests as "master" before serving up kawaii (cute food) with smiley-faced beverages; the Yodobashi-Akiba gadget store of toys, Lego blocks, miniature cars, weird watches, roving vacuum cleaners, and funky toilets; the anime shops featuring *One Punch Man*, *Dark Souls*, *Bloodborne*, and *Berserk* merchandise; manga outlets that make old *Pokemon*, *Digiman*, and *Dragonball* media seem as ancient as *The Epic of Gilgamesh*; and the Super Potato gaming store, arcades dizzy with illuminated dance floors, and trading-card shops where your brain can catch its breath, so to speak. I even thought I might try out a go-cart street adventure dressed as a cartoon character, though going as *Sailor Moon* didn't seem a reasonable substitute for my chosen, *Popeye the Sailor Man*.

The word Akihabara evolved from *Akiba*, a god who controls fire and whose myth is said to have been born in a local shrine after a fire swept through this part of Tokyo in 1869. It then became a center for tradespeople and crafters before evolving into Akihabara Electric Town, following World War II, when it established itself as a black market for electronic products. This period in its history prepared it to merge with the post-war industry of early computerized games sold adjacent to the Akihabara metro station. And finally with the development of more sophisticated games and the stories they told, coupled with internet technology which exported this civic microcosm to the online world, Akihabara became what it is today: a visual smorgasbord of manga, anime icons, cosplayers, and everything else occupying space in the Otaku multiverse.

It is a cosmos that draws people like my friend Alice, a legendary member of Lisbon, Portugal's cosplay scene, an Otaku fan, and a traveler to Akihabara who hopes to return there soon. She knows the territory well: the stories, genres, characters, settings, and themes, though she is careful to point out that Otaku's dark, hyper-sexualized underbelly doesn't appeal to her. "I like the media where there is no hint of sex or romance at all," she says. "And stuff like Vampire Knight and Tokyo Ghoul aren't my thing. I mostly do it for the cosplay." Her costumes and presentations are renowned in Lisbon for their attention to detail. "It's a creative hobby for me," she says. "Socially, it lets me interact with people who like what I like, and it's a conversation starter. Also, at the end of the day I need to be proud of something I have created. The costumes I sew and then wear for others to see do that for me. They make me feel like I can do something that's interesting for people."

About returning to Akihabara, she adds, "I would like to go back someday for the memories I have and how the stories and anime products kept me company in not-so-good times." Alice, who I have known for over a decade, told me once that her Otaku interests began as a coping mechanism after her parents divorced. This is a common theme among Otaku fans I have known.

The book *Fandom Unbound: Otaku Culture in a Connected World*, by three Japanese social science scholars, tries to liberate Otaku from its reputation as a cultural space for victims of life events who have become pathological. I used the book in the final years of my teaching career along with parts of my doctoral thesis, *Popular Privation: Suffering in Fan Cultures*. Here, Mizuko Ito, Daisuke Okabe, and Izumi Tsuji make a valiant effort to situate Otaku in the realm of *moe*, the obsession with imaginative things, in which fans seek new ways of being creative against all the backdrops of our era's cognitive, emotional, and social surpluses. There is simply too much stimulation coming from too many directions to expect new generations of consumers to be traditional. Imagination and morality must take on unfamiliar modes of expression, and a new tribalism made up of self-determined kins and clans, united by play and transcendent forms of amusement, is what is left. And so, we have Otaku. And Akihabara.

My visit there ended in noise and light, followed by a long metro ride through Tokyo's underground to the part of the city where my hotel was located. Fittingly, I was seated across the aisle from a young mother and her daughter, both sporting Hello Kitty logos. How entertaining, I thought, as the train clattered and twisted through the tunnels.

"The Otaku Prayer" which follows has circulated in recent years throughout the Otaku multiverse on a number of platforms. By including it in the book, I do not mean to conflate it with other magnificent prayers herein, though I have retained it for two of its statements: "We thank you for drama and sadness," line seven, and "We thank you for the haters," line thirteen. Both statements emanate from a deep core within Otaku culture which preserves the personal containment of suffering and the acknowledgment of being misunderstood and unaccepted within traditional human contexts. The same story is achingly present in lines 1–6 and their below-the-surface articulation of sexual and gender confusion through the objects mentioned: *yuri, yaoi, ecchi, hentai, lolicons*; and through other images in the prayer as well. I refrain from either elevating or criticizing the prayer as juvenile or puerile, though only to emphasize that all fan cultures are about far more than meets the eye. Otaku is but another example.

The prayer:

Dear our Otaku and anime,
We thank you for the yuri, and yaoi,
the ecchi and the hentai,
the lolicons and Tokyo Ghoul,
for blood and love, lust to must, sub and maybe dub,
We thank you for yuri on ice as well as lie in April,
We thank you for drama and sadness,
We thank you for AMV and tvs,
We thank you for manga and fairy tales . . . ,
We thank you for school life and romance,
heartaches and zombies to Vampire Knight,
to Servamp and . . . zombie school,
We thank you for the haters as well because we have people
    to laugh about,
because half of us are like the children of whales and dumb . . .
    and strong . . .
and the Otaku say Amen.

Chapter 24

Mermaidish

"Teach me to love myself unconditionally and to practice self-care without reservation."

- A FOLKLORIC PRAYER -
COPENHAGEN, DENMARK

BACK AGAIN IN EUROPE, COPENHAGEN seemed an ideal location for a conference on mermaids. Its watery landscape of lakes, rivers, ocean, and misty rainfall invited lots of mythologizing in October 2017's conference, *Mermaids, Maritime Folklore, and Modernity*. Put on by the scholastically adventurous Island Dynamics group out of the Shetland Islands, whose stated purpose is to promote island studies for the benefit of researchers and policy makers, the conference was a knowledge traveler's delight; so much so that conferees couldn't help but drool at the idea of attending a future ID event in Svalbard, the arctic island where the world's seed banks are stored.

But here in Copenhagen the talk was about fishermen's villages and Michelin-starred restaurants, Soren Kierkegaard and Hans Christian Anderson, used bookshops by the dozens, and the Christianshavn hippie commune which a group of us boated out to on a breezy afternoon. That same day, we visited a fountain commemorating the Norse goddess Gefion driving a plough behind her four sons who served as oxen, and of course the bronze, bare-breasted Little Mermaid statue seated on a reddish-brown rock above churning, choppy seawater. I recognized the statue from one of its many global copies I had seen on trips to Solvang,

California, a Danish town near Santa Barbara. In Solvang you can see the statue before making your way to Paula's Pancake House and its inspired menu of flapjacks.

After a few days of mermaidish conference chat, I slipped away to meet up with my friend Adjeksenila from Sao Tome, Africa, whom I had met through my wife in Lisbon. The bright, talkative *Nila* was in Copenhagen taking in the city's renowned academic culture and the freedom she had found in learning. "Sao Tome is the city of my soul," she said over lunch at an Asian restaurant by a swan-graced lake. "It's about my soul, and Lisbon is the city of my heart. But Copenhagen is the city of my freedom. I've been here four years and now see myself as a citizen of the world. I'm not locked into anything or anyplace. I have a notion of where I came from, my roots, but I want to connect with people around the world. I'm ready to move on if doors open somewhere else. If not, I'm happy to stay put."

Nila spoke of adjusting to Danish life, which was "opposite to everything in Sao Tome or Portugal," she said. "Everything happens earlier in the day. Wake up earlier, eat lunch at noon instead of 2pm, eat dinner two or three hours sooner, and be in bed by the time I used to finish the evening meal." And about the cold weather: "It's not an issue. I have to dress for it and have learned there is no such thing as bad weather, only bad clothing." She spoke admiringly of the family who employed her as a nanny, saying how they had taught her "how a family should be," and how "they really believe in me." But all roads seemed to lead back to what she was learning from academic life. "People here are highly educated," she said. "Learning is its own reward. I'm taking as many classes as I can to acquire more knowledge."

Before parting ways after lunch, Nila was still talking, caffeinated from being so amazingly alive, I thought. "And the rhythm of life is different here," she concluded. "I have a better chance of maintaining a work-study balance and still have time for myself. I don't feel I'm ever in a rush. And I love nature here and long walks around the city. There is a delightful balance to life in this place which is very freeing. I feel free." Then she was off to a class somewhere, as I returned to the mermaid conference. The afternoon sessions were deep into watery discourse.

Let's talk about mermaids.

The myth by way of Hans Christian Anderson is a familiar one, more or less. Raised by a widowed father, a grandmother, and five older sisters, a curious little mermaid celebrates her freedom at fifteen by swimming up to the ocean's surface. She spots a handsome prince, saves him from drowning, gets legs from the sea witch's potion, doesn't get the prince after all but can't bring herself to kill him even though she's been rejected, and eventually gets the human soul she desired as a result of her good deeds, with the promise of going to heaven. Disney's 1989 animation altered parts of the original myth, published by Anderson in 1836, and the darker, sadder original is often the one preferred by fans who see it as more true to life.

Contemporary mermaid fans and fan-scholars have a lot to say about both the original and the updated versions: that they serve as antidotes to the state of the world; that we all need magical creatures like mermaids, unicorns, and the array of characters in *The Lord of the Rings* and *Harry Potter*; and that we have a felt need to return to the sea, a metaphor for returning to idealized settings before one can progress to a virtuous existence. Then, in the Freudian-feminist depths of fannish discussion is the view that mermaids are queer symbols, trans icons, and gay manifestations, often energized by biographical accounts of Hans Christian Anderson's bi-sexuality, and that *The Little Mermaid* may have been written in response to the author's failed attempt to win the love of an attractive public servant in 1830s Copenhagen. Indeed, one Edvard Collin just might be that unattainable handsome prince from the story.

My own experience, however, with mermaid fans has tended to lead me along a different oceanic trajectory: one of feminine spiritual empowerment amid the swirling currents of tranquility and idealism. Seemingly, the images in the following "A Prayer to the Mermaid," which speaks of "deep emotional waters," "clearing and purifying," and protecting "the ocean and the earth," roll with a tide of *woman* seeking an inner swell of empowerment for knowing herself and making the world a better place. Offered to the public by *Spiritual Mermaid*, the prayer comes to us accompanied by this statement: "Prayer is the oldest form of energy work. When you pray, you seek to connect energetically. Call on the energy of the mermaid to connect with her essence."

And the prayer:

> Beautiful sea goddess,
> I call on you to assist me in moving toward all that I am,
> as I leave behind what I am no longer.
> Guide me in the way of swimming gracefully,
> even while I abide in deep emotional waters.

Lead me in using water as a tool for clearing and purifying,
> and show me
how to remove any energetic blocks binding my mind, my space,
> and my being.
Teach me to love myself unconditionally
and practice self-care without reservation.
Instruct me on self-reflection as a way to evolve into the fullness
> of who I am.
Direct me on how to protect the ocean and the earth.
Impart to me your pearls of wisdom and your secrets
to inner as well as outer beauty.
Advise me on how to use my power for all that is right and good.
Bestow upon me your ways of connecting with intuition,
> vision and empathy,
and their uses as tools in my life.
I give gratitude for your example and your enlightenment.
Thank you for working with me.

Chapter 25

Jamie Fraser Unceasing

"Be this soul on Thine arm, O Christ."
- AN *OUTLANDER* PRAYER -
LINLITHGOW, SCOTLAND

BACK ON DRY LAND IN Scotland, summer 2019, I joined a cluster of *Outlander* fans for lunch at Mason Belles Kitchen on High Street, Linlithgow.

We had just finished a walking tour of Linlithgow Palace, which functions as Wentworth Prison in the addictively gritty, all-boundary-pushing television series. Six of us sat at a table reading menus offering creative Scottish fare, and after we ordered it became evident that one young woman in our group was carrying all eight of the *Outlander* paperbacks by author Diane Gabaldon in her backpack. We were part of Rabbie's Tours, enjoying a day trek of scattered Outlander filming locations a little north and west of Edinburgh. Doune, Blackness, and Midhope Castles; the Mercat Cross at Culross; and the Linlithgow Palace were all on the agenda. The day itself sparkled weather-wise.

As the senior member of the group, I said to the young woman with the backpack that I hadn't seen anyone so booked-up since Harry Potter days. I shared that it wasn't unusual then to attend an HP con in Salem or Saint Petersburg to see kids and adults carrying all the books. Hardbacks stacked like cairns would appear on flat surfaces or in corners, and you could tell by their condition that they weren't only read, they were inhaled. Ravenous fans do that: they breathe in the original, then exhale poached remains through fan fiction, fan art, and chat.

"Well, what are you reading?" the young woman said. "What is everybody reading?"

Our food was yet to arrive, so we circled the table. A couple of travel guides surfaced as well as some light reading not relevant to the day's activities. One woman, middle-aged I guessed, said she only reads off her tablet, and she was "internetting" as much as she could about Sam Heughan, the actor who plays Jamie Fraser in *Outlander* on television. "He gets bullied a lot in real life," she said, "by people accusing him online of all kinds of things that are untrue. Goes with the territory, I guess."

As we had just toured the fictional prison where Jamie is chained, raped, and tortured by the sadistic Captain Jonathan 'Black Jack' Randall, someone mentioned that her mother stopped watching the show after that. "She said she became Claire (Jamie's wife) at that point and couldn't handle what she was seeing," she said. "So, she stopped watching altogether." I chimed in saying that there did seem to be a fine line in those scenes between realism and sadomasochistic indulgence, and that my wife and I didn't need to see all the flashbacks.

"The psychological torture was worse than the physical torture," said the other male at the table. "I'm not sure I needed to see any of that."

"That's the difference between reading the books and watching the series on tv," said the girl with the backpack full of books. "And I was reading an interview with Diane Gabaldon who said that books are great because people don't always picture what they read. They can know what happened without actually having to see it graphically."

"I just found that," said the woman scrolling on her tablet. "March 1, 2016. *Explore Entertainment*. She (Gabaldon) says, and I quote, '"People who read do not form a visual image from what they're reading. They just don't. They follow the events and get the resonance with the language' ... etc etc etc."

When our food arrived, it was my time to talk books. I mentioned I had just finished *A Cook's Tour* by Anthony Bourdain, which closes with a cheeky chapter on Scottish cooking (fried pizza and haggis, but also the best beef, seafood, and wild game in Europe), and that I had just begun *Royal Sex: Mistresses & Lovers of the British Royal Family* by Roger Powell. The early pages were about James I, son of Mary Stuart, aka Mary Queen of Scots, and his many male companions, which the author attributed to his fatherless existence and his craving for male affection. Ironically, it was here in Linlithgow, at the palace, where Mary was born. Small world.

After lunch, we walked back to the tour van to meet the rest of the group, and were off to more *Outlander* locations. What I would love to have discussed over lunch, or at any other time, was the vivid religious backdrop of *Outlander*. How religion and popular culture feed into each other was a big topic twenty years earlier, but on this day in 2019 it seemed odd to bring it up. The data on religious affiliation among millennials seemed clear enough: they don't go to church, and they don't like to say they're members of any particular faith. But they pray as much as any generation of young people before them, according to the Pew Research Center. "Though young adults pray less often than their elders do today, the number of those who say they pray every day rivals the portion of young people who said the same in prior decades," Pew reported in 2010. So, this was more an issue involving generational differences, with the obvious corollary being that we pray more as we grow older. I could have brought that up at some point but didn't.

By any measure, prayer is common in *Outlander*, as are references to the Bible, Christian rituals, and major figures in historical Christianity.

The outstanding fan site, *Outlander Lists & Timelines*, catalogs everything *Outlander* in the way annotated novels used to explain minute textual details within a given story. It documents, for instance, more than fifty biblical references and their specific contexts, such as Claire's enlistment of Psalm 22:14 (KJV) to help Jamie cope with his prison rape: "I am poured out like water, and all my bones are out of joint: my heart is like wax; it is melted in the midst of my bowels." The site goes on to catalog thirty religious figures including monks, friars, priests, nuns, and at least five Protestant ministers; and twenty-four saints, the likes of John the Baptist, Augustine of Hippo, and Francis of Assisi. Christian rituals such as marriage ceremonies, confessions, masses, sacraments, and vespers, not to mention pagan dances and the blood vow that accompanies the wedding of Claire and Jamie, round out a story so infused with religion it feels as though it might have been conceived in a convent.

About prayer in Outlander, the fan site lists fourteen actual "Prayers and Graces," offered mostly by the long-suffering and Christ-like Jamie. From the *Crofter's Grace*, said before eating a meal, to the prayer for Claire's time-travel safety at the standing stones, Jamie seems a man of passionate, unceasing prayer. In battle, he offers the *Soul Peace*, a traditional *Carmina Gadelica* prayer accompanying a fellow warrior's death, and the *Soul Leading*, which petitions God to lead a soul to Jerusalem, the City of Heaven. These prayers emerge with a spontaneity that has *pray without ceasing* wedded to them. They don't come from some "pious little niche" in an obscure corner of Jamie's life, as the Catholic priest Henri Nouwen once described the false interpretation of unceasing prayer, but from an individual who doesn't separate God from daily life. "Unceasing thinking is converted into unceasing prayer, moving us from a self-centered monologue to a God-centered dialogue," Nouwen adds. It seems that this theme appears in Jamie's character, in spite of, or perhaps because of, his endless suffering.

The Carmina Gadelica's Soul Leading is the death blessing included here:

> Be this soul on Thine arm, O Christ,
> Thou King of the City of Heaven.
> Amen.
>
> Since thou, O Christ, it was who bought't this soul,
> Be its peace on thine own keeping.
> Amen.
>
> And may the strong Michael, high king of the angels,
> Be preparing the path before this soul, O God.
> Amen.
>
> Oh! the strong Michael in peace with thee, soul,
> And preparing for thee the way to the kingdom of the Son of God.
> Amen.

Chapter 26

Opposing Forces

"Prayers follow behind to heal the harm."
- A HOMERIC PRAYER -
RUINS OF ANCIENT TROY, TURKEY

Rissy and I, a couple from Singapore, and a tour guide left Istanbul for ancient Troy one sleepy, sleety morning in January, 2015. On the multi-hour journey, our Turkish guide, for undisclosed reasons, couldn't seem to degrade America and the West enough, until he asked the Singaporeans what their favorite country was, and they said definitely the United States, with France coming in second. "Oh well, then," the guide said. "We did like Barack Obama, I'll give you that, and I've never been to France."

Such was the banter that morning as the van motored across the gray landscape of western Turkey, with frequent views of a colorless Sea of Marmara and its freighters visible through side windows. I had wrapped up a forgettable conference on public space at Bilgi University, and Rissy had flown in from Lisbon to take in Turkish history that she, a historian herself, had never seen. We both came alive while traipsing through Istanbul's mosques and museums, including a dreamy cruise up the Bosphorus through the heart of what once had been the Ottoman Empire. But now it was time to get out of town, and Troy was closer than Ephesus.

"Seriously, I could have been that Iraqi guy who threw his shoes at George Bush-2 in Baghdad," the guide continued. "I was all for America getting the shoe treatment during that war, which as far as I can understand was about Bush-2 avenging the hit Saddam Hussein put out on Bush-1. That's what you go to war for? It's bullshit."

"And we're paying for this?" I whispered to Rissy. "In more ways than one."

Fortunately, the banter stopped when we arrived in Tevfikiye for coffee and a restroom break. Then, in a few minutes, we were at Troy itself, marveling at the gigantic replica of the Trojan Horse placed near the archaeological site. We climbed its steps and snapped selfies in a cold drizzle. The brown wooden edifice seemed more popular culture than serious history to us; more "Achilles Last Stand" by Led Zeppelin; more "Troy" starring Brad Pitt; more *Iliad, Odyssey*, and *Trojan War* by Marvel Comics; and more Homer and Zeus via the video game universe than a symbol of how Troy fits into human cultural history. It was fun, though.

Once inside the archaeological site the mood changed. Excavated foundations of gates, towers, walls, a palatial complex, an ancient cul-de-sac, and houses revealed an authentic place lost in time until its rediscovery in the 1800s. On raised land the ruins looked out toward a broad, flat plain that once lay beneath Aegean seawater and now separated the city from the modern town of Canakkale. As with other ancient sites, archaeologists and historians tend to visualize Troy through numbered levels of stratigraphy. Troy I, for instance, existed as far back as 3000 BCE, when its initial stone settlement was built. Then, Troy II (2500–2300 BCE) and Troy III, IV, and V (2300–1750 BCE) paved the way for Troy VI (1750–1300 BCE), which was likely the city of Homer's *Iliad* and a thriving place of commerce and culture. The year 1334 BCE, give or take, was a possible dating of the Trojan War and part of Troy VI or VII, though later dates of the ten-year war were offered by Herodotus and Eratosthenes. Homer is said to have written both the *Iliad* and the *Odyssey* centuries later, 800–700 BCE, which was also a time of declining culture and architecture in Troy, though the city was inhabited, at least intermittently, until 301–320 CE, when it falls silent. It remained that way for 1500 years until excavations of 1860 and 1871 brought it back to life.

Of course, it has always been alive through Homer, and Homeric Troy echoes across time in the way the Psalmist David of the Old Testament sustains the living memory of ancient Jerusalem. Many people know at least something of Homer's story: how the Greek states' high king Agamemnon sought to avenge the marriage of his brother's wife Helen, who had eloped with the Trojan prince, Paris. Years of fighting ensued until the Greeks' ruse of leaving the city while secretly employing soldiers inside a huge horse structure made of wood, which the Trojans hauled into the city as a war prize. The soldiers then slipped out covertly, opened the city gates, and ushered in the army of the Greek state collective, the Achaeans, who slaughtered the residents of Troy in a final bloody conquest.

My sixth-grade class read both the *Iliad* and the *Odyssey* under supervision of our teacher, Mrs. Campeau, who kept us honest through oral quizzes in front of the class. I much preferred the *Odyssey*, which like the New Testament book of *Acts*, narrated a journey and therefore became a travel story. But the *Iliad* was also respectable to boys at that time for its war narrative, and playing *army* after school each day was a constant in the wooded tropics of southern Florida. We'd come home with poison ivy rashes on our exposed skin, making us look as though we really had been at war and were authenticated in that way.

Rereading the *Iliad* today, I'm more likely to focus on Homer's portrayal of gods and goddesses and their complicated relationship with humans. They mock and mimic us in their superficial arrogance, showing little empathic understanding of life in the suffering earthly state. An early *Star Trek* episode, "Who Mourns for Adonis?" portrayed Apollo as the last of an alien race which had traveled to earth and set themselves up as gods in ancient Greece. Gigantic and powerful but lacking in human ingenuity, the last of their race is easily destroyed when at Captain Kirk's directive the starship Enterprise fires phaser bursts into Apollo's power source, bringing about his end. True to the show's insightful literary template, Kirk is relieved that the alien is destroyed but regretful that humanity has lost its sources of sacred ritual and morality as dictated by the myths of ancient Greece. It's worth revisiting Homer for that reason alone: he reminds us that sacred things possess their own elegance, and searching for God, in humility through prayer and submission, rewards the seeker.

There is a lot about prayer in Homer.

In the *Iliad*, prayer arises from the desire to bring the power of gods and goddesses into the human realm through purification and humility. Prayer is effective when respect is offered, vows are reverent, and repentance is sincere. Sin is its opposing force, moving faster than our prayers can stop it, but prayer can minimize the harm it causes. And the gods bless our prayers and petitions, reminding us that when we ignore them, sin exacts a high price even unto death. Says Homer:

Nay, even the very gods can bend,
and theirs withal is loftier majesty and honor and might.
Their hearts by incense and reverent vows,
and drink-offering and burnt-offering men turn with Prayer,
so oft as any transgressed and doeth sin.
Moreover, Prayers of penitence are daughters of great Zeus,
halting and wrinkled and of eyes askance,
that have their task withal to go in the steps of Sin.
For Sin is strong and fleet of foot,
wherefore she far outrunneth all Prayers,
and goeth before them over all the earth making men fall,
and Prayers follow behind to heal the harm.
Now whosoever reverenceth Zeus' daughters when they draw near,
him they greatly bless and hear his petitions;
but when one denieth them and stiffly refuseth,
then depart they and make Prayer unto Zeus the son of Kronos,
that sin may come upon such a one,
that he may fall and pay the price.

Chapter 27

GERTRUDE AND SYLVIA

"Breathe peace into the horror chambers of the heart...."
- A WAR PRAYER -
SHAKESPEARE & COMPANY, PARIS, FRANCE

THE LAST TIME I VISITED Paris was bittersweet.

Rissy's Avozinha Hilda, who had raised her since childhood, lay dying in a poorly lighted Portuguese hospital room. She seemed at peace, though, displaying her calm recognition of the inevitable with courage and acceptance. As I took a final look into her kind eyes, and embraced her a last time, an airport shuttle arrived to take me to Lisbon International, and I was gone.

The following day, Rissy phoned me at my hotel room in Auteuil to say Avozinha had passed and funeral arrangements were being made. My role at a long-scheduled Paris conference kept me from returning, though I carried reflective thoughts about Hilda the entire week. She was a lovely person. And like many members of the generation that witnessed the duration of the twentieth century, she possessed a calm, survival mentality based on dodging unchosen circumstances and observing events beyond anyone's control. In Portugal, that meant witnessing the fascist rule of Antonio de Olveira Salazar, the Civil War in neighboring Spain, the Carnation Revolution which ended fifty years of dictatorship, the communist seizure of private property, wars and rumors of wars in the Portuguese colonies across the world, and the eventual demise of the five-hundred-year empire which once nurtured national pride but ended in the sadness of regret.

In Paris, the busyness of the conference gave me needed distraction. After it concluded, I had several more days to do what I do best: wander aimlessly, like a pilgrim without a home who doesn't have a care in the world. Wandering has always been a pleasant pastime for me, and there is no better place to do it than Paris. As I walked through St. Germain one evening, I remembered my first time in the city of lights. It was a cold Spring that year, and I had dropped down from Scotland with my first wife for warmer weather that never happened. With a north wind blowing all week, there was no outdoor cafe culture to enjoy, no healing rain, no reflective mood, and a feeling that Paris was uncharacteristically closed. It was actually warmer and more inviting in Edinburgh when we returned there, but my deteriorating marriage limited the enjoyment of anything and anywhere at that time, and all that was left was the recognition that things were falling apart.

The bittersweetness of this time in Paris, however, fit the mood of the city, which is its most beautiful when things are happy but imperfect. Everything was liminal: my state of consciousness, the transitional quality of the Christmas-New Year week, the weather that was neither warm nor excessively cold, and the subdued light that couldn't be described as bright but in no way was dark, either. In this pleasant, late-December state of being, I walked past the Eiffel Tower, through the Louvre, above the Seine, and across broad expanses of the city, in which everything felt open and inviting. I entered Notre Dame Cathedral and sat in a center row for two hours listening to a children's choir piped in from somewhere, its magnetic, meditative glow refusing to let me leave. When I finally mustered the strength to get up and exit, I walked away as if suspended on some kind of holy air current carrying me to my next landing place.

That destination lay on the other side of the river bridge joining the cathedral to the Left Bank bookstore immortalized in twentieth century literature: Shakespeare and Company.

I'm going to remember this day, I thought, while approaching the green and gold facade familiar to Lost Generation fans everywhere. Films such as *Midnight in Paris, Before Sunset,* and *Julie & Julia,* had given the bookstore wide recent recognition, but its more durable image occupied permanent space in the minds of readers who longed for that golden literary age of F. Scott Fitzgerald and Ernest Hemingway, James Joyce and

T.S. Eliot. Outside the store, with its tree of vintage lights reflecting in the windows, one had to wonder what patrons were thinking as they strolled about dreamily in the lighted nightscape. Content to browse through racks of books placed outside the front door, no one seemed in a hurry to go anywhere but into their own minds and romanticized memories. Genuine illuminative moments of ritual are rare in life, and surely this was one to savor.

The store, in this location, belonged to George Whitman, who had died at 98 about a year before my visit. A large white plaque near the entrance commemorated his role as proprietor. By available accounts, he was an interesting man of books, extensive travel, and American military service, who brought his thousand-volume collection to Paris in the 1950s, where he ran the store and lived above it in a small apartment. It was the era of the Beat Generation, his clientele and social circle including William Burroughs, Allen Ginsberg, Henry Miller, Lawrence Durrell, as well as the George Plimpton crowd who crafted *The Paris Review* literary magazine. Whitman had named the store Le Mistral but changed it to Shakespeare and Company in 1964 to honor the Bard and also to revive the earlier store name established by Sylvia Beach, at a nearby location, in the 1920s. So enamored was he with the memory of Beach, he named his only daughter Sylvia Beach Whitman, who was born in 1981 and is now the store's manager.

Where once upon a time I might have gushed over the original Shakespeare and Company by reveling in the memory of the Fitzgeralds and Hemingways, I'm more inclined these days to revisit the lives of the Sylvia Beaches and Gertrude Steins from that influential 1920s stage.

Beach had opened the original location as a bookstore/lending library in 1919, moving it to a larger facility in 1921. She had been born in Baltimore as Nancy Beach to a Presbyterian minister, Sylvester Beach, in 1887, and had acquired her first taste of Paris when Sylvester became assistant minister of the American Church there. Her mother was the daughter of missionaries to India. They lived together in Paris for four years until the Reverend Beach returned to America to become minister of the First Presbyterian Church of Princeton, New Jersey. Name-changed Sylvia followed but then went back to Europe, first to join the International Red Cross in Spain and later to study French literature in Paris. After she opened Shakespeare and Company, she became a magnet for Lost Generation writers, most notably James Joyce for whom she published *Ulysses* in 1922 when no one else would touch more than snippets of it. To her, Joyce was a rare genius who could do no wrong, even though he pilfered money from her cash drawer on occasion and never offered her a penny of the $45,000 advance he received when Random House republished *Ulysses* in 1934.

She was friends with Gertrude Stein, and Stein's partner, Alice B. Toklas; and better friends with bookstore owner Adrienne Monnier with whom she lived for over thirty years until Monnier's suicide in 1955. They, every last one of them, from the literary and artistic contingent residing in Paris during the first years of the twentieth century, to the dispersing crowd of likeminded intellectuals in subsequent decades, were defined by war and what George Orwell once called "that evil time" into which they all had been born. The resulting devastation of mind and spirit was their context. Beach had joined a Red Cross mission to Serbia during World War I, where her first-hand witness of famine and death convinced her that war could never be justified for any reason; that is, until the Nazi occupation of Paris during World War II, when she was arrested and interned in eastern France.

Stein, on the other hand, managed to avoid arrest despite being Jewish and owning loot-worthy art by Pablo Picasso and Henri Matisse. She was the one who after World War I gave us the term, *lost generation*, which Hemingway subsequently conflated with Ecclesiastes 1:4 (KJV) as the foundation for his novel, *The Sun Also Rises*: "One generation passeth away, and another generation cometh; but the earth abideth forever." Stein's own book, *Wars I Have Seen*, later combined insights into both world wars to speak again of depressed, futureless generations. "It is very striking," she wrote in her semi-grammatical style; "they do not live in the present they just live, as well as they can, and they do not plan. It is extraordinary that whole populations have no [prospects] for a future, none at all."

Having once studied under American psychologist William James, she would have been familiar with James's thoughts on generations of sick souls and healthy minds, whom in her own mind could be projected into the wartime sensibilities of the writers and artists she nurtured. War was like dance, she said, always going forward and backward in meaningless repetition; also, that war was more like a novel than real life. "It is a thing based on reality but invented . . . a dream made real . . . but not really life," she wrote. Its ultimate destructive power, she added, was its annihilation of truth. "The times are so peculiar now," she summarized, "so mediaeval so unreasonable that for the first time in a hundred years truth really is stranger than fiction. Any truth."

As I stood outside Shakespeare and Company that late afternoon in December, a million images raced through my mind, as though I were watching a wartime black and white newsreel from a past life I had read about but hardly knew in any real sense. I was in a pleasant Paris funk as the light of day receded. Then darkness fell, and I would rather have joined in the prayer, "World War One - One Hundred Years On," posted by Church of All Saints Bingley, than staying lost in my own thoughts.

> O God,
> The memory of World War I haunts us.
> Stories are handed down from one generation to the next,
> and the suffering and sorrow and senseless horror
> fills the pit of our stomach and paralyzes.
> The earth cries out for blood spilt of one brother [or sister]!
> How cries the earth over thousands!
>
> O God,
> The war to end all wars!
> Today we bow our heads and weep for what is lost and unlearned
>   lessons,
> And humanity's continued loss.
> Breathe peace into the horror chamber of the heart,
> Breathe peace into perverse minds,
> Breathe peace into hands that violate.
> Teach us to respect and celebrate life,
> And life wrought through a wooden cross,
> Whereon shame is named,
> And Love's Power released.
> Peace to nations,
> Peace to man, woman, and child.
> Peace to all, O God!
> For your love's sake.
> Amen.

Chapter 28

GRACED

"I will remain in the world no longer ... and I am coming to you."
- CHRIST'S PRAYER -
GRACELAND, MEMPHIS, UNITED STATES

FROM THE TEMPLE-LIKE SHAKESPEARE AND Company in Paris to the shrine-like Graceland in Memphis, USA, I move back in time to an earlier travel experience in which, as ever, personal reflection leads to prayer.

In 1989, I was traveling in the American deep south with my first wife, long before the collapse of our marriage. Fried like green tomatoes from the August heat, and burned out from a few too many visits to literary and historical places, we decided to give Graceland a go, though neither of us were big Elvis fans.

In Memphis, we checked into a motel on Elvis Presley Boulevard, showered, and took sleepless naps. Jets were rising and falling directly overhead, close enough to make the walls vibrate. We put the air conditioner on high, which replaced jet sound with the rush of cool air, but in sleep's absence we soon were up and heading back out to the oven-like car. It was late afternoon, a hundred-plus Fahrenheit, and we drove to Graceland with a damp towel over the steering wheel.

We walked through the tourist center, the estate, and Elvis's private jet. Television sets, too numerous to count, loitered like watching eyes throughout the house, and halls of glittering memorabilia seemed worthy of Smithsonian treatment. The film about Elvis's life, however, was disappointing, at least in light of my endless desire to know how the early years of a person's life influences their later life course. What little I knew about Elvis centered on his church background, and I wanted more about root connections with his later life, good or bad. He was known to say that his religious upbringing had "nothing to do with his music," unknowing that such smokescreens commonly fall flat in their ignorance of attachment theory. In reality, his music had everything to do with his childhood faith.

At the garden gravesite we were surrounded by reverent pilgrims, some of whom were weeping, and I was reminded of how impassioned fan-disciples can be when trying to place the lingering image of their icon against the backdrop of its disappearance into the unknown. Every word, musical note, and visual memory of the subjectified hero floods the valley of one's mind like a swelling river overflowing all banks of conscious emotion. Elvis's pilgrims came each year by the thousands, of course, to feel. During Elvis International Tribute week that year, twelve thousand had showed up for the annual candlelight procession past the grave. When they returned home, they built shrines to their fallen icon: Elvis hotels, Elvis restaurants, models of Graceland, guitar-shaped swimming pools dedicated to Elvis, and more.

As we walked from the grave that day, I thought about the Elvis restaurant-shrine I had visited in Israel six years previous. Located on the highway that connected Tel Aviv with Jerusalem, a huge statue of Elvis welcomed travelers into a space packed with photographs, busts of Elvis, kitschy felt wall hangings, and framed concert tickets. On the same highway were holocaust sculptures, war monuments commemorating the Israeli state, and ancient ruins culminating in Jerusalem's Old City and its sacred historical universe. Elvis among all that seemed to create a bizarre mix, a Las Vegas Strip-like profaning of holy meanings on display in random contemporaneity. In truth, though, it was a scene ahead of its time in its conflation of meanings, indistinguishable one from another in the context of personal taste and preference. People make meaning based on how they want to make meaning, not because they may have been taught otherwise through the valuations of scholars and institutions. Indeed, the founder of the Elvis American Cafe, now in business for over forty years, said that he equated Elvis with Jesus and believed Elvis, too, would have founded a new religion if he had come two thousand years ago. Many, of course, would say that he did establish a new religion made from devoted fans, though as previously stated about pop culture icons I wonder if the numinous element is really there en masse as it is in the major religions.

Theoretically, I should have been more of a fan myself. Then, I would have a better answer to the Elvis-as-religion questions. My identification with him, however, was limited to what I knew of his past. He was a loner, by many accounts, as am I. He was closer to his mother, Gladys, than to his father, Vernon, who once went to prison for altering a cheque, necessitating uncomfortable jail visits from mother and son. My dad was a good man who never went to prison, but we were separated emotionally much of our lives while my mother and I shared an unbreakable bond. Elvis was a self-taught guitarist, as am I; a compliant student in school, a holder of menial jobs like delivery truck driving, a reluctant military man, survivor of a failed marriage, father to a daughter, and had a lifelong desire for a brother. I identify with all of these metrics in what has been a mostly normal life.

Identification based on religious upbringing is also a connection. As Sunday school, choir singing, Bible studies, youth ministry, and dating girls from church were central to Elvis's early life in southern evangelicalism, so was mine. Once our family had moved from Michigan to Florida after my father's disastrous accident as a police officer, we integrated ourselves into Southern Baptist tradition. That meant allegiances to standard iconic beliefs in biblical inerrancy and individual conversion, but also common restrictions to sins of the flesh through drinking, dancing, and anything approaching premarital sex. Our social lives as children, outside of public school, were based on Sunday school events, *training union*, prayer meetings, Wednesday night church suppers, and church retreats. The world beyond was always held at a distance, though every kid I knew badly wanted to escape into it at the first opportunity. Many of us did escape in our various ways, though we're naive to think we didn't carry our theological baggage with us. We return to idealized components of it eventually, too, hoping that it's still there in some form and that our new baggage of thought and experience acquired over a lifetime somehow accommodates it.

Elvis dodged his own set of exclusions and strictures, imposed on him by the southern Pentecostalism of Mississippi and Tennessee, through a musical stardom approached by few others in the history of popular culture. He really is *The King* in this regard with only Michael Jackson, perhaps, as his distant second among solo performers in rock. As the star without a peer, his meteoric career was a marvel, though he famously fell prey to the standard vices of fame which brought him so low that even non-fans weep over his fatal, barbiturate-fueled heart attack.

What made it so sad was that he feared it would happen but seemed helpless to avoid it. Arlene Sanchez Walsh's book, *Pentecostals in America*, states, "Elvis feared contamination by the unsavory elements of the music business but became subservient to . . . its glamorization of excess, and its banal acceptance of self-destruction."

That old Pentecostalism was still there through all of it, though. As Walsh adds, "Elvis took the most dynamic parts of Pentecostalism's embodied performance . . . and created what I call a religious miscegenation of sound and culture . . . ." He was a little bit country, a little bit blues and black-church gospel, a lot rock and roll, and a whole lot of Pentecostal faith and worship looming in the background. His five Christian albums (*His Hand in Mine, How Great Thou Art, You'll Never Walk Alone, He Touched Me, He Walks Beside Me*), spread out over two decades, makes that clear. And one day when he realized his life had fallen apart in a permanent unravel, he still believed, says Walsh, that "God had ordered his steps even if he didn't know why."

He prayed.

In her 2002 book, *Prayers of Elvis*, Madeleine Wilson wrote that the "Hillbilly Cat/Memphis Flash" not only still believed, he prayed privately and publicly, including "simple prayers of the young innocent boy . . . then throughout his life, to the anguished prayers of an isolated, troubled" man. Perhaps his prayers were like the tormented statements of King David whom in Psalm 18:4 (NIV) cried, "The ropes of death entangle me; floods of destruction sweep over me." Or maybe they were pleas for forgiveness, as in the song "An Evening Prayer" from his 1972 album, *He Touched Me*, where bathed in a prayerful, lyrical balancing of confession and humility, he sang another songwriter's words as his own in passionate authenticity.

However, I like to think that prayer for Elvis forged a deeper imprint than he had previously known or disclosed, and that toward the end of his life he so identified with the suffering Christ that he prayed Jesus's own words from the Gospel of John, chapter 17. As Christ pleaded to the Father for mercy on behalf of himself and his present and future followers, so Elvis likely would have found a place of rest in joining the Lord's words uttered just prior to his own death. This, of course, requires an enormous leap of critical guesswork, yet his most ardent fans would understand the theoretical joining of Elvis with Jesus in his final hours, not because he thought he was equal to Christ but because he could identify with the intercessory pleas of the praying Christ.

In John 17: 6–11 (NIV), Jesus prays,

I have revealed you to those whom you gave me out of the world.
They were yours; you gave them to me and they have obeyed your word.
Now they know that everything you have given me comes from you.
For I gave them the words you gave me and they accepted them.
They knew with certainty that I came from you, and they believed
that you sent me.
I pray for them.
I am not praying for the world, but for those you have given me,
for they are yours.
All I have is yours, and all you have is mine.
And glory has come to me through them.
I will remain in the world no longer, but they are still in the world,
and I am coming to you.

PART FIVE

Chapter 29

Father-Son Roadmap

"Build me a son whose wishes will not take the place of deeds."
- A FATHER'S PRAYER -
HANS L'ORANGE FIELD, HONOLULU, UNITED STATES

THE FIRST THING I NOTICED at Hans L'Orange Field near Honolulu were two large flags, suspended vertically from a high chain-link fence. The United States flag on the left, and to its right the flag of Japan, ruffled softly in a balmy Pacific breeze. Identical in size and shape, the stars and stripes, and the rising sun floating in its sea of pure white, symbolized equality, national pride, respect, and the celebration of difference. Forgiveness was the scene's outlier, but I had no reason to think it was not there, too.

Behind home plate, a group photo was being taken under a horizontal banner announcing in neon green letters: "SUPER SENIOR BASEBALL MATCH BETWEEN US AND JAPAN," with a smaller subtitle, "Field of Dreams 2007 in Hawaii." I counted thirty-seven standing players and another twelve sitting in the foreground grass. Not everyone was smiling, but with men of advanced age it's sometimes hard to tell. Case in point: my dad, sixth from the left in the back row, appeared to scowl, though in fact I knew this event was a highlight of his life, and inside his soul was grinning.

The two teams then lined up between home plate and third base for each country's national anthem and the introduction of players. Members of the Japanese "Over the Rainbows" squad gave a little bow after each player was introduced, while the American "Kids and Kubs" team tipped their caps when their names were called. Ages were not announced, though the minimum on each team was seventy-five, with some being ten or more years older, including my dad who was a few weeks shy of eighty-eight.

The players then reassembled to face each other and shake hands. Journalists from print, broadcast, and streaming news outlets observed. Families smiled from the grandstand, and then under a powder-blue December sky and with the scent of freshly cut grass permeating the air, the Over the Rainbows took the finely sculpted field while the Kids and Kubs prepared to bat. The week of games and formalities continued in more or less the same pattern, while evenings were spent in buffet suppers with interpreters recruited from the local universities. The players seemed to favor Tomoko, a Japanese-Hawaiian interpreter with a welcoming smile and silver chain earrings. I had flown in from California, determined not to miss a minute of the spectacle. To witness the coming together of men who had fought against each other in "The War," yet who now had agreed to face off in friendship on the baseball field, was too important not to shoot my entire travel budget that year. Of even greater personal fulfillment for me was the fact that the event would be my dad's final hurrah on the diamond and possibly my last chance to be a devoted son.

Baseball.

It was, beyond travel, the only thing we ever bonded over.

The bond was forged when I was a small boy growing up in Detroit, and my dad was in his thirties. Indeed, the first thing I clearly remember him saying happened one afternoon as I was hanging with neighborhood boys in the basement of our house. We were doing who knows what when suddenly Dad howled upstairs, shouting, "Eddie Yost just hit a grand slam homer!" That was it. He was watching his beloved Detroit Tigers on black and white tv and couldn't contain his excitement. That might also have been the moment I decided to join him in front of the screen to watch the games and become a lifelong fan. In that same basement, he taught me to bat left-handed like his hero, Ty Cobb, even though I was naturally right-handed. We played catch in the backyard, saw live games downtown at Tiger Stadium, discussed favorite players, and lived and died by the final scores. As the decades progressed, we were still at it, speaking by phone about the Tigers in the World Series, player retirements and deaths, and favorite memories of The Team.

Baseball was our lifeblood in other ways, too. After Dad had recuperated from a severe back injury as a policeman and moved our family to

Florida, he became my Little League manager. Then, throughout middle and high school when I played infield on the school teams, he attended every game, cheering me on from the grandstands. My interests in competitive baseball, however, began to wane in my late teens, replaced by music, literature, arts and sciences, and of course, travel. The baseball drop-off greatly disappointed him, and one day while sitting in the car he looked me in the eye and said, "I feel like I can't count on you anymore." This created a rift in our relationship that persisted for a long time, until he himself joined a competitive senior league when he turned sixty. I saw this as an opportunity to heal the rift. Whenever possible I flew in from where I was living to watch him play first base for the Three Score Club and later for Kids and Kubs. This brought both of us a lot of joy for nearly three decades, culminating in the Hawaiian tournament I was now attending.

The first three games against the Japanese team were satisfying but uneventful. During Thursday's game four, however, Dad stumbled badly after an at-bat, injuring both knees, an ankle, and perhaps mostly his pride, and then he removed himself from the lineup. When I went to check up on him in his dugout, he said gently, "I can't do it anymore." That was the last time he ever played. He lived another eight years, but there was no baseball in his life, and that enduring connection was over for both of us. The following day I found him lying in bed, alone, staring at the ceiling of his Honolulu hotel room. He was going to watch the Friday game from the dugout, and later in the day a group trip to Pearl Harbor was planned for both teams. That night, he returned to the hotel limping and somber.

On Saturday, though, an amazing thing happened. A final, formal banquet took place at an oceanfront restaurant, and large, round tables accommodated blended groups of American and Japanese players and immediate family who had attended the event. After a meal including popular dishes from both countries, a master of ceremonies opened the floor for testimonials of which there were many. Interpreters assisted non-English speakers. Dad gave a moving account of his time in Japan and Okinawa during the war, and mentioned that after he made his postwar return to the United States, he missed the Japanese friends he had made. He wanted to stay there for the rebuild under General Douglas MacArthur, but was sent home instead. I was beaming with pride in the seat next to him. Other testimonials included gestures of forgiveness for the attack on Pearl Harbor and the atomic bombings of Hiroshima and Nagasaki.

As the evening ended in tearful goodwill, a middle-aged Japanese man who had been sitting at another table introduced himself to Dad as Junichi. He had flown in from Tokyo to honor his father who had passed before the tournament. After hearing Dad's testimonial, he wanted to thank him for possibly being part of the humane treatment of his father who had been a prisoner of war. He said without it, his father might not have survived, which meant he would never have been born. Whether true or not, this opened up a conversation that lasted until nearly everyone had left the banquet room, and Junichi stayed in touch through cards and email for the rest of Dad's life. It also opened a new channel of communication for Dad and myself: his personal World War II history. I asked him new questions about old topics each time I visited him, which he delighted in answering, and I learned countless details of his story which had never before surfaced.

It became our final father-son bond. He died in 2016 at the age of ninety-six, and on my annual US visits I still stop at his gravesite in the Bushnell military cemetery in Florida where he rests in tranquility beside my mother.

The following prayer was composed by General MacArthur for his only son, Arthur MacArthur IV, born into the famous MacArthur military family whose roots go deep into American history. Prayers are sometimes more like wishes, and this prayer presents a father's wish-list of virtues he would like his son to possess: courage, humility, compassion, humor, remembrance of things past, and others. Whether or not these specific virtues resonated with the son, or how he felt about living truncated within his father's personal ideals, seems another story. Born in 1938, he bounced around the Philippines with his mother as his father was leading the war effort in the Pacific, eventually winding up in the safe confines of Australia. He moved with his family to Tokyo during the reconstruction and then to the United States after his father was dismissed by President Truman over strategic disagreements. In America he attended baseball games and circuses, loved music and drama, and majored in English at Columbia University. Then, he began to withdraw from public life, and an Associated Press story about him was headlined, "MacArthur's Son Shuns Military Life." He lived for many years alone in a New York City hotel, declined interview requests, and resided finally in Greenwich Village under an alias.

What kind of son was he? What kind of a father was Douglas MacArthur? Where did my dad and I locate ourselves on the exceedingly tangled father-son roadmap? Such questions are hard to answer for men, though we can always wish. And we can pray, as did MacArthur while stationed in Australia:

> Build me a son, O Lord,
> who will be strong enough to know when he is weak,
> and brave enough to face himself when he is afraid;
> one who will be proud and unbending in honest defeat,
> and humble and gentle in victory.
>
> Build me a son whose wishes will not take the place of deeds;
> a son who will know Thee —
> and that to know himself is the foundation stone of knowledge.
>
> Lead him, I pray, not in the path of ease and comfort,
> but under the stress and spur of difficulties and challenge.
> Here let him learn to stand up in the storm;
> here let him learn compassion for those who fail.
>
> Build me a son whose heart will be clear, whose goal will be high;
> a son who will master himself before he seeks to master other men;
> one who will reach into the future, yet never forget the past.
>
> And after all these things are his, add, I pray,
> enough of a sense of humor,
> so that he may always be serious, yet never take himself too seriously.
> Give him humility,
> so that he may always remember the simplicity of true greatness,
> the open mind of true wisdom,
> and the weakness of true strength.
>
> Then, I, his father, will dare to whisper,
> "I have not lived in vain."

Chapter 30

CANDLE POWER

"Gods . . . you are near to my life, to my problems, my family . . . my future."

- AN ICELANDIC PRAYER -
KEFLAVIK, ICELAND

AS AN AMERICAN STUDENT AT the University of Edinburgh in decades past, I often flew Icelandair to Scotland with free stopovers in Iceland offered by the company at that time. Most of the visits were in winter, and I was always stressed from wrapping up a semester of teaching in the United States while gearing up for the submission of my doctoral research at Edinburgh. So, I was never on the chilled oceanic island for longer than a few days, which is a big travel regret. The place is otherworldly.

Conversations with travelers on the long flights were frequent, especially before Christmas when dopamine levels were high and good times in Reykjavik were anticipated. One couple from California, seated next to me in economy class, said they never went anywhere else for the holidays. No relaxing beach vacations. No tropical excursions to paradise. No funky Mediterranean holidays in Greece or Italy. Just Iceland. Their preference for the Nordic winter experience had started years earlier, and why mess with a good thing?

Then, there was a conversation about *wheels* with a woman who used winter travel to scout new locations for the Ferris wheels she leased throughout northern Europe. She wanted to put one in Iceland, though transporting it up from the UK where she stored them in a field might prove tricky. "I'm on my way to Edinburgh, where there is always a Ferris wheel at the winter carnival on Princes Street," I said. "Oh, that's one of mine," she said, glowing. "We've been there going on fifteen years. There's a lot to the business. You have to stay up on design and technology, or someone else takes your place. Right now, there's a company in Sweden that has some radical new wheel. We're a bit nervous."

On the ground in Iceland, then out of the small terminal, I taxied to either Keflavik or Reykjavik taking in as much undefiled winter air as my lungs could hold. Chatoyant, jewel-like stars shimmered overhead and enlisted the crescent moon to light up night landscapes seeming to be more imaginary than sensory. Arriving at a hotel, I was already under some kind of yule spell that says drop your bags and check in fast because the action is outside in the cold, which really isn't cold but rather like a crisp, refrigerated blanket that prickles the skin while the rest of the body stays warm. It wasn't as if the shops, bars, and restaurants weren't inviting with their welcoming candle-in-the-window glow. It was just that you wanted to stay out in the walking lanes with the unmistakable feeling that you'd never be more alive than you were at that moment in icy time.

Apparently, only time itself freezes in Iceland.

Because my visits were disappointingly brief, I have often turned to Icelandic travel literature to remind me of what I missed and how much I want to return. The best of the recent books would have to be *Names for the Sea: Strangers in Iceland*, by Sarah Moss. Of re-read quality is "Winter," a chapter one might use if teaching a course in the uses of color and light to a person with synesthesia. One person's silky gray might well be another person's milky indigo, but Moss manages to persuade us that her descriptions are reliable to anyone who sees through their mind's eye. Verbs themselves create cosmic motions: a waning sun "sidles over the horizon"; winter light "drains from the sky"; "stars wheel through days and nights." And then there are the colors: "There's pallor in the southeastern sky, but out to the northwest, over the sea, the sky is navy, full of cold stars." We see the "false pink promise," black on white "moon shadows," and land that "glows like well-polished furniture in candle-light," all of which surely are Iceland in winter.

At one point, Moss goes home for a holiday visit to England where it is cold, convenient, and measured before returning to Iceland "to be warm again." Candles, too, add to that warmth, as per my own observations there. Many candles in many places.

Candles in winter, though, are about more than warmth and soft light. They ignite romance and soothe senses, according to the National Candle Association. They decrease distraction and are therapeutic, according to Aleteia, a society for Catholics. They symbolize the eternal light of Christ for Christians, restfulness for Jews during Shabbat, respect and deference for Buddhists, Ying and Yang for Taoists, according to the interfaith Patheos group. In Islam, says Patheos (and which I know from personal observation), candles accompany Eid al-Fitr, the celebration that follows the month of fasting in Ramadan. I vividly recall a restaurant full of candles in Tangier, Morocco where celebrants were enjoying their first breakfast in a month as Rissy and I ordered dinner. Candles seemed to unify all of us in a welcoming atmosphere, which was also one of the times in my life of travel when I saw how much pure joy exists among celebratory Muslims.

How would religions even exist without candles? one is inclined to ask.

A short vignette. One early morning in Keflavik, I walked down the long hallway from my hotel room to the dining area where breakfast was served. Candles were placed strategically on wall shelves, in corners, near the buffet, and on dining tables, creating a subdued ambiance. The only unnatural lights were the small round bulbs that illuminated a buffet table packed with cold cuts, cheeses, and a variety of baked goods. Alone in the eating area, I poured a freshly brewed coffee, placed a few items on a plate, and sat down at a table. A charming, talkative girl of about seventeen, I estimated, appeared from the kitchen, and I now reconstruct our conversation from memory.

"Welcome to Iceland," she said. "Are you arriving or leaving?"

"Heading off to Scotland in a few hours," I said. "It's lovely here. I want to return sometime."

"It should be light by about eleven. I hope you enjoyed your stay at our hotel."

"Very nice. Even the kids running through the hallways all night," I said, jokingly.

"Ha ha," she laughed. "Those might have been the Yule Lads. We have stories about mischief-making kids who come at the holidays to steal things and create general havoc."

"Hmm, I thought they were just rowdy kids having a good time. Is that some kind of a Lutheran story?"

"Oh, we're not Lutherans like everyone thinks," she said. "We like our own gods, like Odin, Loki, and Freya. We pray to them sometimes. Some of us are Asatru."

"Asatru?"

"It's our ancient religion, before the Lutherans and the Catholics came here. Well, have a safe flight. Come back sometime. Summer is best." And she disappeared into the kitchen.

I returned to my room, packed, and soon was in a taxi on my way to the airport a few miles from the hotel. The sun did come up between eleven and noon, though it was never very bright. My taxi driver said enjoy it now, it'll be gone by three-thirty. I never got to see it set and was on my plane by one o'clock. In the intervening years, the amateur historian in me has grown increasingly interested in the pre-Christian world, not just in Iceland but everywhere. I maintain an active Christian faith, but I do enjoy learning about ancient beliefs and practices that may have shaped aspects of monotheism and my own belief in one God. At the same time, I do not begrudge anyone for the beliefs they hold, or the prayers they offer. Somehow, they are heard. Somehow, they repair the damage caused by disbelief and the resulting spiritual void which traps the human mind in its own terminal neuroplasticity.

The following "Candle Prayer," from *Odin's Gift* in Iceland, speaks of faith, hope, and love in a Nordic mythological context:

> Gods, I come before you to light this candle.
> I know that a candle is not a great sacrifice,
> It is almost nothing of me,
> Almost nothing of my work,
> Almost nothing of my money.
>
> It is only a sign
> That I want to remain in your presence
> For a few moments in silence.
>
> It is a sign that I have come because I know
> That you hear and see me,
> That you are near to my life,
> To my problems, my family,
> My work, my surroundings,
> And my future.
>
> This candle is a sign of trust

And my faith in you, my Gods.
I trust that it can rekindle my own heart's fire.
When I go now, this candle remains
As a symbol of my presence,
Until it has consumed itself.
Receive it as my sacrifice,
Receive it as my prayer,
Receive it as my silence,
And as a sign of my love.

Chapter 31

CHANNELING LUCILLA

"St. Jude, patron saint of lost causes, pray for me...
my husband, my marriage."

- A PRAYER OF REGRET -
THE COLOSSEUM, ROME, ITALY

WHILE SPENDING A DAY AT the Colosseum a few years ago with Rissy, I found it impossible not to see the world's most famous classical monument through the lens of *Gladiator*, the 2000 film directed by Sir Ridley Scott and starring Russell Crowe. Its soundtrack ear-wormed its way into my brain for the entire day, as did the indelible memory of scenes featuring Crowe's Maximus Decimus Meridius, Joaquin Phoenix's Commodus, and Djimon Hounsou's African tribesman, Juba.

I was not surprised. Through years of teaching a media psychology course with an emphasis on fandom, I had frequently shown relevant clips from the film, such as Crowe's decapitation of a foe while shouting to an adoring audience, "Are you not entertained? Is this not why you are here?" And then there was Derek Jacobi's Gracchus, speaking to his fellow Roman senators about Commodus's sought popularity with the masses: "He'll give them death, and they will love him for it."

That day, while examining as much of the ancient amphitheater as possible, furnished me with the all-important prospect of seeing face to face what I had been teaching about for so long from a distance. It was hot and dusty among the travertine stone walls and staircases, but my historian wife and I didn't want to leave, our imaginations stimulated to the point of meditative suspension that, as mentioned, doesn't come very often and stays until we decide to squelch it.

The visit was also a time of clarification brought about by an awareness of changing times and societal trends. If I were to teach that same course now, twenty years after the movie was released, for instance, I would choose other clips and a different perspective. I would likely, or only, offer to students Lucilla's story as the most relevant plot point for our times. Fleshed out by Connie Nielsen, Lucilla walks a daily tightrope between her brother Commodus's incestuous desires, his threats to the safety of her young son, Lucius, his consuming efforts to have her former lover Maximus killed in the arena, all of it packaged in a world that, for her, exists far beyond any forms of amusement or entertainment contained by the Colosseum. What would Lucilla say about her place in that world? Would she see herself as a victim, a willing participant, a maker of mistakes that led to her own predicament for which she was at least partially to blame, a helpless pawn offering no avenues for escape? Hard to say.

And isn't that the point? We don't have close to enough information about either the internal or external lives of women in the ancient world to answer those questions adequately.

In the specific contexts of Rome, the Colosseum, gladiators, sex, violence, and death, we do have a few snippets of women. We encounter Eppia, for instance, the Roman senator's wife who allegedly ran off with the gladiator Sergius to the Nile River in Egypt. She was said to have forsaken her husband, sister, weeping children, and country for a man with a deformed face, a deep helmet scar, an ugly growth on his nose, and a leaky eye. What was the attraction? Was the perilous voyage across the sea with her lover a fair exchange for her entitled life in a Roman villa and her seaside spread at Antium with her family? We don't know because the narrator of the vignette, Decimus Junius Juvenalis (commonly known as Juvenol) doesn't allow Eppia to speak, preferring instead to use her as an example in his satirical attack on pagan Rome. To Juvenol, she merely belonged in his diatribe on adulterers, seducers, and unfaithful wives. He calls his satire, "The Ways of Women."

We also encounter Faustina, the empress of Marcus Aurelius and mother to Commodus, whom like Eppia may have found love in the arms of a gladiator. One account holds that after Marcus Aurelius visited soothsayers about the alleged infidelity, they suggested he have the gladiator killed, his wife bathed in the dead man's blood, and then have sex with her. Again allegedly, the emperor executed the advice and raised Commodus, whom in turn showed enduring interest in the gladiatorial violence of the Colosseum. On a less-macabre stage, there was also Valeria, who was said to have seduced the Roman General Lucius Cornelius Sulla sometime in pre-second or first-century Rome BCE at a gladiator fight. Plutarch, Sulla's biographer, said that Valeria had exited a back row where women commonly sat, approached the general, brushed off his cloak, and placed her hand on his shoulder in obvious flirtation, receiving a marriage proposal in return.

Much scholarly doubt, of course, accompanies the stories of Eppia, Faustina, and Valeria—not to mention that of Angelica, former girlfriend of goldsmith Benvenuto Cellini, whom according to Cellini himself was unsuccessfully re-wooed in a dark arts ceremony held secretly at the Colosseum, releasing a legion of bad demons—and yet the stories have survived. As with Ridley Scott's film, the place just seems to massage the imagination while one is in Rome, similar to how Scotland's Loch Ness keeps visitors searching for the monster. We really would love to hear from the women, though. What might Eppia say about Juvenol's general contempt for women which painted her into so egregious a corner? Would she say something about the contrast between her suffocating life of privilege and her survivalist escape through a condemned man serving punishment as an outsider from society? Would Faustina counter her blood myth with a retort about the cosmology of perverted desire in Rome, which featured bizarre images such as the sculpture of a gladiator in combat with his own phallus which had the head of a biting animal? Would Valeria speak about the insult of being relegated to the back rows of the Colosseum only for being born female?

Or would all three women offer sincere regrets for engaging in behavior unbecoming and contrary to their true selves? When Lucilla arranges Maximus's escape from prison in order to overthrow Commodus, Maximus says, "You risk too much." Lucilla responds by saying, "I have much to pay for." Who, for the love of righteous confession, isn't listening now?

The historic silencing of women is tragic not only because the stories of virtuous, victorious lives are lost to us, but also because we have been deprived of confessions made by women coming to terms with their own mistakes, in their own words, unfiltered by satirical, condescending men. Had the Juvenols and Plutarchs of the Roman gender politic stepped aside to allow the Eppias and Faustinas to speak, needed historical balances would have been restored for a world that looks back and sees only misogyny.

Far removed from that ancient imbalance, we have "Pray for Me, for I Am an Adulteress," a prayer offered by a contemporary woman, Julia, and posted on the *Pray with Me* website. Feeling lost and in need of mercy brought on by her marital unfaithfulness, Julia's confession is addressed to Saint Jude of Lost Causes, who may have been the canonized Jude of the New Testament whose book precedes the *Book of Revelation*. In any case, her "human sorrows" echo in the eternal quest for the forgiveness of sins and the hope for grace that follows:

> I've failed as a wife, almost each of the six years we've been married,
> not to mention the (almost) six years of dating before we wed,
> I have crossed the line and this time it was the ultimate line.
> I know it will take a miracle from some other realm that impacts this
>   human one,
> for my husband to back down from divorcing me.
> I have no reason to deserve to be with him,
> he has given me so many chances and like the ridiculous woman I am,
> I have blown each and every last one of them.
>
> Saint Jude, patron saint of lost causes, pray for me.
> Pray for my husband, my marriage.
> I can barely believe I'm actually praying to a Catholic saint right now
> (on a computer no less).
> I am no longer Catholic but believe in the saints as higher beings,
> So, with this belief I have to trust that you, Saint Jude, whatever/
>   whoever you
> are out there in the reality we people on earth just can't comprehend,
> I beg of you, have mercy on me and restore my husband's heart
> to the beautiful, warm, passionate thing it was before I got my hands
>   on it.
> I believe in penance but also that it comes in the form of reincarnation.
> I just pray the rest of this life is peaceful for my dear combat veteran
>   husband;
> he's done so much for me, the least I can do is pray.
>
> Thank you for listening to my human sorrows. I am truly grateful.

Chapter 32

SISTERS OF ECCE HOMO

*"I dare not ask for improved memory,
but for growing humility...."*

- A NUN'S PRAYER -
ECCE HOMO CONVENT, JERUSALEM, ISRAEL

I HAVE BEEN A PERIODIC visitor to Jerusalem, traveling to the holy city as a pilgrim, and for other reasons, in 1983, 1985, 1990, and 2007. I would like to go back one more time, with my wife or possibly my daughter, to see them empowered by the history, humanity, and spirituality of the place as only a meditative journey within the ancient walls can do.

When I recall my own sojourns there, I mostly remember the nuns at the Ecce Homo Convent, now known as the Ecce Homo Pilgrim House. Built over some interesting Roman pavement from the first century CE, the nuns' dwelling place reaches high above the Muslim Quarter of the city, which means their day tends to be structured around the five calls to prayer from an adjacent mosque. The amplified muezzin recording vibrates the windows of the convent, which bothers some residing pilgrims, though the nuns don't seem to mind. In fact, as Sister Bernice told me one evening on the open rooftop in 1985, she liked to use the call as her own reminder to pray unceasingly under the stars.

How I first came to Ecce Homo in 1983 tasks my memory. Possibly, I had followed a friend, Zelma, from the archaeological dig we were on. A large group of us were earning academic credit, or simply life experience, by excavating the ruins of an ancient biblical city, and with the expedition camp closing on weekends we dispersed in many directions. Zelma, an interesting woman many years my senior, had become a conversation partner at the dig, and I remember seeing her at the convent. She was from somewhere in the American south, and on a biblical materiality quest to complement her life of Bible reading far removed from its geographical source. Her annual visits to "the land" had a healing effect on her body as she approached seventy, I recall her saying over breakfast at the convent. In any case, in 1983 I was staying in a pilgrim's cubicle by night and exploring the Old City of Jerusalem by day.

Two years later, I returned for a month while on assignment for *Aramco World Magazine*. My job was to develop a Jerusalem follow-up to an article exploring the travels of English-language authors to other parts of the Middle East. At Ecce Homo, I expected to occupy a cubicle again but was given a beautiful room overlooking a garden when I was assumed by the staff to be a visiting priest. I informed the prioress about this mistaken identity, but she allowed me to stay in the room until a real priest arrived. My days were spent in the convent library and in wandering around Jerusalem photographing staircases and monuments mentioned by authors who had visited in the 1800s.

Then, in 1990 I returned again to the holy city as the faculty leader of sixteen evangelical university students receiving summer course credit. We were booked into The Institute of Holy Land Studies (now Jerusalem University College) on Mount Zion, which was necessary since daily lectures were held there. The entire experience, however, seemed culturally narrow in the protected confines of the Institute, and I would rather have seen the students de-evangelicalized and de-Zionized at Ecce Homo in the Muslim parts of the city. I was unable to pull it off, though, even as I worked hard to show them a broader approach to faith than the evangelical one. I have tried most of my life to de-program myself from the power-order cult of American evangelicalism which masquerades as Christianity.

Seventeen years passed. I was living in southern California in 2007 when Terry, a friend from Santa Barbara, asked if I would accompany her to the Holy Land. She offered to pay my airfare, so we flew from Los Angeles to Tel Aviv, taxied up to Jerusalem, and checked into the convent. All the nuns I had known from the previous visits had moved on or passed away, but the open spirit of hospitality and cultural accommodation was still present, and Terry thrived in it. I would see her each day in the library or out on the breezy rooftop, open Bible on lap, inhaling the spiritual essence of Jerusalem. By night, I introduced her to old friends in the city such as Nassir, a Palestinian man still making the best pizza in the Old City at his place on the Via Dolorosa. Terry was so taken by his charm that she traveled solo one day to the West Bank to meet his family. Modestly dressed but uncovered, she found herself put upon by male bus passengers on the way back but survived.

On the days following, we moved about the countryside as tourists, taking in the Dead Sea, Masada, Jericho, Galilee, and more, though what Terry most wanted was to return to Jerusalem for spiritual journaling at Ecce Homo. That was when I realized again how important Jerusalem is as a destination, especially for sojourning women seeking a liminal state of being that can serve as a rite of passage from something to something they had never known in any previous life experience. Trapped in suffocating careers but desiring real work, or in lifeless marriages craving real intimacy, they seek a transitional channel from the mundane to the deep. Perhaps they've grown so weary of habitual mind games fostered by being responsible for everyone else's well-being, they wake up one day to realize they have been caught in the spokes of an endlessly rotating wheel whose centrifugal force keeps them from transitioning to the freedom of mind every human being needs to feel whole. Perhaps nuns know this dynamic best.

Growing up, I didn't know any nuns myself. Catholic neighbors in Michigan, however, gave me caricatures of nuns as bossy disciplinarians teaching in the local Catholic schools, and caustic jokes from anti-Catholic sources supplemented the caricatures: *What is black and white and black and white . . . ? A nun rolling down the stairs.* Our Baptist church did little to counter this mentality, though much later in life many Protestant traditions began to accommodate Catholic spirituality through the writings of Thomas Merton and Henri Nouwen. And, of course, there were theological nods to Saint Augustine, Thomas Aquinas, and other church fathers for their shaping of the Christian mind. Yet, any roles women might have played historically in this mindset emerged slowly if at all, and nuns seemed to occupy a silent space in some sealed environment neither necessary nor relevant to faith.

In 1524, Martin Luther wrote a letter to nuns from his residence in Wittenberg, Saxony. Freed from their vows to the Catholic Church seven years after the Reformation, the nuns had asked Luther for any thoughts he might have that would justify their actions. He wrote back saying there were two solid reasons they could forsake their vows: one, where "men's laws" and their own "conscience" were being manipulated in such a way as to destroy their "freedom of choice;" and two, where they wished to be in "marital union" with a man, accompanied by the desire to "bear children." He added, "Suffice it to say that no one needs to be ashamed over how God has made and created [them], not having been given the high, rare mercy to do otherwise." Now, five hundred years later, one wonders whether Luther might do some table-turning, saying it's okay for women to free themselves from the suffocating circumstances of modern life and to find spiritual liberation in unexpected places, such as in a convent.

The nuns of Ecce Homo, according to their website, seem to be happy enough. Sister Bernadette arrived from Australia and says that she "knows what it means to be different. I took my freedom and went my own way until the whisper from this faithful God grew stronger." In the heart of Jerusalem, she feels "challenged daily to be a woman of peace; to seek deeper joy, and to make greater efforts to create space" for the other nuns to live in freedom. Sister Trudy, also from Australia, has lived at the convent for fifteen years and enjoys "walking with sisters who come here to study in 'the land.' I praise and thank God for this call, and I continue to hear the voice behind me saying, 'This is the way, walk in it'" (Is. 30:21 NIV).

Two Canadian nuns speak of being healed in the deep identifying presence of Jerusalem. After eighteen years at Ecce Homo, Sister Lucy sees "how necessary reconciliation and healing are in complex situations. Often the strong words of Isaiah come into my heart and mind: 'You cannot rejoice for Jerusalem if you have not first mourned with her'" (Is. 66:10 NIV). Sister Rita, who entered the convent in 1997 after caring for her ill mother, says, "I've discovered that in life you take in all that will help you grow, to be alive, to live worthwhile and contributing lives. God was present in both the joys and the harder moments of my life . . . no matter the struggle, obstacle, or mood." Having their "mood" transformed from that which existed in burdensome past lives into a lighter, joyful present might be the best way to describe these nuns.

The "Old Nun's Prayer" offered here is said to have been discovered in an English church, and is possibly from the seventeenth century, though many believe it is more recent. Light, tongue-in-cheek, and from someone who knows how to laugh at herself, the prayer doesn't take anything too seriously and incorporates the mood of ultimate self-acceptance:

Lord, you know better than I know myself
that I am growing older and one day will be old.
Keep me from the fatal habit of thinking I must
say something on every subject and on every occasion.

Release me from craving to
straighten out everybody's affairs.
Make me thoughtful but not moody;
helpful but not bossy.

With my vast store of wisdom
it seems a pity not to use it all;
but you know, Lord, that I want a few friends at the end.
Keep my mind free from the recital of endless details,
give me wings to get to the point.

Seal my lips on my aches and pains;
they are increasing and love of rehearsing them
is becoming sweeter as the days go by.
I dare not ask for grace enough
to enjoy the tales of others' pains,
but help me to endure them with patience.

I dare not ask for improved memory,
but for growing humility and a lessening cocksureness
when my memory seems to clash with the memories of others.
Teach me the glorious lesson that occasionally
I may be mistaken.

Keep me reasonably sweet;
I do not want to be a saint; some of them are so hard to live with,
but a sour person is one of the crowning works of the devil.

Give me the ability to see good things in unexpected places
and talent in unexpected people,
and give me O Lord the grace to tell them so.
Amen.

Chapter 33

Good Hope

"What misery it would be to suppose our friends . . .
were annihilated at death."

- A VOYAGER'S PRAYER -
MACAU, CHINA

BUT FOR THE FACT THAT she was not Catholic, Harriet Low also might have made a good nun. She had a service mindset, seemed at peace with being single, and was at heart a spiritual adventurer. Her articulate journal of travels in southeast Asia, primarily Macau, left us with a vivid portrait of a young American woman lost in unfamiliarity but with a hunger to know what lay beyond the comforts of a guarded life. She was, in the early 1830s, moreover, an innocent abroad three decades before Mark Twain's, *The Innocents Abroad*, and through her eyes we see not only a clear and colorful Macau but also the perilous journey by sea to get there and then get home again.

In 2010, it was hard to see anything on the ferry from Hong Kong to Macau. Strong north winds had mountainous, tossing waves on the South China Sea lashing against the boat's windows, keeping the jammed-in passengers in foamy gray suspense all the way. By the time we docked in Macau, a few were seasick, no doubt wishing they hadn't been munching on those Portuguese egg tarts for sale in the commissary. I was one of the lucky ones to have skipped breakfast that day, though I too bolted for dry land once the hatches were opened.

Out in the streets where the air was moist and the ground stable, I walked past the casinos that rival those in Monte Carlo and Las Vegas, stopping to photograph the gigantic, gilded lotus rising above the red granite of Lotus Square. A symbol of Macau's prosperous economy, the monument was part of the celebration in 1999 which marked the end of Portuguese sovereignty over Macau and its ceremonious transfer to China. In Portugal, we talk a fair amount about this because it was the final piece of the empire to go. Outside Portugal, only historians and attentive travelers know much of anything about our five-hundred-year empire which extended to Brazil, many of the islands in the Atlantic Ocean, Angola and Mozambique in Africa, parts of the Indian Ocean and the coasts of India and Sri Lanka, and a large swath of the western Pacific Ocean from East Timor north almost to Japan. Even the discoveries of Australia and New Zealand are part of the discussion if you believe *Beyond Capricorn* by Peter Trickett, the book arguing that the Portuguese were there, exploring and mapping, in 1522, more than two hundred years before England's Captain James Cook made his big public splash.

Walking through old Portuguese Macau, I could have sworn I was at home in Lisbon. Its wavy, cobbled streets, small shops filled with Portuguese delicacies, and Baroque architecture painted in pastel tones, charmed me like an afternoon stroll down Lisbon's Avenida da Liberdade. A tranquil rain started to fall as I reached the monumental staircase of Saint Paul's Church, its facade standing enormous and solitary in the background. Built by Jesuits between 1602 and 1640, the entire church stood for two hundred years before it caught fire during a typhoon in 1835 and everything but the facade was lost. It, too, was slated for demolition out of safety concerns but was eventually restored and fortified, making it one of the seven wonders of Portuguese origin.

Harriet Low refers to the great church in her journal, and little did she know it would come crashing down mere months after leaving Macau for America in 1834. She had arrived in late September, 1829, barely out of her teens, looking for adventure. Her sponsor was the East India Company, the British trade group founded under Queen Elizabeth 1 in 1600 as the English, Portuguese, Spanish, Dutch, and French were all staking claims in Asia over the trades in spices, silks, and tea. It's not clear from the journal exactly what Low did for the company, other than enjoying the off-hours leisure activities for which it was known. Also, she had a beloved aunt and uncle, apparently employed by the EIC in Macau, and that was likely her reason for going there. She was the second of twelve children, born in Salem, Massachusetts, and a lone image of her placed in the journal reveals a confident woman dressed formally with an open book in her lap.

Shortly after leaving Salem, she knew she was into something very real. One of her first observations was of the ship trying to make its way through the treacherous Atlantic headwinds blowing from the southeast, and how she had been saved from the dangers that surrounded her. Thirty-five days in, she said, "I pray . . . that I may daily learn to put my trust in that Being who is continually watching over me. I hope that I shall not always live a useless life, but by a good example (if nothing more) I may do something for Him who has done so much for me." Seventy-nine days in, after the ship had successfully rounded the bottom of Africa and navigated the Indian Ocean, she noted that they were almost to Java and was struck by how far from home she had sailed. She talked about the "wave to wave" monotony of the journey and the uncertainty of her life, writing that any prospects of future happiness for her lay hidden in the future. A three-week stop on dry land in Manila revived her, but again at sea she wrote, "Sick all day. Squally, rainy, uncomfortable weather, and a heavy, irregular sea [has] made us all sick. I was stretched out on the floor all day, or in my trough . . . ."

At the four-month point the ship arrived in Macau, which Low described as "beautiful" and "romantic." She liked her house and garden, set amid Macau's grid of narrow streets, and five days later she was invited to her first evening event: "the night of the ball," she wrote. "We went at 8 o'clock [and] enjoyed ourselves very much, and did not return until 3am, the first time in my life I was ever out so late." Clearly, life was good for a twenty-year-old, though in time she grew frequently annoyed by many things: the ogling of men, the confusion of spoken languages, the Chinese, the Portuguese, the lascars from unfamiliar places, the Catholic Church and its public processions. "Our bigoted little Puritan," as the journal's editor described her, wrote, "It is now Lent, and they have many of these processions. When I see these things, I thank my God that I was born where they worship Him in a more Christian way."

By the following year, however, that same little Puritan was growing up. She enjoyed walking "to the steps of the Cathedral" and listening "to the rich tones of the organ," which seemed to caress her into a state of self-reflection. Then one day she entered the church during a mass, writing, "For the first time [I] approached the altar and partook of the holy sacrament. May it be the commencement of a new life in me." At that point, and in the years ahead, the focus became one of shedding childish illusions and moving toward a more mature faith than her American conservatism had provided her. "I often ask myself why I was born, and for what purpose I was sent into the world," she wrote. "This morning was spent in self-examination, to see if by any means I could think myself worthy."

The dye seemed fairly cast at that point, and the balance of her five years in Macau consisted of acknowledging silly foibles and superficiality, accepting what might never change (like being a permanent "spinster"), dreaming of home, and most of all trying to be a better Christian. "I earnestly hope that the love of such a [deeper faith] will grow with my years and strengthen with my strength, for I am very sure that it is the only consolation in adversity, and the securest refuge in times of disappointment and trouble."

She had grown close to her aunt, and to her uncle whom she described as "my father in feeling," and when the time came to ship out with them for home, the uncle grew gravely ill. He was failing badly on board, though he accepted his condition without complaint, eventually dying as the ship reached Cape Town, South Africa. Low described a "dreadful chasm" she had fallen into, which contained "the sick and dying bed of my dear Uncle. I pray that it may make a lasting impression on me ... and I pray also that my end may be calm, peaceful, and happy like his."

After leaving Cape Town, the journey home was plagued by swarming cockroaches in the sleeping quarters of the ship, rotten weather, frustrating head winds, and halted progress, so that Low felt she would never arrive home. She did, however, and the journal ended abruptly on the 21st of September, 1834, with these words: "I cannot explain how I feel, it is a sort of all-overness, and yet it appears to me that I am going to a strange place, as I have been to so many before."

A postscript was added by her daughter Katherine, who eventually published the journal in 1900 as *My Mother's Journal: A Young Lady's Diary of Five Years Spent in Manila, Macao, and the Cape of Good Hope from 1829–1834*. In the note, Katherine Hillard said that her mother, the "spinster," eventually found happiness with "the Hon. George S. Hillard from Boston," moved to England, and gave birth to eight children. After he died on a visit to America in 1859, Harriet Low remained in the US where she "preferred to spend the rest of her life among her own people," until her death in 1877. No mention was made of her ever traveling again.

Though she spoke often about praying, no prayer exists in the journal. Yet, the heartfelt confession offered at the moment of her uncle's death seems prayerful enough to take as such, so I include it here:

> "If I am not made better by such lessons as these, what am I made of? Oh God, grant that each may make a deep impression, let not the remembrance ever be obliterated, and may they serve to make me wise unto Salvation.

> "Was in my own room by myself all day thinking much of my dear departed Uncle, and fancy him enjoying a Sabbath in heaven, with angels and the Spirits of the just made perfect. What a delightful thought! How dreadful it would be to be deprived of the hope of immortality. What misery it would be to suppose our friends, both soul and body were annihilated at death, [and] how foolish indeed it would seem to form ties today which tomorrow were to be burst asunder and leave us today on a wearisome life, without the hope of being reunited.

> "But thanks to our Father in heaven and our Lord Jesus Christ, we have that hope to lean upon and which will support us in the hour of adversity and urges us to press onward in a moral and religious life that we may be ready when we are called."

Chapter 34

FORESEEING A DIVIDED NATION

> "O powerful goodness... accept my kind offices to
> Thy other children as the only return in my power for
> Thy continued favors to me."
>
> - A DEIST'S PRAYER -
> PHILADELPHIA, UNITED STATES

THE MACRO HISTORY OF WHITE America has never engaged my imagination the way the country's micro histories of ethnicity and race have. I get little from it and would rather journey through the vintage black musicscapes of Mississippi, the historical communities of Asian immigrants in California, or any Native American places, from Seminole country in south Florida to the Puyallup culture of Puget Sound.

Still, like many Americans I have taken the obligatory eastern seaboard trip as both child and adult, the latter perhaps to see if I had missed anything important from the first time. Plymouth Plantation, Boston's Freedom Trail, Gettysburg, Washington DC, Charleston, Savannah, battlefields and monuments, memorials and gravesites, all are taken in accompanied by the feeling that one visit is, or should have been, enough. More than enough, perhaps.

The lone exception for me might be Philadelphia, in general, and the Benjamin Franklin sites, in particular. Traveling to places where historically iconic people lived forces one to think about those icons, and I have never minded being obliged to think about Franklin. At

Independence Park I remember walking through the excavated home site which revealed the stratigraphy beneath his house. Levels of earth corresponding to Franklin's years in Philadelphia had been marked out and detailed with the archaeologist's primary text: broken pottery. Facing the balk, one could see buried items possibly belonging to Franklin himself, and more importantly, the man unknown to anyone but his immediate family. His wife Deborah; a son, Francis, who died young; another son, William, who opposed his father's revolutionary instincts by siding with the British as a loyalist; and a beloved daughter, Sarah, who named her son after her father, were all part of the story. It's a good story.

My original reading of Franklin's autobiography, in fact, was a major event in my informal education. Amazingly, it sits on a shelf here in Lisbon, having been through the transoceanic move plus earlier moves to Toronto, Chicago, Minneapolis, Los Angeles, Edinburgh, and indeed a few other places. I had picked it up as a teen in Florida, where I read it during early mornings as frogs bellowed and croaked in the backyard by the drainage canal. That little book had given me a hungry mind that made me want to settle down and learn. The dullness of my high school brain and the endless report cards with "not living up to his potential" inscribed across the back, suddenly sharpened into a wild curiosity. More, the autobiography had presented me with a pattern of spiritual development that turned me inward. Franklin's generous recollection of events such as his baptism in Boston's Old South Church, and his father's singing of "Psalm tunes" to him when he was barely out of the cradle, made my own background of "family worship" and "ambassadors for Christ" seem not as weird as it once had.

My emerging doubts about everything, too, seemed suddenly okay. Franklin's trajectory toward unbelief pressed in on him as a teen who had become a disputer of church doctrines. He began to value work and study more than going to church and became known as an infidel and atheist to his friends. Later, he viewed himself as an emerging deist, which he understood as an expression of Christian belief stripped of its suffocating doctrines. He wrote, "My parents had early given me religious impressions, and brought me through my childhood piously in the dissenting way. But . . . after doubting by turns of several points, I began to doubt of revelation itself. In short, I soon became a thorough deist."

He lived happily and productively that way. Only occasionally did he feel the need to return to church for instruction he could not get apart from it. His silly attempt at moral perfection had shown him the futility of trying to be "good" in a world that led one in other directions if he strayed too far from base. Yet, when he returned home, as it were, he did not find moral instruction. He found, instead, a church wallowing in its doctrines; more interested, he wrote, in "making people into Presbyterians" than in creating moral citizens capable of using their faith to make a difference in the emerging republic. It's doubtful that Franklin ever returned to church after that. He made his own way theologically, reciting one of two daily prayers as a way of maintaining a connection to the deity while going forward with his life. And when pressed to offer a creed, Franklin spoke of a God who made all things, who governed the world by his providence, who rewarded virtue and punished vice, who had given humans an immortal soul, and who was reachable through prayer.

He never stopped believing in prayer.

Independence Park in Philadelphia is, of course, home to Independence Hall, where in 1787 as the Pennsylvania State House it harbored America's Constitutional Convention, also known as the Philadelphia Convention. Gracing its green and gray interior is as good a place as any to meditate not only on the founding of the American government but on the spiritual and practical concerns that made it possible. Of enduring, and dare I say timeless, interest is Franklin's speech to the delegates in which he pleaded for opening all business with prayer. Seeking "in the dark to find political truth," he reasoned, should follow the act of "humbly applying to the Father of lights to illuminate our understandings." "Divine Protection," he added, had been sought from and provided by God during the skirmishes with "G. Britain," and "have we now forgotten that powerful friend? Or do we imagine that we no longer need his assistance?"

Said the 81-year-old Franklin: "I have lived . . . a long time and the longer I live, the more convincing proofs I see of this truth—that God governs in the affairs of men. And if a sparrow cannot fall to the ground without his notice, is it probable that an empire can rise without his aid?" He worried that without prayer, an eventual confusion of "Babel" would result, and that future voices would become "divided by our little partial local interests" and "our projects will be confounded . . . ." The solution: "I therefore beg leave to move—that henceforth prayers imploring the assistance of Heaven, and its blessings on our deliberations, be held in this Assembly every morning before we proceed to business, and that one or more of the Clergy of this City be requested to officiate in that service."

Franklin's motion was seconded, but it was not approved. The note he scribbled below his speech read, "The Convention, except three or four Persons, thought Prayers unnecessary!"

One may feel confident, though, in believing that Franklin's daily prayers continued to be repeated, as they had throughout his long life:

> O powerful Goodness! Bountiful Father! Merciful Guide!
> Increase in me that wisdom which discovers my truest interest.
> Strengthen my resolutions to perform what that wisdom dictates.
> Accept my kind offices to Thy other children
> as the only return in my power for Thy continued favors to me.

***

> Father of light and life, thou Good Supreme!
> O teach me what is good; teach me Thyself!
> Save me from folly, vanity, and vice,
> From every low pursuit; and fill my soul
> With knowledge, conscious peace, and virtue pure;
> Sacred, substantial, never-fading bliss!

Chapter 35

My Racial Timeline

"Forgive me for hiding behind a façade
of racial progressiveness...."

- A PERSONAL CONFESSION -
DETROIT, UNITED STATES

DETROIT. SUMMER, 2008.
After collecting my daughter in Minneapolis, we traveled east by car through Wisconsin, rode bikes around vintage Mackinac Island in Michigan, and headed south to the Motor City, where I promised her a Major League baseball game and the best Coney Island hot dog she'd ever have. Promises fulfilled.

Seeing my birthplace, boyhood school, and first church were more of an attention challenge for a twelve-year-old, but when our conversations turned toward race, she perked up. I had at times referred to the Detroit riots of 1967 to talk about race in general, which must have struck a chord because she had many questions and is today a special education teacher in an urban school.

Ironically, that July week in 2008 was also when the race-relevant movie *Gran Torino* was being filmed in Detroit. Hoping to get a glimpse of Clint Eastwood and crew in Highland Park, Warren, and Grosse Point Park, we drove around the blocked locations and failed to see anything but scrums of techies in t-shirts hoisting film equipment. When *Gran Torino* arrived in theaters later that year, however, the Detroit in the film was exactly the city I remembered from childhood. Weed-fringed sidewalks, rusting fences, aggressive blue-collar workers, and vacant urban emptiness encapsulated the film in Detroit attitude and gesture. Protagonist Walt Kowalski, played to scary perfection by Eastwood, could have been any number of Detroiters I had known through my parents, most of whom were racists by isolation from, and superficial interaction with, minorities, but not in the depth of their souls. When Kowalski gets to know people, he judges them by their personal character, not by their race. I saw this often as a kid.

We checked into a dingy motel on Jefferson Street, downtown. It had received a 1.9 rating for its musty, broken, nonfunctional, and noisy anti-qualities, but it was safe, the reviews said, and within walking distance to many places. "Grandpa used to walk these streets as a cop," I said to Megge, so maybe we were seeing a little of what he saw back in the day. Greektown, Corktown, Mexicantown, Lafayette Park, the Eastern Market, and a mostly isolated River Walk were on our agenda, along with a few restaurants cited by Lonely Planet. When we walked onto Rosa Parks Boulevard, the namesake being the brave Alabama woman who refused to surrender her segregation-era bus seat to a white person, I mentioned that this was once 12th Street, ground zero for the '67 riots. And I proceeded to tell the story.

In 1967, we had already been living in Florida for five years. The broken back my father suffered as a policeman had healed as much as possible through spinal fusion surgery, and we returned to Detroit that summer mainly to appease my mother, who had not yet adjusted to life in the buggy, muggy tropics.

After a Saturday night party with relatives, we woke up Sunday morning to the sound of police sirens and a huge plume of smoke rising over downtown. Television news crews were already on top of it, reporting that a police raid on an unlicensed "blind pig" bar had touched off a riot. Eighty people in the bar plus two local vets who had returned from Vietnam were arrested. Outside on 12th Street, an agitated crowd watched, and a bottle was thrown at a police officer by the son of the bar manager. Stores were then looted and set on fire. The riots continued for five days with state and federal troops called in. When the conflict subsided, forty-three people were dead, thirty-three black, ten white, mostly from gunfire by police and National Guardsmen, a few by store owners. A four-year-old girl was among the dead.

"It was very sudden and very weird," I said to Megge. "A curfew was imposed, the lights went out, businesses went dark, and we couldn't go anywhere or do anything in the city, so we went back to Florida earlier than planned."

"Did you talk about it?" she asked.

"I don't remember anyone in our entire circle of relatives, friends, or churchgoers, saying much about it at all," I said. "I only remember my uncle Rookie telling his teenage son, my cousin Gary, not to drive his car downtown. I remember that because he was an affable, gregarious man, who had suddenly become serious, saying "don't drive there" over and over again. There was no attempt among any of us to understand, empathize, relate, connect, or discuss. I remember silence and fear. Mostly silence."

Since that father-daughter trip to Detroit in 2008, I have at different times tried to construct a racial timeline to better understand my relationship with African Americans, especially, over my life. Socrates' prime directive, that "the unexamined life is a life not worth living" has always seemed important to me, though I wish I had applied its wisdom to race much earlier than I did.

The first time I saw a black person happened at our house in Detroit when I was six or seven years old. With Dad in the hospital, my mother had hired an African American man, Ben, to paint the trim on our house, which was peeling badly. Mom called me into the kitchen, where she had poured out a glass of Vernor's ginger ale over ice, and she told me to go outside and give it to Ben. "You call him Mr. Ben," she said, "and Sir." With her watching from a corner window, I did as she asked. Mr. Ben was dressed in white painter's clothes and a Detroit Pistons cap. Standing on the ladder under the eaves, he said, "Oh, that looks mighty good, thank you," and he drank the ginger ale quickly. After he handed back the glass, I stayed there for a long time not saying a word, just watching him paint. Then, I went back in the house.

Two years later, at my new school in Florida, the school handyman was known to us as Mr. Fred, a quiet African American man from Harlem Heights in Fort Myers. As children we thought well of him, though none of us ever spoke to him. There was nothing to say and no reason to speak. Later, in junior high and high school, there were African American students, two black baseball coaches, and an African American math teacher, all of whom I had little personal contact with, though had they been white I almost certainly would have known them better. Same story, basically, in my undergraduate program at the University of South Florida and, indeed, during graduate school at Northern Illinois

University. Interaction was superficial or strained in all cases, and yet I lived my life happily, under the illusion that I was racially progressive in my own mind.

When I finally took a good look at my unimpressive racial timeline, in which I saw myself hiding behind comfortable, insular silences from childhood to adulthood, I decided to make changes, though I was already in my teaching career, and sometimes in life we're a little late. Nevertheless, I went out of my way to enjoy my African American students and colleagues whenever possible, and to get to know them personally in contexts of equality and friendship. I drew as much African American content as possible into my courses, from Richard Wright to Alice Walker to Metz Lochard, including regular field trips to places like the Center for the Preservation of Democracy in Los Angeles. Occasionally, however, my efforts backfired, as when I attempted to facilitate a discussion of the n-word in *The Adventures of Huckleberry Finn* and lost a valued African American student in the process. Even attending the funeral of this student's parent failed to undo the damage I had caused, and it's a regret that sticks with me to this day.

Silence. Fear of connecting. Arrogance. Conceit. Indifference. Insensitivity. Privilege. Those are my sins, and more when I look at myself. They are sins to be pitied, sins that have made white Americans desperate, tired, and unloved across time, toward which redemption seems hidden in some distant place, unavailable and unreachable. Pray for us. I had also never imagined that "Prayer" by the African American poet, Langston Hughes, seemed more applicable to white people living lives of racially isolated comfort and prosperity than black people struggling in difficult lives lived under enduring oppression and racism. Hughes speaks of exhausted people living in tired environments, made so by the feeling that their deeds have rendered them unloved, even by God.

As I have grown older, I have often thought how much I would have benefitted all those years ago by going regularly to a priest for confession, as traditional Catholics have done for centuries. Had I done so, my prayer might have resembled the confession I offered a while back to the Catholic website, Absolution Online. Choosing the "Internal Sins" option and its virtual confessional booth entitled, "dwelling with complacency," I offered my confession:

Holy father, please hear my confession.
When I look beyond the surface of my racial timeline, I see complacency,
cowardice, denial, and hypocrisy. My own.
Forgive me for these sins, I pray in earnest.
Forgive me for hiding behind a façade of racial progressiveness,
and the pretense of living free from bias and prejudice directed toward
sisters and brothers I should have befriended but chose to ignore.
I walked away from them with my nose in the air.
I walked away because of how they looked, how they sounded, how they
presented themselves in ways unfamiliar to me.
And because walking away was easy.
Forgive me most of all for my paltry attempts at making anti-racial statements,
which at the time seemed noble and purposeful, yet over time have been
shown to make me seem righteous when I was not.
My hypocrisy is that of self-righteousness masquerading as
racially-accommodating public acts designed to make me look better, wiser,
and more enlightened than I really am.
I ask for your forgiveness, Lord, and for genuine healing that will allow me
to see others through the eyes of our Lord and Savior, Jesus Christ.

PART SIX

Chapter 36

UNPROTECTED

"I'm falling apart. My past no longer protects me."
- A PRAYER OF DESPERATION -
CHERNOBYL, UKRAINE

TRAVELING THE UNSPECTACULAR ROAD FROM Kyiv to Chernobyl, I sat back in my bus seat and thought about how my Ukrainian grandmother, Maria, used to pronounce Ukraine in her thick east European accent. She called it "U-kray-ina," which is the Romanized pronunciation, and she had little to say about it other than recalling hazy memories of places and people left behind during World War I. She had emigrated solo to America at seventeen, bounced around the Rust Belt for a few years, fended off bad men, and wound up in Detroit where she married my Polish-Ukrainian grandfather, Victor, and raised a family. My parents often urged me to tell her interesting story when I was an undergraduate journalism student. I wish I had listened.

The week before heading up to Chernobyl in 2013 had been spent at a philosophy conference put on by the National University of Kyiv. After daily sessions concluded, there was plenty of time to comb through Kyiv's gardens and cathedrals, and even to get robbed outside a McDonald's around midnight. How lucky was I to have been carrying only a few euros and pocket change. "Thugs can spot an American instantly by how you walk," warned the conference hosts. I did listen, but the lure of a Big Mac and fries was hard to resist. "You can keep passport," smirked one of the thieves in his best Gary Oldman voice.

On the bus, I unfolded a map of Ukraine depicting a bleak Chernobyl with radiating circles extending over Kyiv and the Dnieper River, and then clockwise over Belarus, Russia, Moldova, Romania, Hungary, Slovakia, and Poland to complete the roundel. Each country, and even more distant ones, had received at least traces of nuclear radiation from the infamous meltdown during spring, 1986. It happened on a Saturday in late April when the number four reactor at the Chernobyl Nuclear Power Plant exploded, followed by a reactor-core fire that burned for nine days, releasing airborne contamination throughout the region. Two plant operators died instantly, plus twenty-eight more in the time following from acute radiation syndrome. Within two days, forty-thousand-plus residents of neighboring Pripyat were evacuated, and a few days later the fire was contained, though not before enough radiation had been released to cause the eventual deaths of thousands from cancers and related diseases.

A radial six-mile exclusion zone was later increased to nineteen miles, and that was where we were headed. The German tourist sitting in the next seat was showing off his bright yellow dosimeter, which he planned to use for radiation detection once we were in the zone. Even after all these years one can't be too careful, he seemed to be saying, which was quite an understatement as some estimates held that the area within the exclusion zone would not be habitable for twenty thousand years. When we arrived there, I periodically heard the scratchy sound of the dosimeter as the man pressed it close to random objects. It sounded like super-fast Morse code, echoing in the deserted structures we were now walking through.

Up close, Pripyat was even more of a wasteland than that depicted by cinematographers who had filmed it for docudramas. Eerie multilevel apartment buildings with glassless windows; staircases smothered by twisted, overgrown roots; and decaying sports arenas were a twilight zone residing within an apocalypse that resisted even graphic-novel narration. A rusting amusement park scrambler standing near a corroding Ferris wheel projected broken appendages, which made it look like a giant insect from a 1950s B-movie. And then there were the children's toys, many of them, left behind in the evacuation: dolls lying on bare earth, in empty classrooms alongside open textbooks, positioned with hands raised as if in the act of questioning a departed teacher; discarded teddy bears on skeletal bed frames; a rusting toy truck sitting on a cracked cement pillar.

Some accounts of Chernobyl included scientific timelines of the unfolding disaster, with minute-by-minute technical detail for use by workers tasked with the prevention of similar accidents occurring in the future. A more simplified timeline focusing on the human drama was offered by *USA Today*, inclusive of the following moments: February 1986, a Ukraine public official says publicly that the odds of a nuclear meltdown at Chernobyl were 1 in 10,000. April 25, 1986, an emergency water-cooling system is tested in the event of an accident. April 26, an explosion blows a thousand-ton lid off its base, releasing radiation and producing a second explosion. April 27, evacuations begin around the plant and extend out six miles. April 28, a public statement is finally released by the Soviet Union acknowledging the accident but offering scant details. May 1, May Day parades go on as planned throughout the region despite the presence of dangerous, drifting, radioactive clouds. May 14, Mikhail Gorbachev, the Soviet president, enlists thousands of "liquidators" to clean up after the accident, many whom succumbed to nuclear radiation and died from excruciating pain and deformities.

Twenty years later, in 2006, Gorbachev admitted in his memoir that Chernobyl, more than anything else, was the likely reason the Soviet Union had collapsed.

Back in Kyiv, after that emotionally exhausting bus tour, I returned to my hotel and collapsed myself on the bed. Sometimes you're not up for what you see, and what your mind does with it, when you travel to places like Chernobyl. Face-down on a pillow as I drifted off to sleep, I remembered my snarky high school teacher, Mr. Springer, whom at graduate commencement shouted at me from across the football field. *"Hey Pawley,"* he yelled, *"what are you gonna do with your life?"* I thought for a moment, then said, *"I'd like to see the world." "What if you don't like what you see?"* he barked. *"I don't know,"* I said. *"I can still learn things."*

Sometime later I sent an email to my friend Nataly, who headed the Oriental Studies Circle at the National University of Kyiv. I asked her about Chernobyl. What was it like living so close to such a major catastrophe? What do Ukrainians say about it? Do you discuss it at the university?

She surprised me by saying she'd never been there and had no plans to visit.

"It's contemporary history, useful for rethinking the world order," she said. "It was one of the key factors of the fall of the old USSR and the appearance of new states in eastern Europe. Here, it moved people from admiring atomic energy to becoming part of anti-nuclear movements. And it's a cultural symbol."

A cultural symbol?

"In a strict cultural sense," she added, "there are the movies, computer games, and books which shape policy of memory about the catastrophe. But they're not Ukrainian in origin. Also, there are Christian icons showing Jesus Christ protecting people from Chernobyl." She quickly pulled up three such images and sent them. In one, a sitting Christ holds five weeping children with nuclear fires burning in the background. In another, a huge Christ, larger than the nuclear reactors, ministers to tiny victims seeking protection. In a third image, Christ is in heaven, standing on a cloud with Mary and a Christian knight holding a sword and shield; below is a devastated earth with white-robed people wearing gas masks.

I asked Nataly, who is steeped in studies of philosophy and religion, if those disciplines nurture memory for her, or do they foster a kind of forgetfulness which relocates the painful past into some distant place where it exists but is released only when it can be used to make a point?

"During crises, philosophy tries to find an alternative way for society," she said. "Of course, it may serve the state and its policy of memory, but ideally it should be critical and leave the choice to remember or to forget to the individual. The individual is always free to use the tools of philosophy to lift or destroy himself or herself."

"What answers exist for you personally?" I asked.

"I think that there are no direct answers but an eternal search for them," said Nataly. "I'm trying not to follow popular passing trends but to be honest with myself and to keep searching. As one great mind, Bertrand Russell, said, 'I will never die for my views, because I might be wrong.'"

In 1997, the Nobel Prize-winning journalist and oral historian, Svetlana Alexievich, published *Voices from Chernobyl: The Oral History of a Nuclear Disaster*," which extracted brutal reflections on the event, mostly from former residents of Pripyat who survived it. The reflections are not prayers, though some can be recast as such. In fact, when the book was published in the UK, the title was changed to *Chernobyl Prayer: A Chronicle of the Future*. A Ukrainian psychologist, Pyotr S., offered a reflection which has stayed with me since that day spent wandering through Pripyat and the nuclear facility at Chernobyl. It focuses on a man's desire to forget bad things in his life caused by war, which he does and is protected by his ability to forget. But then Chernobyl happens, and he realizes he's no longer protected. I present it here reset from paragraph-form to prayer lines, and I imagine hearing the voices of my Ukrainian ancestors imploring God not for answers to suffering but simply to draw him into the deep emotional centers of those who have witnessed the unthinkable.

> Then why do people remember?
> So, they can determine the truth?
> For fairness? So, they can free themselves and forget?
> Is it because they understand they're part of a grand event?
> Or are they looking into the past for cover?
> And all this despite the fact that memories are very fragile things, ephemeral things.
> This is not exact knowledge,
> it's more like a set of emotions.

***

> I wanted to forget. Forget everything.
> And I did forget.
> I thought the most horrible things had already happened.
> The war.
> And that I was already protected, now that I was protected.
> But then I traveled to the Chernobyl Zone.
> I've been there many times now.
> And understood how powerless I am.
> I'm falling apart.
> My past no longer protects me.
> There aren't any answers there.
> They were there before, but now they're not.
> The future is destroying me, not the past.

Chapter 37

METERED MIGRANTS

"But God of all, I am shaken in that faith, when I read of what is happening on the threshold of my country."

- A BORDER-WATCHER'S PRAYER -
TIJUANA, MEXICO

AS I TRAVEL IN MY mind back to Tijuana, Mexico, which was a short drive from Los Angeles when I lived there for a decade, I think first of poetry rather than prayer: specifically, the feral, fatalistic verse of Luis Alberto Urrea and his collection of border moments, *The Tijuana Book of the Dead*.

About the conflation of poetry and prayer in studies of both subjects, attempts at drawing differences can be elusive. Basic statements such as "poems are written for audiences . . . but prayers are written for God" (www.themillions.com) tend to lock up the subject in an oversimplified box until it pops the lid and escapes its binary chains. Broader statements such as Leah Silvieus's *Hyphen Magazine* comment in 2019 speak more about similarities than differences. "I feel like poetry, much like prayer, is that state of searching, of a willingness to surrender to the unknown, to feeling through the dark," she says. Or, listen to Jean Valentine, author of eleven poetry collections: "There's a likeness between poetry and prayer that is not so much thanks or supplication, but the more unconscious activity of meditation or dreaming."

Language "forges a shape," adds *Poetry Magazine*'s Mary Karr in "Facing Altars: Poetry and Prayer," for articulating emotion, especially that of torment, whether the torment takes the shape of poetry or prayer. Perhaps it is appropriate, though annoying, to say that we'll only know when something is a poem or a prayer when what we have encountered is one or the other. Such a frustrating thought might even lead us back to the nineteenth century French theologian and literary scholar, Henri Bremond, who once argued that " . . . while poetry may point in the direction of prayerfulness, only prayer itself, with its requisite divine grace, leads us into the higher realms of mystical prayer." I can live with that, though I'll allow that good poetry can be quite prayerful. Urrea's poems, from the opening, "You Who Seek Grace from a Distracted God" to the title cut, "The Tijuana Book of the Dead," with "Arizona Lamentation" and "There is a Town in Mexico" in between, carry tormented, beseeching moments surely heard by God.

The last time I visited Tijuana was in 2006 when I traveled there with Akiko, my friend from Japan with whom I shared a season of vulnerable, post-divorce melancholy. Crossing the Mexican border at 9am was a dream; re-crossing the American border at 9pm, a nightmare.

I vividly remember that five-lane traffic jam on baked pavement that hadn't cooled. Border lights looked like artificial orange stars against a backdrop of billboards, and I forget how many hours we waited for our first glimpse of heaven, otherwise known as San Diego. The visit had not been special for any reason other than the fact that Akiko could now say she had been to Mexico. We spent most of our time in the Centro district, dodging grabby merchants, dining on local cuisine, and drinking Corona light beer in air-conditioned cantinas. The stately Tijuana Lighthouse was a visual refresh as were views of Colorado Hill sloping down into a taupe valley, and we had a good conversation about border towns while sitting in the shade of a high-rise at Zona Rio. But then it was time to make our way back, and wouldn't San Diego's Gaslamp District be nice for a late dinner.

At some point, I mentioned to Akiko that residents of southern California refer to Tijuana simply as TJ. It is heard often from people heading there for medicinal bargains and souvenirs like sombreros and flamenco dresses. Also, the city is a mainstay in popular music, all the way from Herb Alpert to Lil Wayne. Everyone seems to have a TJ story or know a little about it, especially its connection to the round-faced Franciscan monk, Junipero Serra, who established his Alta California mission just north of the border. Of course, the flip side of Tijuana is its reputation for crime, drugs, violence, cartel wars, and of late, the highest per-capita rate of corona virus cases in Mexico. It is also one of the cruelest places anywhere for migrants seeking asylum in the United States: a dream frequently dashed by the enforcement of *metering*, the US policy of allowing fewer and fewer asylum applications to be accepted.

A 2019 report by NBC News told that story.

"Lidia," wrote Daniella Silva, "wrapped her arms around her six-months-pregnant belly, as she waited anxiously with her daughters, ages 2 and 4, and her husband . . . at the El Chaparral crossing on the US-Mexico border." The family had fled the street gang that had killed her father, brother, and cousins in Honduras, joining a caravan of migrants for the brutal walk/bus-jostle north. They had one suitcase holding everything they owned. A month passed until they arrived in Tijuana where they bounced between local shelters under the constant threat of more gang violence. Lidia, headachy and vomiting, while caring for her asthmatic children, was sure she would be killed in this city where over two thousand others had died the previous year. Migrants, pressed against other migrants, waiting for their case numbers to be called, knowing they might be metered out of the system at any point, left to fend for themselves in Tijuana, completed the picture. In time, Lidia and her children were granted asylum, though her husband was detained for unknown reasons. When last asked by Silva how she was doing, Lidia replied, "mal": badly.

I learned much about immigration from the hundreds of Latino students who honored me by signing up for my courses in California. They were a constant joy to teach and learn from, though many hid unhealed wounds from seeing their families ripped apart by the immigration process itself or the aftermath of trying to adapt to America's harsh racial landscape of exclusion and reward. Almost always, I deduced, some family members lived undocumented and under a Damocles sword of being deported, so they could never really take part in the American Dream. They were excluded. One student, name withheld, told me that her father came to the US at nineteen with his brother, worked in the roofing business, married, lived in a crowded house with relatives, and finally, twenty years later, received his green card. His wife, however, remained undocumented, as did all the women in the house, and unable to work. So, nothing changed, ever, as keeping their gasping lips above water, economically, became a permanent condition.

On July 4, 2020, this same student posted the following message on a social network: "Today, I don't celebrate independence. I mourn a nation who so fervently holds onto a way of life that does not respect all people. As an American, I feel deep pain. I have seen first-hand the systems that oppress people. As a white Latinx woman, I know what it is to fear the system, but I have never feared being murdered by it. For all people of color on this stolen land, I mourn because all of our people have been mistreated. It's not a nice way to live, to feel like you don't have a country. Until we can all hold onto the promise of the American Dream as ours, I'm going to continue to mourn on the 4th of July. No justice, no peace."

I wonder, is it possible that people use the ubiquitous ether of social networking as a substitute for messaging a seemingly unreachable God who grows increasingly silent in a world, indeed a universe, where not even murmured responses can be detected? Sooner or later, everyone encounters this silence. It sends us back to all the borders of life whether in Tijuana or the hoped-for crossing into heaven; over and over; to Lidia's story, to my student's post, to Urrea's poetry, or to all who continue to pray, regardless of whether answers are forthcoming.

The prayer, "An Encounter with Silence," by Leo J. O'Donovan S.J., is an example:

> Loving God,
> I come before you to pray for my brothers and sisters,
> Your children and members of Christ's body,
> at the southern border of the United States today.
>
> What we read of their suffering
> seems nothing less than a Passion for thousands.
> Little children crowded into cells
> where they scarcely have room to stand.
> Without decent sanitation or food,
> separated from their families,
> the older ones taking care of the younger.
>
> God of mercy,
> I believe that you live within whatever and whomever I am,
> the ground of my existence, its gracious cause and hope,
> its true future, its blessed promise of eternal life.
> I could not always have said so much.
> But now through your grace I do believe it.

But God of all,
I am shaken in that faith,
When I read of what is happening on the threshold of my country.
Are not the women and men and children there also the vessels
of your eternal presence?
Many of them, most perhaps, from what we call the Northern Triangle,
have indeed been baptized.
But your incarnate Word is addressed to all of them.
Your spirit of freedom hovers over all of them.

Who will speak your Word and give your Spirit to them now?
How will the freedom and responsibility,
the integrity and compassion Christ came to secure for us all,
come now to our country and its leaders
in this time of squalor and rejection,
if those are even words strong enough for what is happening?

Can I continue to believe
that you are more interior to my soul than I am to myself
without confessing the same truth for every soul
on the border in Arizona and New Mexico and Texas?

Oh, gracious God, you are silent.
But give us, I beg, the words and wisdom,
the courage and yes also the tact,
not to speak empty words about your presence,
while others of your children,
your children and ours,
are suffering what seems worse than death.

Chapter 38

GAPS TEMPORARILY UNBRIDGED

"... help us, God, to feel the suffering of every Bedouin parent."
- A RABBINICAL PRAYER -
PETRA, JORDAN

RABBI RACHEL BARENBLAT BEGINS HER "Sukkot Prayer for the Bedouin" with these words: "Once our people wandered in the desert sands."

The statement prepares the way for a prayer of identification which theorizes an ancient linkage between the persons praying and the persons being prayed for and about. Further employing phrases such as "our Bedouin neighbors" and "our nomadic ancestors," as the rabbi does, emphasizes a sense of deep identification, or *consubstantiality* as previously mentioned, the literal joining of substances: the substance of who we are with that of someone else. It's a common dynamic within the human imagination, whereby we imagine that we know a media celebrity or fictional character, for instance, and they in turn know us. Whether it exists in real life and real time, however, is another question, and throughout life we may at different times wonder whether or not it is possible to become consubstantial with other people, especially across cultures, no matter how hard we may try.

In 1990, I flew into Amman, Jordan with sixteen American students who had signed on for my six-week study tour of Jordan, the Palestinian Territories, and Israel. Our Royal Jordanian flight from New York City touched down at night, and we booked into a downtown hotel in Amman. After much needed sleep, we met for breakfast the following morning, and I noticed how chipper and rested everyone seemed, for which I was grateful. All the trip prep worked, I thought to myself, which was often the case for these adventures. Spring semester had concluded, and we had three weeks to do nothing but prepare for unfamiliar settings, languages, foods, people, and expected annoyances common to all travel. Adequate advance work had a way of permeating an entire trip with purpose and resolve, and this one had certainly started right.

The bus ride from Amman to Petra further fed the anticipation. Passing through sun-drenched Jordanian landscapes of sandy desert coloring seemed peaceful and inviting. Jet lag had not yet set in, so no one was sleeping. One young woman, Joyce, noticing the indoor-outdoor design of desert houses, got out of her seat and whispered in my ear that someday she was going to move here. I wouldn't blame you, I said, as I recalled for her the first time I had felt the desert magic of the Middle East. It had happened seven years earlier, in 1983, while on an archaeological dig which had transformed my life. Clarity, for lack of a better term, had resulted, and in my mind I often returned to that moment through prayer and meditation. I was so alive, so clarified, as though I had suddenly grown self-aware and inwardly at peace.

We arrived in Petra and disembarked. Students were visually familiar with the look of the rose-colored stone city from having seen *Indiana Jones and the Last Crusade*, the third film in that franchise. It appeared the previous year, and the final scenes narrating a fiction about Christ's Holy Grail had been shot in Petra. "You have chosen wisely," says a centuries-old Templar knight who watches Harrison Ford drink from Christ's humble cup, receiving eternal life in the process.

The Siq, a passage through a marvelous striated gorge, was the only way into the city, and we passed through it on rented donkeys. Once inside, we became speechless among ancient ruins carved into the sandstone mountains. Nabataeans, a Bedouin people from the borderlands of Syria and Arabia, had once controlled trade routes in the region, leaving behind a theatre, a Great Temple with monumental staircases, a monastery carved immaculately into a hill, tombs, gates, pillars, and read all about it online or in your travel guide. Rome annexed the city in 106 CE. Byzantines followed two centuries later. By 700 CE., Muslims had moved in, followed four centuries later by invading Crusaders under Baldwin 1 of Jerusalem, until the Crusaders themselves were routed by the Arab, Saladin, in 1187, returning Petra to the Muslims. Then, for five centuries the city fell silent to the world until it was rediscovered by a Swiss archaeologist traveling through the Middle East in 1812. He correctly identified it as the historical center of the Nabataeans.

Today, the B'doul people of Petra claim to be descendants of the Nabataeans. They once made comfortable homes in the many adjacent caves, until they were forced to abandon them when the city was claimed by UNESCO as a World Heritage Site. They were then forcibly relocated to Umm Sayhoun, their appointed, cement-block village nearby, where they reside still, making daily return trips to their souvenir stands in Petra. We collected a few items ourselves before leaving that day, and I still have the Bedouin sand bottle I purchased. Six shades of desert sand, poured through a funnel into a concave bottle, had been sculpted with a bent coat hanger to show mountain scenes carefully arranged by a Bedouin artisan. It is beautiful, original, and distinctly Bedouin.

Appreciating Bedouin people and culture is a constant among Westerners who have observed, lived with, written about, and filmed in Bedouin Arab lands. Knowing, really knowing, Bedouins, however, is another story. Classic movie lovers, for instance, will recall Sir David Lean's epic, *Lawrence of Arabia*, and its mostly-true portrayal of the English army officer, T.E. Lawrence. Through acts of courage and cultural identification, inclusive of camel riding and donning Bedouin attire, Lawrence unites the Bedouin Arab tribes against the occupying Turks in World War I. He respects his new Bedouin friends, and they him, but do they ever really know each other? Toward the end of the movie, a frustrated Lawrence pinches his white skin and says to his Bedouin friend, Sherif Ali (played by the Egyptian actor, Omar Sharif), "That's me. What color is it? That's me, and there's nothing I can do about it." Ali protests, but Lawrence says, "You lead them. They're yours. Trust your own people, and let me go back to mine." Finally, the cruelest cut of all comes from the Arab Prince Faisal, who says of Lawrence, "He is *almost* an Arab."

On theme but closer to our time is the book, *Married to a Bedouin*, by Marguerite van Geldermalsen. As a twenty-something backpacker from New Zealand, van Geldermalsen found herself in Petra, romantically wooed by its Bedouin culture and a handsome Bedouin man, Mohammad. After a brief courtship, they fell in love, married Bedouin-style, had children, and enjoyed a protected life in a cozy Petra cave. Along the way, van Geldermalsen spoke of waking up with the sunrise and healing silence, sipping sweet tea and baking fresh Bedouin bread, taking long walks through oleander-covered canyons, and watching a full moon slip behind the Crusader castle after a stroll under starlight through the Siq.

"I was welcomed and accepted by everyone," she said, as she became an integral "part of something larger . . . and I was going to be a Bedouin woman from now on."

Sadly, however, Mohammad died from kidney failure, brought on by "uncontrollable blood sugar levels," in 2002. Days of mourning passed, followed by months of "going through the motions of my life," van Geldermalden wrote, and while life went on, "my reason for being there had gone." With her children, she then moved away, as her final statement concluded the memoir: "I wasn't in Petra for the mountains or the history—or even for the culture. Without Mohammad to hold me, I am no longer married to a Bedouin and . . . I have become a nomad once again." Echoing through her story, moreover, was a sense of never fully integrating into Bedouin life or fully identifying with Bedouin neighbors living in close proximity. She didn't say why this was the case; she simply adapted to life in a peaceful, interesting place, with her reason for staying there being the love she shared with her husband. "I can see now how lucky I am," she said years later, after relocating to Australia. "I met Mohammad and got to know him in his own world, in his own home, alone." It was not her own world, though, and apparently never would be. Consubstantiality hadn't held her there, and she was gone.

For curiosity's sake, I asked about van Geldermalden while in Petra. I had originally read her story, as an article, in a 1985 issue of *Aramco World Magazine*, and I thought students, too, would benefit from meeting her. She was still living nearby in Umm Sayoun at the time, though no one seemed to know her whereabouts that particular day. We would have had many questions, for sure.

The questions I would have for Rabbi Rachel Barenblat might revolve around the effectuality of praying across cultures for people one doesn't really know. Can prayer be a bridge to deeper identification and understanding, or is it more of a rhetorical effort to say "I care," and now God has to finish the work?

In any case, prayer is better than no prayer, as the soul reaches out in the hope of joining with otherness.

> Ribbono Shel Olam, Master of the Universe—
> Shekhinah, Whose Wings shelter creation—
>
> Once our people wandered the desert sands.
> Now we merely vacation in rootlessness

While our Bedouin neighbors perch
Without permission, their goats forbidden to graze.

Time after time the bulldozers tear down homes
And playgrounds, uprooting spindley olive trees
To make room for someone else's future forest,
As though saplings mattered more than children.

As we sit beneath palm fronds, corn stalks, pine boughs
Decked with gourds and strings of lights, as we
Invite our nomadic ancestors to join us
For tea and conversation, help us, God

To feel the suffering of every Bedouin parent
Whose children wake from demolition nightmares;
To recognize the merit in their love
Of living lightly on the land.

Once our Temple—God's sukkah, a house
of prayer for all peoples—was razed by hate.
Holy One of blessing, move us now to protect
Those who live in temporary circumstance

Which is all of us who dwell on earth.
Help our hands and hearts to bring repair.

Chapter 39

The Inevitable Response

"Guide us to the straight path. The path of those on whom you have bestowed your grace, not of those who earned [your] wrath...."

- A QUR'ANIC PRAYER -
JERICHO, PALESTINIAN TERRITORIES

WE RETURNED OUR DONKEYS AND left Petra in sizzling afternoon heat. Sleepy silence on the bus prevailed all the way back to Amman. With jet lag setting in, another night in the hotel was welcome, though early the following morning we set out on the road again, bleary eyed as we headed for the West Bank.

Crossing the unexpectedly small Edmund Allenby bridge over the Jordan River put life or something like it in those tired eyes as various checkpoints featuring passport confiscation by armed soldiers intimidated a few students. Others, however, seemed excited by this real-world moment, and whatever tension it may have caused ended when the passports were returned. The span known as the King Hussein Bridge in Jordan, and the Al-Karameh Bridge to Palestinian Arabs, popped and creaked as we rolled slowly over it, and shortly we were on the other side.

My insistence that the study trip include the Palestinian Territories had been met with apathy as visits to Nablus and Ramallah, and later even Bethlehem and Hebron, evoked yawns. To be fair, it was the time of the first Intifada by Palestinians demonstrating against the Israeli occupation of their lands, which at that time had just passed its forty-year mark, and businesses were shut down almost everywhere. The eerie quiet was bothersome, though a salty, satisfying float in the Dead Sea revived the group. Conversations were happening again, we'd soon be in Jerusalem, and all seemed well.

Then suddenly, *crack!*

As our bus rolled toward Jericho, a fist-sized rock, hurled by a teenage boy from a crowd of teenage boys, struck our front window, shattering most of it. Our driver said it would be unsafe to continue, so he contacted the tour company and ordered another bus.

The ensuing hours provided time for reflection as we sat in the shade of date palms in quiet, ancient Jericho. Everyone had something to say, and I spoke of my West Bank sojourns in 1983 and '85. The Israel-Palestine template had been burned into my consciousness by that time, I shared, so much so that key dates provided a structure of memory for thinking about the conflict. It included 1896, when Theodor Herzl published *Der Judenstaat*, which called for the creation of a Jewish state. It then moved to 1917 and the *Balfour Declaration*, in which the British called for a Jewish homeland on Arab territory. In 1922, the old League of Nations stepped in to approve the British plan to use Palestine for the Jewish state; and after more years of mass protests by Palestinians over Jewish Zionists streaming into the land, accompanied by revolts squelched by the British and the army of hotel-bombing Zionist terrorists known as the Irgun, the stage was set for war. The war of 1948 established Israel. The war of 1967 took additional Arab land in the Golan Heights and Gaza Strip after Israel was attacked by Syria from the north and Egypt from the south. And the war of 1973, which occurred on Yom Kippur, the Jewish holy day, killed and displaced a lot of people. I ended my very incomplete list of dates at that point by saying at least one good thing had happened since 1973. That was the US presidency of Jimmy Carter, whom working with Egyptian president Anwar Sadat and Israeli Prime Minister Menachem Begin, had orchestrated peace between Israel and Egypt.

There were other glimmers of hope, too, for this troubled land, though one immutable truth remained: things had never gotten better for the Palestinians. Even now in 2020, this is still the case.

Our new bus arrived in early afternoon. We could see it from a distance, heading up the Jericho highway through optical waves of heat that made it appear liquified like a rolling bar of melting chocolate. Then in cool AC, we were on the road again. Our travel agenda remained fairly in-tact with visits to the desert oasis of Ein Gedi and the Qumran Caves, where the Dead Sea Scrolls had been found by a Palestinian boy looking for a lost animal in the late 1940s. The final stop was the mountaintop fortress of Masada, where extremist Sicarii Jews had leaped to their deaths in advance of siege-minded Romans who were hunting them down in the year 73 CE. We descended the fortress by hiking down a snake path in late afternoon and were back in the bus headed upland across precarious geography toward Jerusalem.

There is a lovely Jewish prayer for the Palestinian people, full of compassion and goodwill, from the reconstructive Judaic organization, Ritualwell. Its hopeful, empathic rhetoric preserves a moment that is both spiritually reflective and forward-looking:

> In the name of Elohim, the most merciful. May the Palestinian people receive the healing powers of our prayers. May they be granted safety, success, love, security and hope. May they enjoy the fruits of freedom and equality that they—and all humans—deserve.
>
> As Jews, we pray for their well-being. We remember that the Holy Land is a shared space, and pray to see the day when Jews, Muslims, Christians, Druze, and all religions will live there together in peace.
>
> We hope for the day when Palestinians may return. We pray together with their Jewish neighbors that they can rehabilitate their history and rebuild what could be the best place on earth. A place of many cultures and true equality.
>
> We pray that Palestinians will be able to live lives free from violence and oppression. And we ask God to help us build bridges of peace with them. "Let there be light. And there was light." May we be the light that brings peace and hope to our Palestinian friends and to all the world. Amen.

Criticizing such a beautiful prayer, or any sincere prayer for that matter, is a fool's game. However, it should also be noted that such a prayer would very likely fall on deaf ears in the Palestinian territories. A backstory of questionable assumptions exists here, led perhaps by the statement, "We remember that the Holy Land is a shared space." It seems improbable that the occupied would ever be moved by an occupier's gesture like this. Palestinians, who were pushed off their land in successive purges, have for so long suffered under institutionalized occupation and the costs it imposes, that one wonders if any idea of "shared space" is anything more than an occupier's attempt to assuage their conscience.

Also, hoping "for the day when Palestinians may return" is an equally noble-sounding invitation for the descendants of the removed to return to their ancestral homes located in what is now Israel. But that would require a peace deal, which for the first time ever provides real justice for the Palestinians, and no one has any idea what such a deal would look like. How would Jerusalem be divided? How would refugees be granted their complete "right to return?" What sorts of financial restitution would be made? These are practical questions requiring a forthright political will that has never been allowed to develop. In its absence, the Palestinians are dominated by military checkpoints, constricted movement, and an economy stifled by decades of unfair treatment by higher powers who don't listen.

Finally, wishing that the Jews and Palestinians might find time and space to "rehabilitate their history" is an elusive dream met by the most common response anyone has ever heard regarding the conflict: "They have been fighting forever, and that will never change." I heard it from my father, mother, relatives, friends, pastors, teachers, and media my whole life. The assumption, moreover, that historical longevity precludes modern change tends to hide the fact that Israel-Palestine is a contemporary conflict, barely a century old. The problem, therefore, is not historical scars; it's more one of fresh wounds which get painfully poked every time the Israelis build another West Bank settlement. Both family trees are rooted in ancient soil, if you will, but one enjoys an orchard-like existence while the other struggles to stay alive.

The fine prayer to "Elohim, the most merciful," is compassionate but severely limited by the immense oppression of its human context. I do not know what prayer is being shared among Palestinians at this moment in time, though among its eighty-five percent Muslim population on the West Bank, I might imagine hearing *Al-Fatihah*, the prayerful opening of the Qur'an, which seeks the guidance and mercy of God to find and walk "the straight path." Its passion emanates from its few words of hope and their hint of injustice lurking in the background:

> In the name of Allah, the Most Gracious, the Most Merciful.
> Praise be to Allah, the Lord of the Universe.
> The Most Gracious, the Most Merciful.
> Master of the Day of Judgment.
> You alone we worship, and you alone we ask for help.

Guide us to the straight path.
The path of those on whom you have bestowed your grace,
not of those who earned your wrath, nor of those who have gone astray.

Chapter 40

AMID THE RESIDUE OF OCCUPATION

"It is the Good Friday of sorrow and bitterness, of abandonment and powerlessness, of cruelty and meaninglessness that this ... people experienced as a result of unrestrained ambition that hardens and blinds the heart."

- A PRAYER FROM POPE FRANCIS -
MUSEUM OF OCCUPATIONS, TALLIN, ESTONIA

DIAKONIA, THE SWEDISH INTERFAITH DEVELOPMENT organization, defines *occupation* as "a form of international armed conflict that arises when a territory, or parts thereof, come under the authority of foreign hostile armed forces, even if it is met with armed resistance." Expanding this legal definition involves recognizing "central notions" of moral value, which include administering the occupied territory "for the benefit of the local population," "maintaining the status quo" in said territory, refraining from acting "as sovereign over" the occupied nation, and working to "protect, respect, and enhance the rights of the protected occupied population."

It distresses one to realize how otherwise respectable nations have failed on all moral points in their various occupations: the French in northwest Africa, the British in India, the United States in Native American territories, and Israel in Palestinian lands, to name just a few. But shouldn't these failures be tolerated if occupying powers ultimately bring about positive, progressive change in the nations they occupy? Such a question implies that ends-justifies-the-means thinking is okay, though it ignores the levels of permanent ruin some nations have fallen into because of how they have been occupied. Have Native American nations recovered? Have South Africans? Have Palestinians? In these contexts, one has to wonder if occupation is ever justified, and under what circumstances. That should be the yardstick for praying into a bruised, suffering world of places and peoples who were crushed by occupation and never found a way to get back on their feet.

The Baltic nation, Estonia, seems an exception, though only Estonians can say for sure if the stable footing they seem to be on is real and permanent.

On a placid morning in August 2013, I boarded a two-hour ferry from Finland to Estonia, landing in the city of Tallin around noon. It was a one-day trip, which tells you almost nothing about such an interesting place, and I was in and out of noted places like a digital travelogue streamed to people high on crystal meth.

Tallin itself is a vibrant watercolor of church spires, cone-topped roofs, cobblestone foot passages, gates, gardens, markets, and public squares with good al-fresco dining. The cuisine consists of well-prepared dishes from eastern Europe's rye-bread-and-pork belt and is washed down with plenty of good beer and vodka. After lunch upon arrival, I had Toompea Castle to visit, plus a boutique artisan section known as Telliskivi Creative City, a Russian Orthodox Cathedral with black onion domes under gold crosses, and two small museums. To make sure I didn't lose my return ferry across the Gulf of Finland late in the day, I had to choose between the KGB museum in the Viru Hotel and the stand-alone Museum of Occupations. I chose the latter.

In Europe, sometimes it feels as if there is a small museum on every street corner. Certainly, collecting and displaying is a basic human desire, and museums curate cultural heritage artifacts as a way of organizing them for ease of observation and interpretation. But "the art is in the edit," says Stephen Rosenbaum of *Forbes Magazine*, suggesting that all the minuscule arrangements and redactions determine whether or not visitors *get* the story the museum is trying to tell. Good curators look for "unusual linkages" and "unexpected themes," Rosenbaum adds, and they are "mixologists," who "see around corners" to create a mix that transcends "a handful of related items set side-by-side."

The challenges faced by the curator's mix at Tallin's Vabamu Museum of Occupations and Freedom stemmed from the immense task of telling the story of Estonia's three occupations: the first by the Soviet Union, followed by the German occupation, and followed yet again by the return of the Soviets, all occurring within a fifty-year timespan, 1940–1991. Repression and crimes against humanity weren't easy themes to present, the goal being to narrate what is unforgettable to Estonians. Indeed, the museum is housed in an irregular structure of glass walls, as if to say nothing is hidden here, look inside, and don't forget what you see.

Things hard to forget, even for a half-day visitor, included the following: a wall of cold steel Soviet prison doors set behind foundation rods. The doors are set up like decaying monoliths of differing heights, creating a jagged image of cold cruelty. Then, there was the enormous sculpture of parallel locomotives, one with the Soviet Red Army star replacing the headlamp, the other featuring a black Nazi Swastica also where the headlamp would be. On both sides of the trains were lines of old suitcases representing the forced evacuation of Estonians kidnapped, imprisoned, exiled, or murdered. In the museum's basement was a huge sculpted head of Vladimir Lenin with terrifying eyes and mouth, disembodied from its torso as if housing only an evil brain removed from sense and emotion. And finally, to provide a needed audio dimension, there were recordings of Estonians, some who experienced all three occupations, telling horror stories and meditating on the preciousness of freedom and the resulting hopelessness when it is gone.

At the end of the curatorial trail, of course, is a happy ending: the liberation of Estonia. But as stated, one might have reason to wonder if the happy ending is really happy and if it is a permanent ending.

In Estonia and places like it, according to Neil Taylor in *Estonia: A Modern History*, "the past takes an increasingly disturbing grip."

Such a "grip" includes the memory of Estonian President Konstantin Pat's radio address in June 1940 warning his people that ninety thousand Soviet troops had begun their invasion. "The Red Army has just crossed our border," he stated. "Please do not resist, as resistance is futile . . . ." Within exactly one calendar year, sixty-one thousand "Estonians had been murdered or deported," Taylor writes, even as the "charades" of popular elections were held to hand over control of Estonian commerce and infrastructure to Moscow. Libraries were cleared of intellectual thought, newspapers became voices of Soviet propaganda, and the Estonian flag had to be smaller than its red flag replacement, forcibly sewed by local seamstresses. The German occupation brought some cultural relief, though it was even harder on anyone who supported Jews under newly installed swastikas flapping in the wind. Then, after the Nazis fell, the Soviets returned in 1944, staying for the next forty-seven years, re-imposing their controls and collectivism, until their second occupation finally ended in 1991.

When the museum opened in July 2003, after a record-cold winter in Estonia, the ceremony included champagne, violins and cellos, speeches on the symbolism of occupation, and the placing of a time capsule. Estonia's president said this was both a commemoration and a warning "to remain on the lookout for future threats." The Estonian prime minister added, "This is the past, not the present . . . where future generations will see what must never be repeated." Other voices spoke about the fragility of freedom and democracy, and a local priest recalled all that had been taken from Estonians through foreign occupation, but all they still had: their soul. "We have been vanquished, but we haven't been broken," he said.

The ceremony ended with the sprinkling of holy water.

Fifteen years later in September 2018, Pope Francis made a four-day visit to the Baltic nations of Lithuania, Latvia, and Estonia. With their histories of occupation pervading his thoughts, he offered the following prayer:

"'My God, my God, why have you forsaken me?'" (Matthew 27:46 NIV)

> Your cry, Lord, continues to resound. It echoes within these walls that recall the sufferings endured by so many sons and daughters of this people . . . and those of other nations who paid in their own flesh the price of the thirst for absolute power on the part of those who sought complete domination.
>
> Your cry, O Lord, is echoed in the cry of the innocent who, in union with you, cry out to heaven. It is the Good Friday of sorrow and bitterness, of abandonment and powerlessness, of cruelty and meaninglessness that this . . . people experienced as a result of unrestrained ambition that hardens and blinds the heart.
>
> In this place of remembrance, Lord, we pray that your cry may keep us alert. That your cry, Lord, may free us from the spiritual sickness that remains a constant temptation for us as a people: forgetfulness of the experiences and sufferings of those who have gone before us.

In your cry, and in the lives of all who suffered so greatly in the past, may we find the courage to commit ourselves decisively to the present and to the future. May that cry encourage us not to succumb to the fashions of the day, to simplistic slogans, or to efforts to diminish or take away from any person the dignity you have given them.

Lord, may [the Baltic nations] be a beacon of hope. May they be a land of memory and action, constantly committed to fighting all forms of injustice. May they promote creative efforts to defend the rights of all persons, especially those most defenseless and vulnerable. And may they be for all a teacher in the way to reconcile and harmonize diversity.

Lord, grant that we may not be deaf to the plea of all those who cry out to heaven in our own day.

Chapter 41

PICKING UP THE LIE TRAIL

"May the Lord cut off insincere lips,
every glib tongue that utters deceit."

- A PSALMIST'S APOCALYPTIC PRAYER -
MUSEUM OF COMMUNISM, PRAGUE, CZECH REPUBLIC

ANOTHER SMALL MUSEUM, AND ONE to approach intentionally rather than casually, is the Museum of Communism in Prague.

The genius of any good single-topic museum is that the entrant encounters a story fully presented, free from the distraction of competing narratives. Crowds tend to be small and quiet, admission prices are low, and mental exhaustion can be minimal, depending of course on the subject matter itself. With Prague's Museum of Communism, the seriousness of the topic resounds, yet one leaves feeling as though she or he has digested a factual account rather than a soul-immobilizing novel.

After being blown around by Prague's March wind in late winter 2012, Rissy and I finally found the place through a trial-and-error street search. Where was it, we wondered, as our map and phones seemed to get us close but not on target. Oh, there it was, next to a fast-food restaurant, its small entry sign suddenly in view. On the sign was a Russian doll with vampire-like fangs and the words, "Museum of Communism is here! 1st Floor, Next to Casino, Na Prikope 10, Prague."

We learned that an American businessman, Glenn Spicker, had opened the museum in 2001 after having spent $28,000 on approximately one thousand artifacts. Spicker then recruited a documentary filmmaker,

Jan Kaplan, to design the museum as a succinct three-act tragedy. Act 1 focused on ideals of communism such as state control of the economy by a dictatorship. Act 2 explored the reality of life under a communist regime, and Act 3 unraveled the nightmare of surviving a police state. Spicker wanted to incorporate a local perspective into the tragedy but found Czechs tight-lipped about their past, which involved a Nazi invasion in 1939, a Soviet invasion in 1945, and the Czechoslovak Communist Party by 1946. "The nightmare for Czechs," he would later say, "was really the knock on the door," and the sudden awareness that "you were being listened to" and now you were about to be interrogated. By that time, the communist takeover was in full swing.

Commentators have discussed the manipulative skill of the communist infiltration in what was then Czechoslovakia during the years 1944–48. The strategy involved playing on the centuries-old Czech fear of Germany while unleashing propaganda that framed the Soviet Union as Czechoslovakia's only geographic protector. Being simultaneously exhausted by Nazi maltreatment, the Czechs were desperate for any kind of hope, and when the propaganda machine offered the slogan, "Government of the people, by the people, and for the people," they took the bait. The communists corrupted the leaders of the Czech Social Democratic Party, removing their political foes, and eventually there wasn't enough resistance to save the central European republic from falling.

Rissy and I strolled past the obligatory images of Marx, Lenin, and Stalin; past pictures of jubilant workers in wheat fields with graceful birds overhead; past smiling adolescent pupils studying in well-equipped classrooms, soldiers in uniform, soldiers and common workers clasping hands and giving shoulder hugs; past neatly pressed Red Army uniforms and propaganda boards saying "Against Capitalism and the USA"; and past a brass wall plate with the words, "One death is a tragedy, one million deaths is a statistic (J.V. Stalin)." The star feature of the museum was an interrogation room with its aged sign, "VYSETROVNA INTERROGATION OFFICE," a functional quarter of creepiness with a radiating vibe seeming to say, except for the luck of where and when you were born, this could have been you.

"I can't even imagine the knock on the door and the voice on the other side telling me to report," I whispered, making three close-fisted knocks that seemed to echo through the empty museum.

It was likely that Rissy was closer to imagining such a scenario. Growing up in Portugal, she had as a child witnessed the country's decade-plus flirt with communism, starting with the overthrow of the fascist Salazar regime in 1974 and ending in 1986 when it joined the European Economic Community (now the European Union). There were no knocks on any doors that she remembers, but hammer-and-sickle symbols were everywhere.

"There was no democracy," she said. "Many people were put out of their homes by the communists, who seized their private property, and anything that had been profitable was suddenly nationalized." If it wasn't valuable, it was sometimes burned to the ground, like the houses of Rissy's grandparents and great grandparents, who were also called fascists. Factory owners were exiled to Brazil, and farmers were removed from land that had been in their families for generations. Something as simple as building a garage for your car was impossible because the local city councils had joined *The Party* and forbade private ownership. "That happened to my uncle," said Rissy. "Mostly, people were just afraid. Conversations were muffled, political discussions were nonexistent, even streets were renamed. And the slogans, like 'Long live the people's power' and 'Reagan go home' after Ronald Reagan's state visit in 1985, are remembered," she added.

"George Orwell called communism 'a hate world, a slogan world,'" I offered.

How different it was growing up in America, I thought, where my whole understanding of communism was second-hand. From the black-and-white tv images of Nikita Krushchev's "We will bury you" speech in 1960, seen on the same small screen that broadcast *Leave it to Beaver* and *The Andy Griffith Show*, to Mrs. Campeau's reading of *Animal Farm* to our sixth-grade class, communism was never more than a distant concept older people talked about, as nonthreatening as a polio vaccination. Later in life, however, through reading and rereading Orwell, as well as books such as *A Higher Kind of Loyalty* by Chinese journalist Liu Binyan, who suffered under the lies of Mao Tse Tung's China, I realized that you can know a thing through representation: in print, in cinema, even in a good museum. But you have to pick up the story and follow where it leads, not where you think it might lead, or where you might want it to lead, but to that place where truth emerges at the end of a long, confusing trail. With communism, that truth is, as Psalm 12 (CCB) illuminates, deceit: lies uttered by "insincere lips" and "glib tongues" devoid of any murmur of faith or godliness.

Help us, O Lord, none of the godly are left,
the faithful have vanished.
Everyone lies; with flattering lips they speak from a double heart.
May the Lord cut off insincere lips, every glib tongue that utters deceit.
Many say, "Our strength lies in our tongue,
we know how to speak, who will lord over us?"
The poor are despoiled and the needy suffer; now I will save them, says the Lord.
"I will give them security."
The promises of the Lord are sure and lasting—
silver refined in the furnace seven times and freed from dross.
Hold us, O Lord, in your keeping;
Protect us always from this generation,
for the wicked prowl on all sides,
and the basest are exalted.

Chapter 42

ETTY HILLESUM

"At night, too, when I lie in bed and rest in you, O God, tears of gratitude run down my face."

- A HOLOCAUST VICTIM'S PRAYER -
AUSCHWITZ-BERKENAU EXTERMINATION CAMP, POLAND

AUSCHWITZ.

My day there began and ended in silence, with a lot of silence in between, which is undoubtedly the best way to do the infamous concentration camp as a traveler.

What was there to say, to fellow passengers on the bus, to visitors at the cold steel and brick camp, or even to God? I couldn't think of anything, anyway.

It was December 22, 2008.

The religious studies conference at Jagiellonian University had ended the previous night with a dinner in Christmassy Krakow. As attendees went their separate ways, I stopped at a local bus station to buy a morning ticket, and at 8am the bus pulled away into an icy Polish landscape.

No one said a thing.

What, frankly, can one say about Auschwitz, or indeed about the entire Holocaust, that hasn't been said twelve million times before? That's twice for every Jewish person who was murdered during the twentieth century's most genocidal chapter. At some point in one's life, one realizes that Norman Finkelstein's book, *The Holocaust Industry: Reflections on the Exploitation of Jewish Suffering*, had to be written. The industry is and has been, without question, an exploitative goldmine. However, it must be added that a story so big and so full of emotional horror was bound to mix with the perfect blizzard of the century's exponentially growing media culture, thereby creating a below-the-surface, iceberg-like canon of cultural production that still resists quantification.

Upon arrival at Auschwitz, I stepped off the bus and joined an orientation session in the entry building of the camp. A guide was talking but his listeners weren't, even when he asked if anyone had questions. Soon we were walking under the familiar Arbeit Macht Frei ("Work Makes You Free") sign, whose words seem to float, suspended between bent steel bars which run parallel to each other.

The tip of that massive Holocaust iceberg had to be Steven Spielberg's 1993 film, *Schindler's List*, I thought, while wandering through the cold. How could anyone forget the disassociated girl in red running in her innocence across the black and white cinema-scape? Or the murdered woman engineer shot in the head for warning Amon Goeth of a fatal construction flaw? Or the crematorium ashes falling like snow on Auschwitz at night? At least forty other feature films, moreover, were made about the Holocaust in the 1990s alone, not including documentaries which number about a hundred by casual count, a calculus possessing subcategories. One currently making the rounds as of this writing is the original 1945 *Nazi Concentration Camps*, a ghastly preserve of visual evidence used at the war crimes trial of twenty-one Nazi bosses.

In silence, we walked along cold, wide foot paths, past colorless brick baracks which had originally been used to house the Polish army. The Waffen SS head and occultist, Heinrich Himmler, chose the facility himself to accommodate the *Final Solution* inhabitants who arrived on trains to be tortured and eventually executed. We stopped at Block 11, where the standing cells, in which freezing prisoners stood up for nights on end with a small hole for breathing, were located. The death wall, rebuilt after the war, was also there. It was covered with frozen flowers commemorating the many who had been executed by firing squad.

And the museums. Eighty-four Holocaust museums and monuments exist in the US alone, with twenty-four in Germany, seventeen in Ukraine, fourteen in Israel, thirteen in France, eleven in Russia and Poland, and single-digit numbers spread across the world. They serve as travel destinations in and of themselves. Indeed, the day after my Auschwitz visit, I received an email from an American colleague who wanted to know if I would recommend that she visit the camp with her Holocaust literature class the following summer. My answer was that I would not. Based on personal experience with students at the Yad Vashem World Holocaust Remembrance Center in Jerusalem years earlier, I had concluded that the eternally sombre Holocaust experience was not a good fit with the student travel mentality. You might be able to do it in low winter, I added, but even then, you'll have to find a way to extract genuine reverence from superficial frivolity.

I myself was not immune from the problem, I realized, after exiting Auschwitz-1 for Auschwitz-2, otherwise known as Birkenau. As a freezing wind whistled through the barbed wire and watchtowers, I found myself humming Jimi Hendrix's cover of Bob Dylan's song, *All Along the Watchtower*, complete with guitar riffs. Despite a certain relatability to lyrics emanating from a conversation about inescapable mental confusion between Dylan's joker and thief, I thought this is hardly the right conflation to be making in the place where trains brought people along cold straight railroad tracks directly into the gas chambers. Holocaust music would have been more appropriate, such as the gypsie lament, *Auschwitz*. Translated from the Romani language, the song stamps out an image of stark reality about a prison, a lover, a famine, hunger, and an evil Auschwitz prison guard. Included in Hitler's "enemies of the race-based state," it is estimated that at least a few thousand Romani died at Auschwitz.

At Birkenau, the guide knew all the specifics. The dates: 1939, when Germany invaded Poland, massacred Polish Jews or placed them in ghettos; 1940, when Himmler chose Auschwitz; 1941, when he expanded the facility and the first prisoners were gassed with the cyanide-based pesticide, Zyklon-B; 1942, when the genocidal Final Solution commenced its three-year run of unspeakable terror; 1945, when it ended as the Germans blew up the gas chambers and crematorium in advance of the invading Soviet Red Army. And the numbers: 438,000 Jews from Hungary, 300,000 from Poland, 69,000 from France, 60,000 from Holland, 55,000 from Greece, and additional thousands from Belgium, Yugoslavia, Slovakia, Austria, Norway. "Only 700 from Norway," said the guide. I believe that is when a few of us broke away from the group in silence, each making our way back to the entry point of Auschwitz-1.

The danger of numbers, dates, and physical details which authenticate an event like the Holocaust is its obvious removal of the individual human story, which tends to get lost in the particulars. Even the sheer number of stories can be a problem. Perusing limited numbers of them, however, can be rewarding, whether the criteria is age, gender, country of origin, or any category of choice that has a chance of revealing a real flesh-and-blood person. Persons were born somewhere and had names. They ate meals, wore clothing, had personalities, studied subjects, worked, came home from work, got fired, owned pets, and had human relationships. My personal preference is to know the names of people and what kind of work they did. Jane Haining, for instance, was a Scottish missionary who tried to save young Jewish girls; she died at Auschwitz in 1944 as prisoner 79467. Edith Stein was a Catholic Jew from Germany who died at fifty in 1942. She had been a nun and philosopher. Tadeusz Tanski was an automotive engineer from Poland who designed the CWS T-1 automobile, dying at Auschwitz in 1941. And Karl Parsimagi was a gay Estonian painter who died at forty, having been sent to Auschwitz because of his sexuality or the fact that he may have been hiding Jewish friends. The list goes on.

I'll rest at the story of Etty Hillesum.

She, too, died at Auschwitz at age twenty-nine, in 1943. Her Dutch-Jewish parents and two brothers were also Holocaust victims. The parents were believed to have died while in transit from the Netherlands to Auschwitz, the brothers perishing in other camps.

Etty studied law and Slavic languages in Amsterdam. She had a chaotic youth and was sexually promiscuous, having numerous affairs, which led her to say in her journal that she was "accomplished in bed" and was "counted among the better lovers" in her Dutch circle of acquaintances.

One of her affairs was with her psychotherapist, Julius Spier, a German Jewish refugee approximately thirty years her senior. Sex may have fueled the physical dimension of their relationship, but spiritual seeking provided a channel through which Etty sought to encounter the inward depth of her soul. She began to commit thoughts to a journal, at Spier's leading, and to internalize passages from the Bible through meditation.

Including Saint Augustine's *Confessions* and Thomas a' Kempis's *The Imitation of Christ* in her emancipation, she emerged with a power that insulated her from despair regardless of circumstance. "The misery here is quite terrible," she wrote, while imprisoned at the Westerbork Transit Camp, which preceded her transfer to Auschwitz; "and yet, late at night when the day has slunk away into the depths behind me, I often walk with a spring in my step along the barbed wire . . . I can't help it, that's just the way it is, like some elementary force—the feeling that life is glorious and magnificent, and that one day we shall be building a whole new world."

Then, on the train to Auschwitz, she wrote that she had her Bible and a few other books to sustain her, and she was talking to God. "Alas," she said, "there doesn't seem to be much You Yourself can do about our circumstances, about our lives. Neither do I hold you responsible. You cannot help us, but we must help You and defend Your dwelling place inside us to the last." That "dwelling place" was never compromised, as far as anyone knows.

Etty Hillesum carried one notebook to Auschwitz, having given eight more to a friend, with the intent of having them published one day. In 1981, they were.

Four years later, in 1985, a monument featuring a stone slab broken by a jagged fracture, titled "An Interrupted Life," was placed on a grassy lawn in her birthplace of Deventer, Netherlands. The portion of stone that follows the fracture slants upward into infinity, uninterrupted as it were, much like the "Prayer from Auschwitz" she left behind:

> You have made me so rich, O God;
> please let me share your beauty with open hands.
> My life has become an uninterrupted dialogue with you, O God,
> one great dialogue.
> Sometimes when I stand in some corner of the camp,
> my feet planted on your earth,
> my eyes raised toward your heaven,
> tears sometimes run down my face,
> tears of deep emotion and gratitude.
> At night, too, when I lie in bed and rest in you, O God,
> tears of gratitude run down my face,
> and that is my prayer.
> Amen.

PART SEVEN

Chapter 43

FINGER PAINTING AND IMMORTALITY

"... all ye other Gods that dwell in this place,
grant that I may become fair within."

- A SOCRATIC PRAYER -
THE SCHOOL OF ATHENS, APOSTOLIC PALACE, VATICAN CITY

BUCKET-LISTING IS A BAD WAY to travel. It emphasizes destination over journey, thereby removing discovery from the process of going point to point on any roadmap. There's no place on earth that I really want to see, moreover, unless I can see it unexpectedly through random sojourning and seeking. I mostly believe this.

If I ever did have a bucket list, however, one destination on it might have been my favorite painting, *The School of Athens* fresco, in Vatican City. When I did finally get to take it in, with my wife in 2011, it was on a trip through Italy, which made the experience even more gratifying as it was part of a journey and not a destination itself. After a sweltering afternoon in crowded, noisy St. Peter's Square, we strolled strangely un-inspired through the equally-crowded Sistine Chapel on our way to the Raphael Rooms (Stanze di Raffaello in Italian), which extended a cool invite to our summer weariness.

The Hall of Constantine was there featuring its visions and battles, as was the Room of Heliodorus with its vivid expulsions and deliverances. The fact that they didn't hold our attention presented us with a vibrant contrast in the Room of the Segnatura, where time suddenly stops, replaced by a sense of wonder so immense, one feels as though some eternal train is collecting passengers and we hold tickets. There, the four frescoes by Raphael told the stories we wanted to hear, visually: poetry in *The Parnassus*, where Apollo sits surrounded by muses as he plays a lira da braccio to accompany his recitations; theology in *The Disputation of the Holy Sacrament*, where debating popes mingle beneath biblical characters who float on a cloud; legal discourse in *Cardinal and Theological Virtues*, where church and secular legality reside under an arch of characters representing the ideals of I Corinthians 13 as well as the cardinal virtues of fortitude, prudence, and temperance; and finally, *The School of Athens* itself, a breathtaking panorama of philosophy and education which invites all viewers to partake in its ancient discursive warmth. Speechless, all I could think of was that after nearly a half century admiring it from afar, there I was standing before it in awe.

The first time I ever saw the painting was in a college humanities course. The instructor, a jovial southern woman from New Orleans who had just returned to America from Italy, was lecturing on Benvenuto Cellini's autobiography, illustrating her ideas with Kodachrome slides of Florence and Rome, where the famous goldsmith had worked. Slides during the pre-Powerpoint era could be monotonous as the projector clicked one after another against the cooling fan's back hum, but when *The School of Athens* suddenly broke into view, I broke with it. Who were all these colorful characters spread intriguingly across the scene? What were they doing? What story was being told? Indeed, following our instructor's lead, we attempted to identify faces in much the same way our generation had once done with The Beatles' *Sgt. Pepper's Lonely Hearts Club* album cover.

Plato, depicted by Raphael as the old man in the center with an index finger pointing up, was all about the philosopher's *theory of forms*, we were told. What we see on earth are only shadows of what exists above us in the spiritual realm. Aristotle, the younger man standing to the right of Plato with his hand held down and flat, says no, reality exists more in what we can see and touch. Pythagoras, in the lower left foreground holding book and quill, emphasized the laws of mathematics as our best sources of knowledge, and to his right Heraclitus, a dark and isolated man, taught that the basis of life was constant change, and don't resist it. Other philosophers, including Parmenides and Plotinus, had their own views of truth and reality, but their presence in the painting could not be confirmed.

God bless that wise and gentle professor. I wonder what became of her.

All these decades later, I am still transfixed by the painting. It speaks through color and gesture, form and mood, in an eternal visual language. Mostly, I want to know more about the philosophers assembled so beautifully by Raphael and why we continue to revere them.

Linda Johnsen's *Lost Masters: Rediscovering the Mysticism of the Ancient Greek Philosophers* sees them as having drawn much of their inspiration from Eastern thought, exported to the West in varying ways. She paints Pythagorus, for instance, as a traveling educational pilgrim: to Mount Carmel for "solitary meditation," to Egypt for science and "spiritual mysteries," to ancient Babylon for "the Brahmins of India" who had immigrated there. How ironic, she notes, that when we think of Pythagorus today, we only recall a "mathematical axiom" he never invented: the Pythagorean theorem. "We've forgotten," she says, "that . . . he was known best as a spiritual master."

Parmenides, she adds, was "drawn to spirituality" and higher states of consciousness, goals achieved through personal purity and self-discipline. Plotinus, who never made it to India, was nonetheless a seeker of Indian wisdom and spirituality, on his way to appreciating reality in terms of "transcendent spirit, cosmic mind, and individual soul." His influence was profound, even on the Christian father, Saint Augustine of Hippo, whom on his deathbed requested a copy of *Enneads*, the collection of writings by Plotinus. "In the face of death," Johnsen writes, "Augustine's sectarian bias fell away" in favor of "the eternal truths of the great mystical tradition underlying all faiths."

Rising above all others as objects of eternal study are Plato and Aristotle, just as Raphael must have concluded in *The School of Athens*.

Plato, in Johnsen's mind, is the man of sobriety who found himself perpetually disgusted by drunkenness and self-serving carnal behaviors in the people he knew. He was "orderly, industrious, and self-disciplined . . . preferring solitude to the company of fools." He was also a brilliant writer but a lousy speaker with a squeaky soprano's voice appealing to no one except Aristotle, his dream student. Aristotle's intellect and curiosity allowed him to look beyond such superficialities on his way toward building a philosophy based on hard facts. While he mourned the death of his great teacher, he had already moved away from the upward pointing finger of spiritual seeking, as it were, and toward the flattened, outstretched palm of verifiable things.

This eternal imprint of Plato and Aristotle on our consciousness endures in many forms. Even, or especially, in places like the Vatican, where discussing what is real and true creates the lifeblood of the community, the two great Greeks remain central. One has only to view the recent film, *The Two Popes* (2020), to witness a cinematic shadow of the undying Platonic-Aristotelian conversation.

The movie tells the story of Pope Benedict XVI (Joseph Ratzinger), who famously resigned from papal leadership in 2013, and his eventual choice of successors, Pope Francis (Jorge Mario Bergoglio) who was elected Pope shortly after. Arguably, Benedict is the Plato of the story: the purely intellectual man of books, culturally out of touch, preserving the unshakable integrity of higher ideals that do not change regardless of their existence *above* a changing world. Francis, on the other hand, is arguably the story's Aristotle: down-to-earth, moderate, a reformer, a fan of sports and popular music, a liberation theologian who likes to be out on the street with common people. We know both men in the present, but we also see Francis through flashbacks to an earlier life as a young man of science, facts, and the simple enjoyment of love and life.

As the story commences, revelatory conversations surface. Benedict suggests that Francis compromises the faith to serve superficial ends. Francis says he can no longer support an out-of-touch church which ignores its own problems, such as clergy sexual abuse, and practices meaningless rituals "while the planet burns." Benedict says God doesn't change; Francis says God does change, like nature. "So what matters is what you believe, not what has been taught for centuries," says Benedict. Their relationship eventually softens through mutual respect, and each man makes a confession of his shortcomings. Benedict confesses that he failed God by "hiding away in books and study" and "not having the courage to taste of life itself." Francis confesses his spiritual emptiness by failing to trust in God completely when his country, Argentina, exploded in a military coup. Broken but also freed and healed, the two popes depart from each other with a new future set before them.

One wonders how Plato and Aristotle would have solved their differences in *The School of Athens*. Raphael doesn't tell us this, preferring instead to preserve their dialogue visually, perhaps saying to the world that it's the conversation that truly matters, not the unsolvable choice between owning what lies above and acknowledging what is verifiable.

One more observation of the painting: how Raphael portrays Socrates. Despite his own enormous philosophical stature, Socrates is painted several human figures to the left of center, where he is shown looking off to the left, using hand and finger gestures while speaking to a group of intent listeners. Some commentators have suggested that Raphael had Socrates listing steps for remembering what is important in life, but I wonder. Creating steps to follow causes people to remember the steps rather than the deeper essence of what is being taught. Surely, that would not have been Socrates' intent, he being as rich a source of pure wisdom as anyone. Benjamin Franklin once wrote that only two people were worthy of being imitated: Jesus Christ and Socrates.

It had to be something different. Linda Johnsen portrays Socrates as the one philosopher possibly worth greater enduring attention than his own student, Plato. He was known to question everything others saw as important, leading them into humiliating self-contradiction, which, coupled with the false accusation of having no "respect for the gods," eventually got him arrested and sentenced to death for corrupting young minds. He "refused to run," however, says Johnsen, and on the last day of his life he "carefully weighed the arguments for and against the immortality of the soul." Why couldn't that have been what he was enumerating with his fingers in *The School of Athens*? one is inclined to ask. In any case, he said that reason alone wouldn't answer the question but that, untied from fear and desire, the soul would be freed at death, abiding "in a permanent state worthy of a divinity."

He drank the poison, his followers wept, and he left this world in tranquility: the state of being "fair within," as his prayer, according to Plato, stated:

> Dear Pan, and all ye other Gods that dwell in this place,
> grant that I may become fair within,
> and that such outward things as I have
> may not war against the spirit within me.
> May I count him rich who is wise,
> and as for gold,
> may I possess so much of it as only a temperate man might bear
> and carry with him.
> Is there anything more we can ask for, Phaedrus?
> The prayer contents me.

Chapter 44

The Touch of a Ragged Hat

"Almighty God, of whose only gift cometh wisdom and understanding: We beseech thee with thy gracious favor to behold our universities, colleges, and schools, that the confines of knowledge may be ever enlarged . . . ."

- A SCOTTISH PRAYER -
EDINBURGH, SCOTLAND, UNITED KINGDOM

EDINBURGH HAS SOMETIMES BEEN CALLED "the Athens of the North." In my seven years there, plus annual revisits, I never once heard anyone use the phrase. But due to the Athenian architecture overlooking the east end of the city, one can see how the description has survived. Calton Hill rises above the main east-west corridor, Princes Street, and is a kind of poor man's Acropolis with Parthenon-like *doric* columns standing since their placement in the early 1800s. Plans for completing this Scottish-version Parthenon were abandoned when the builders ran out of money in 1829, and construction was never restarted.

Something that survived in a more complete form, however, was Edinburgh's city-wide hunger for learning, which is said to have gathered raging momentum around the same time the Grecian structures were built. The University of Edinburgh had existed since the late 1500s but by the 1800s was considered one of the best in Europe. Today, it ranks among the world's top twenty year after year. Smaller academic venues also share the stage, and all who live in the city witness a collective knowledge crave which gives the city its *phenomenology* reputation. In coffee shops, pubs, bookstores, or walking down a street somewhere, you're likely to hear lively academic talk. I probably received more intellectual inspiration from the lady who took out the trash each night at Semple's Computer Lab than I did from my doctoral advisors at New College.

During my time there, in any case, I came to think of Edinburgh in particular, and Scotland in general, as places where academic spirit, and other good things, survive.

Indeed, survival seems an imperishable strain within the Scottish DNA. Sprawling Edinburgh Castle, for instance, has sat atop its outcropping of volcanic rock for at least eight hundred years, yet it remains active today. At night it appears to float above the city, illuminated warmly in a way that anesthetizes its painful history of attacks that left it crippled but never destroyed. From the Longshanks Siege of England's Edward I in 1296 CE, which cleaned out treasures and state records and sent them down to London, to the siege during the Jacobite rebellion of 1745 CE, survival has been a trick of its existence.

The tartan kilt is also a survivor, as is good whiskey and the Scottish bagpipe. Tartan fabric goes back at least to the Celts, who wore colorful checkered cloaks, and possibly even to ancient China where tartan has been found on mummified bodies. The *Falkirk tartan* of 230 CE was possibly the first in Scotland, and after a thousand-plus-year absence from historical record, the tartan reappeared in 1471 CE when the Bishop of Glasgow, who oversaw the treasury of James III, wrote about "blue Tartane," "halve of Tartane," and "doble Tartane to Lyne ridin collars to her lade the Quene." It remains today an accepted form of dress throughout Scotland as kilt makers in Edinburgh turn out traditional and modern fabrics that are quite popular.

Whiskey appears to go back at least to Christian monks who distilled it for medicinal purposes in twelfth-century monasteries, and probably much farther than that to ancient Greece and Persia. Once it became known as *Uisge Beatha* (Gaelic for "water of life") in Scotland, forces of culture and society set out to limit its popularity through taxation, licensing fees, wartime restrictions, and other forms of regulation. Yet, today its survival is marked by more than a hundred active distilleries which serve local and global consumers.

Then, there are the bagpipes. They create the ancient brooding soundtrack of Scotland. Historically, they are thought to have originated in Egypt in a simpler form, possibly brought to Scotland by Roman legions who occupied northern *Britannia* (England) in the farthest reaches of the Empire. The Scottish bagpipe featured a great drone, two tenor drones, a blowpipe, chanter, and of course the bag itself which maintains the sound. The *Piob Mhor* is the Great Highland Bagpipe, though the instrument was also a key part of weddings, feasts, and fairs in lowland Scotland down near the southern border. As a war instrument starting in the 1500s, it was used to inspire fighting men into battle, earning the tag, "vicious," applied by the English both to the sound of bagpipes and to anyone wearing a tartan kilt. The bagpipe's survival on the streets of Edinburgh bears an audible consistency with the visual, tactile Scottish weather drawing the elements of northern British life together in moody resilience.

As much as I love the castle, tartan, whiskey, and bagpipe, however, there is another survivor that stirs the soul within me: the continuing recognition of theology as the backdrop for all learning. University of Edinburgh graduates are still touched on the head by the *Geneva Bonnet* of sixteenth-century theologian John Knox at commencement. Dubious legend holds that the ragged velvet and silk hat was made from Knox's breeches, an unproven story despite its ceremonial importance for nearly two centuries. When graduating students hear their names called at the elegant McEwan Hall, they lean slightly while walking across the stage and are *capped* as graduates. The obvious symbolism is that regardless of which art or science each graduate has studied, their stamp of approval comes from the discourse of theology, the university's root.

I once had an interesting street conversation while standing at a bus stop in the Edinburgh city center. A man who, like me, was a researcher at the university, asked me which school I called home, and I answered, the school of theology. As a light rain began to fall, he said he was studying string theory in the school of mathematics. We got on well as we shared an umbrella, when suddenly he felt free to say he was fine with the university's religious history and had no problem with my school, New College, staying in business. He then added, "But seriously, do people still believe in religious stuff? I mean really believe?" He said this in an honest, nonthreatening way, and I answered, "I think it's about more than belief these days." Just then, his Hanover Street bus arrived and he boarded as I waited for my own, so the conversation never developed beyond that point.

Had it continued, I may have gone in any number of directions. Knowing of his mathematical interests, I may have said something about theology entertaining big ideas, such as the relationship between divine action and quantum physics. Perhaps God works at a level of microscopic quantum things in nature rather than from outside our world as a cosmic overseer. Such an idea leads into the topic of divine activity and evolution: the recognition that God created everything that lives through evolutionary processes. Since I know little about these big ideas, however, I may have instead approached his questions about belief. What does it mean to believe, and what makes people believe in God? I was at the time studying causes of belief in fan cultures, where fans who organize around objects such as sports teams and popular literature, appear to become true believers only after participation in their fan culture reaches a certain point. The more we participate, the more we believe, I could have said, whether participation occurs among fans, church goers, or scientists.

We could have, in any event, had quite a conversation as total strangers standing in the rain waiting for our buses. That is what makes Edinburgh so special, and I don't know of any place in the world where such everyday discourse survives in so many random places and unplanned moments.

The following prayer is taken from the 1929 CE edition of *The Scottish Book of Common Prayer*. Themes such as knowledge enlarged, illumination of mind, divine presence, and being in all ways a humble learner, emanate from Scottish prayer as timelessly as the life-sustaining theology which supports all forms of knowledge and understanding resident in this Athens of the North.

> Almighty God, of whose only gift cometh wisdom and understanding:
> We beseech thee with thy gracious favor to behold our universities,
>   colleges, and
> schools, that the confines of knowledge may be ever enlarged,
> and all good learning flourish and abound;
> bless all who teach and all who learn;
> and grant that both teachers and learners in humility of heart
> may look ever upward unto thee,
> who art the fountain of all wisdom;
> through Jesus Christ our Lord,
> who liveth and reigneth with thee in the unity of the Holy Ghost,
> ever one God, world without end.
> Amen.

Chapter 45

Denouement

"O Educator, be gracious to your children . . . that we may be made tranquil . . . ."

- A SECOND-CENTURY PRAYER -
HADRIAN'S WALL, ENGLAND, UNITED KINGDOM

From Edinburgh, one of many popular day trips involved getting out of the city early and heading south toward the border abbeys, and then on to Hadrian's Wall in Northumberland, England's northernmost county. I thought of it as a tranquility trip to alleviate the stresses of academic life and was sometimes joined by other doctoral students who also needed a break. Doing it alone was even better as solitude, silence, and the feeling of misty landscapes nurtured anyone's desire for peace.

The four abbeys, at Dryburgh, Jedburgh, Kelso, and Melrose, each possessed its own charm and calculus of stories, including attacks by invading English troops over the course of roughly five centuries. They had been founded in the 1100s CE, but by the mid-1500s their run as Catholic places of worship and prayer was ending, replaced by the Scottish Reformation. Retired local tour guide, Nigel Cole, describes them as "medieval ruins which share a broad affinity of origin and denouement," suggesting rather soberingly that regardless of how or where you start, or how magnificent your life becomes, your demise is coming like the final act of a great play, or in this case the last gasp of stately churches.

Nevertheless, strolling through the abbeys was always a pleasant indoor-outdoor experience which nurtured a kind of solemnity from imagining what the elegant structures looked like in their day. Today, their cacophony of churchyard gravestones, wind-eroded arches, exposed foundations, moss covered crosses, deserted cloisters and towers, while infused with melancholy, is also quite romantic. Lovely rivers named Tweed and Teviot flow past, and the wind and rain which compete for one's attention offer a traveler's warm embrace. Ironically, they have a similar effect of a good whiskey by candlelight with a friend. Perhaps in the end, romance is the experience of savoring the moment because you know nothing lasts forever.

The road from the abbeys south to Hadrian's Wall was also a visual treat as it wound through wooded countryside, bubbling streams of clear water, and stony *Masterpiece Theatre* villages. The wall itself, depending on where you joined it, was good for hiking, which I did as recently as 2019 with my wife.

It was also an amazing place to contemplate history. A second-century marvel of Roman engineering stretching across *Britannia* for seventy-three miles (eighty by Roman measurements), it was placed by the Emperor Hadrian to, in his words, "separate Romans from the barbarians to the north." Assembled by the Roman army following the emperor's visit in 122 CE, stonework up to six meters high and three meters below ground formed the partition, and its success as a barricade was followed twenty years later by construction of the Antonine Wall, under succeeding Emperor, Antoninus Pius, for similar purposes.

Both emperors lived with the knowledge of previous conflicts inclusive of the Gallic Wars under Julius Caesar in 55 and 54 BCE; the revolt led by the "warrior queen" Boudicca which killed 70,000 Romans and their supporters in 60 and 61 CE.; and the Battle of Mons Graupius, which slaughtered thousands of Caledonian Confederate Celts in 83 CE. So, wall investment was easily justified by a Roman Empire reaching the heights of its international power. Rome was going to be in Britain for a long time, and yet it was only a few decades after Hadrian that the empire's centuries-long decline commenced, say historians. By 200 CE, its downward trajectory was visible. By 400 CE, it was in a state of near-total collapse, which included Rome's final withdrawal from Britain, in 410 CE. By 476 CE, its own denouement was written like the conclusion to a multivolume historical novel.

But before that sad time arrived, Hadrian's moment during the second century seemed destined to be written as an affirmation in the history of empires and the individuals who lead them. Indeed, as one of the

Five Good Emperors of Rome, a political collective ruling from the final years of the first century to the end of the second, Hadrian was key in preserving both the internal security and external expansion of the empire which extended from the Persian Gulf to the North Sea. Through his elite military, he would no doubt have Romanized what is now Scotland, too, if its land had been more desired. He stopped short, however, opting for a protective wall instead.

It is said that Hadrian wrote an autobiography which was lost to antiquity. Stepping into that unfortunate literary vacuum, however, was the 1951 fictional autobiography, *Memoirs of Hadrian*, by Belgian-born French writer, Marguerite Yourcenar. A page-turner's page-turner, the novel is presented in the first person by a sixty-year-old Hadrian who knows he's going to die but not before writing a long letter to his successor, Marcus Aurelius. The letter covers his travels through the empire, his life as a Roman soldier, his heart condition, his loveless marriage to wife Sabina; his interests in astrology, Greek culture and philosophy, and his *Age of Gold* era of political stability. When we get to the Britannia section, the adventure progresses from a difficult ship crossing to the island, his dream of establishing an empire governed from the west, and regular uprisings of the dangerous Caledonians. For this reason, he tells Marcus Aurelius that he built the wall to safeguard the "fertile" south, adding "a temple to the god, Terminus, as a peace initiative." Finally, in praise of this remote place of sibyls and prophetesses who foretold his own death, he writes, "Everything enchanted me in that rainy land: the shreds of mist on the hillsides, the lakes consecrated to nymphs wilder than ours, the melancholy, grey-eyed inhabitants."

In absorbing Yourcenar's classic, one quickly forgets it is fiction, and when her Hadrian cuts his Britannia visit short so he can tend to empire business elsewhere, the disappointment is palpable. The reader craves more about the nymphs, the melancholy, the wall, and certainly that second-century world of relative calm. It must be said, however, that the so-called calm had to co-exist with at least two major wars, a pandemic which killed an estimated five million, and the disastrous arrival of Commodus, the megalomaniac emperor who was assassinated in 192 CE. Perhaps the calms and storms of history are so interwoven, adjectives are little more than weak attempts at unraveling complex threads too difficult to grasp in their actuality.

The second-century theologian, Clement of Alexandria, might have said as much. His knowledge of the spirituality of his day crossed many borders: Christian, Judaic, Gnostic, the Greeks, and eastern thought available to him, enough to know that what the human soul most desires is tranquility. And though his legacy was eventually given the boot by the Catholic Church in 1586 CE for his broad perspectives, his prayer to an educator God, a compassionate judge who understands the "sea of sin" that makes life turbulent, survives.

> O Educator, be gracious to your children,
> O Educator, Father, Guide of Israel, Son and Father, both one, Lord.
> Give to us, who follow thy command, to fulfill the likeness of thy image,
> and to see, according to our strength,
> the God who is both a good God, and a Judge who is not harsh.
> Do thou thyself bestow all things on us who dwell in thy peace,
> who have been placed in thy city,
> who sail the sea of sin unruffled,
> that we may be made tranquil and supported by the Holy Spirit,
> the unutterable wisdom, by night and day, until the perfect day,
> to sing eternal thanksgiving to the one only Father and Son,
> Son and Father, Educator and Teacher, with the Holy Spirit.

Chapter 46

A Message of Tides

"Prepare me to carry your presence to the busy world beyond, the world that rushes in on me, till the waters come again and fold me back to you."

- A MONASTIC PRAYER -
HOLY ISLAND OF LINDISFARNE, UNITED KINGDOM

ONE MORE PLACE IN MY southern Scotland/northern England orbit needs to be mentioned: Holy Island of Lindisfarne.

The peculiarity of visiting this tidal island is that while it possesses remarkable history and natural beauty, most travelers preface their comments about it with memories of *the causeway*. You leave the main highway about half the distance between Edinburgh and Newcastle, where approaching the island you're suddenly on a smaller road that floods twice a day by deceptively fast, incoming tides. If you get stuck in rushing water that can exceed the height of a large SUV, you can blame the North Sea, the moon, gravity, God, your parents, your spouse, your life circumstances, the hotel that didn't warn you ahead of time, or your own negligence for not planning ahead by reading the local tide schedule. That last item is likely where the blame should fall. But even if you're the one travel party each month, on average, that does find itself submerged, there is still hope in the form of a refuge shelter with steps you can scale until the water recedes. The local islanders refer to it as "the idiot box," but as the proprietors of The Belvue Guesthouse chortle, "It's better to be safe than drowned."

Once securely on the island, you notice the Lindisfarne Castle, perched on raised green-scape and refreshingly compact, unlike fortresses requiring a whole day to wander through. Stones from the nearby Lindisfarne Priory served to construct its infrastructure in the mid-1500s CE after Henry VIII dismantled the priory as part of his campaign to remove England from its Catholic past. Protection from the Scots was its rationale, continued by Elizabeth I who made improvements during her reign a few years later. Thereafter, it went as silent as any other deserted slice of history, eventually ending up in the National Trust during World War II. Today, it's an ethereal backdrop to a solitary stroll along the beach, accompanied by the sound of waves lapping the shore and perhaps a light North Sea breeze.

A walk among the red stone ruins of the priory is an even better meditative experience, especially as you learn details of the island's Christian history in the nearby museum and bookshop. It begins with the conversion of Anglo-Saxon King Oswald and his desire to bring the faith to Northumbria in 634 CE by inviting the Irish Bishop Aidan to set up a priory. Aidan arrived with twelve monks the following year. They lived simply in makeshift houses, established a literacy school, and produced attractive books which set a template for the artistically-elegant Lindisfarne Gospels, produced decades later. They also welcomed women and girls to become educated in Celtic monasticism, producing the energetic teacher and administrator, Hilda of Whitby, who became a respected abbess.

After Aidan died in 651 CE, he was followed by his disciple, Cuthbert, a compassionate hermit of great influence all the way up to Edinburgh, where he is thought to have established the church that now bears his name. Tensions between Roman and Celtic approaches to Christianity had produced ecclesiastical instability during Cuthbert's time, with some believers adopting the broader Celtic inclusion of women in the life and work of the Church. Cuthbert no doubt felt sympathies for this view, though he is said to have emerged more Roman in his faith due to its two-fold emphasis on prayer and silence. He was, like Aidan himself, an ascetic at heart, and spending as much time as he did on Lindisfarne, this perfect place of silence and solitude had shaped his life in God. He died in March 687 CE on Inner Farne Island but was buried on Lindisfarne the same day.

Cuthbert's legacy as an inner-directed saint of fortitude and humility is sometimes described as a cult that influenced even kings of Northumbria and beyond. He was buried and reburied several times, eventually ending up in Durham Cathedral, though it is unlikely that he, as his mentor Aidan before him, would have desired all the attention.

Lindisfarne continued in its monastic ways after both monks were long gone, until a different kind of sea rushed in and covered it in 793 CE: the first invasions by the Vikings. The fictional televised *Vikings* miniseries rightly begins at Lindisfarne, and its murderous plunder of the island and its terrified monks is documented in the annals of the *Anglo-Saxon Chronicle*. Translated from Old English, it describes the catastrophe:

> In this year fierce, foreboding omens came over the land of the Northumbrians, and the wretched people shook; there were excessive whirlwinds, lightning, and fiery dragons were seen flying in the sky. These signs were followed by great famine, and a little after those, that same year on 6th ides of January, the ravaging of wretched heathen men destroyed God's church at Lindisfarne.

This was a tide, so to speak, that would not be stopped until it covered everything in its path, at least until the time of the Normans, who were said to have revived the Lindisfarne Priory sometime after the year 1093 CE. When we walk through those red stone ruins today, we are walking through Norman history.

Here, I wish to express caution as I conflate a fragment of my own personal history with that of Holy Island's, though there seems a message in all this madness. It is a message of being overcome by metaphorical waters, not my own but nonetheless real, in the form of tragedies that rush in and roll over us as an all-encompassing tide which threatens to extinguish the very breath from our lungs.

Specifically, the last time I attempted to visit the island was on the darkest of nights at the end of a family holiday through England and Scotland. Nine of us had loaded into a rented minibus destined for an extended tour of notable sights: Stonehenge, Salisbury Cathedral, Stratford on Avon, Westminster Abbey, and days of wandering about standing stones, walls, and monuments. Heading home along the coast from London to Edinburgh that Sunday, I suggested we bunk at Holy Island and continue the following morning. When we arrived at the island, however, high tide covered the causeway. We u-turned toward a pub along the main highway and had a late supper instead. One in our party said she felt like something was pulling around her neck, making breathing a chore. Later in Edinburgh that same night, we received a call from the United States saying there was no easy way to say it, but her lovely daughter had driven her car into the garage, closed the door, and left the engine running. Suddenly, that metaphorical tide was sweeping over all of us.

At this moment in life, 2020 at this writing, I suspect that every last one of the adult populations on earth can no longer count deeply tragic moments on the fingers of both hands. The suicides of loved ones alone can likely fulfill the count. The son who put a gun to his head in his bedroom, the mother who did it by sleeping pills, or my beautiful childhood friend, Lorna, whom at thirty drove her car to the top of the Sunshine Skyway Bridge in Florida, jumped off, floated in Tampa Bay with a broken back, and shouted to her rescuers, "don't save me," before being pronounced dead at a hospital, are but three of many I have known personally. Or then there was that Sunday morning in Canada when a group of us celebrated a tiny one's first birthday, went off to church, and returned to encounter her crib death by suffocation the sitter had no way of preventing.

And the tides roll in and over.

St. Aidan of Lindisfarne, author of the following prayer, would have said yes, my dear ones, sooner or later you're likely going to be submerged, as most of us are in the human realm. But that same tide that covers us can also be the force which carries us back to God's loving embrace. All will be well, you will see, I imagine him saying. Do not be afraid, do not despair. And follow me in prayer to the God who knows all about the waters of life that rush in, bringing us back to himself and the safety of his love.

> Leave me alone with God as much as may be.
> As the tide draws the waters close in upon the shore,
> make me an island, set apart,
> alone with you, God, holy to you.
> Then with the turning of the tide
> prepare me to carry your presence to the busy world beyond,
> the world that rushes in on me,
> till the waters come again and fold me back to you.

Chapter 47

"Where Were You When I?"

"I shall soon lie down in the dust; you will search for me, but I shall be no more."

- JOB'S PRAYER -
TEL LACHISH, ISRAEL

With the Israeli rainy season over, vegetation that covered the Tel like a grassy veil had dried into a brittle brown, and was easily burned off the surface, exposing a huge, flat-topped mound that resembled a landfill. Cut into its sides were remnants of previous excavations: ancient house foundations, drainage canals, a city gate, a revetment wall, buttresses, staircases, a siege ramp, ruins of a palace fort on top, and a deep trench where about sixty of us would dig for the next two months. It would be a mental feast on Old Testament history, ancient military battles, and God.

It was summer, 1983.

That same year, "The Year of the Bible" as it became known in America, US President Ronald Reagan had made a startling proclamation: "Within the covers of the Bible," he said, "are the answers for all the problems people face." As expected, many criticized him for political posturing in advance of a second term, but the statement seemed appropriate. After a decade of failed presidential leadership, Watergate, Nixon-Ford-Carter instability, the holding of American hostages in Iran, and Reagan's own attempted assassination, America and indeed the world seemed ready to look forward by looking back: to the Bible, to the roots of Judeo-Christian assumptions, to a usable past of biblical teaching on power and authority, and to hard conflicts solved by simple binary solutions.

The Old Testament was, frankly, everywhere at that time. It became a kind of popularized folk canon of selected narratives exploring latent Sunday school memories held by baby boomers. The Ark of the Covenant, Kings David and Solomon, Samson and Delilah, Creation and the Flood, floated along the surfaces, and occasionally in the depths, of popular film, music, television, and magazines. With this canon came a parallel popularization of biblical archaeology and numerous travel-study opportunities in biblical lands. Thus, when the prospect of joining the dig at Tel Lachish was presented to me as a way to earn academic credits at the ancient desert city between Tel Aviv and Jerusalem, I came alive with anticipation. That particular dopamine rush has subsided over the years but never left completely.

We rose each morning at four, awakened by a camp guard pacing through our tent community while beating a drum. The guard was necessary for security, and the dig itself bore the memory of its first leader, James Leslie Starkey, a British archaeologist who excavated Lachish in the 1930s and was murdered while on his way by car from the Tel to a museum opening in Jerusalem. Starkey and his team had done much to uncover evidence of the attack on Lachish in 586 BC by the Babylonian king Nebuchadnezzar, an event recorded in the Old Testament book of Jeremiah, chapter 34 verse 7. Starkey's death in 1938 was followed by archaeological haggling over times and dates of ancient events, and decades later new work was initiated by David Ussishkin, the lead archaeologist of our season of digging in 1983.

After a breakfast of fresh bread and grainy coffee, we were at the Tel by five. Ussishkin's team met us there to explain procedures and objectives, which included seeing the Tel as a layer cake with each layer revealing a different era of history. For Lachish, this *stratigraphy* included at least eight layers, or *levels*, ranging from the period following the Nebuchadnezzar conquest, all the way back to Bronze Age activity many centuries, even millennia, before Christ. Our objective was to further uncover what was known about Level III, the remains of a densely populated city conquered in its heyday by the arrogant Assyrian king, Sennacherib, in 701 BCE. Also documented in the Old Testament, its larger memorialization exists in Sennacherib's own annals, which mentions "forty-six strong walled towns . . . I besieged and conquered by stamping down earth ramps and then by bringing up battering rams, by the assault of foot soldiers, by breaches, tunneling and sapper operations." Lachish was one of the forty-six.

As the sun made its daily ascent, the rich reddish-brown, mud-brick interior of the trench changed gradually to a hot, dusty tan. "People, drink water" and "keep your heads covered" were the most common statements heard, and by late morning we were scraping, combing, and brushing pottery fragments and formations of stratified earth in intense desert heat. On days when intact pottery, or something containing ancient writing, were unearthed, the supervising archaeologists attempted quick explanations which were inconclusive but offered context. The great reward for all of us was elemental education based on real discovery, and I do not remember hearing a single complaint the entire two months.

Work ended each day at noon when the searing heat had us scrambling back to the camp, which was refreshingly shaded by eucalyptus trees. We showered in cold well water, ate a substantial lunch, and then crashed on our tent cots until dusk most days. The cool of evening was perfect for lectures at a makeshift classroom under the trees, with visiting scholars adding a topical smorgasbord to the mix of archaeology, history, and religion. At the Q and A following one lecture, a student asked if the speaker had read James Mitchener's novel, *The Source*, published two decades earlier but still influential among pop-history buffs. Mitchener, who was also hot during that 1980s micro-era of Old Testament archaeological intrigue, had fictionalized local history, from the Stone Age to the Crusades, in a supernatural story involving a fictional tel in northern Israel, where people from each stratum came alive. A best-seller in its day, the book may have prepped many to study history and archaeology, so the student's question was a reasonable one.

But the lecturer, who was a stratigraphy expert, shut him down fast. "That's fiction," he said. "The archaeology is all wrong, and it's a silly story, too. What we're doing here is real. Please excuse my bluntness." End of discussion.

It may have occurred to me at the time that this dig experience was about physically touching the preserved objects of a mysterious history. Knowing historical narratives of great movements and contexts takes on new meaning when you're pulling arrowheads and scarabs out of the very earth they fell upon and adding them to the story. No doubt, that was true. But thirty-plus years on, I have also come to think of the era as a generational seeking of the unknown, elusive deity of the Old Testament. Was this god, God, and how would anyone begin to comprehend a deity who toggles between mercy and benevolence, wrath and punishment, disinterest yet able to count the hairs on one's head? The world of culture at that time had fresh impressions of the Son, from the far-reaching Jesus Movement of the previous decade, and now was the time to contemplate God the Father in all his personalities.

Old Testament scholars I have known have said that the O.T. deity emerges only from the accumulation of personal characteristics applied to God in the forty-six canonical books. And because the canon is so complex, the deity that emerges is equally complex. In Genesis, he is a creator; in Exodus, a deliverer; in Judges, a judge; in Ruth, a companion; in Nehemiah, a reformer; in Psalms, a shepherd; in Proverbs, a wise teacher. And so on. He doesn't appear at all in the books of Esther and Song of Solomon, and in Ecclesiastes he is the point of reference against which, without him, all of life is a meaningless vacuum; a characterization that has appealed to writers and artists across time.

In the book of Job, which scholars date to approximately the time of Level III in the Lachish excavation, the deity speaks from a whirlwind as though residing within the desert forces of heat and dust which swirl around human lives trapped in existential angst. Job, a faithful man, suffers physical and emotional indignities as part of a wager between God and Satan, the deity seeming not of the mind to explain the situation other than to contrast Job's pain with his own divinity and all-powerful persona. "Where were you when I laid the foundations of the earth?" he says, to which Job is speechless.

He is, of course, restored to health and wealth in the strangest of all melodramas, but his earlier lingering prayer of seeking his creator through timeless questioning endures like the eternal earth beneath his feet:

> What is mankind that you make so much of them,
> that you give them so much attention,
> that you examine them every morning
> and test them every moment?
> Will you never look away from me,
> or let me alone even for an instant?
> If I have sinned, what have I done to you,
> you who sees everything we do?
> Why have you made me your target?
> Have I become a burden to you?
> Why do you not pardon my offenses
> and forgive my sins?

For I shall soon lie down in the dust;
you will search for me,
but I shall be no more.
   (Job 7: 17–21 NIV)

Chapter 48

THE OMEGA VOICE

"Above all, trust in the slow work of God."
- AN EVOLUTIONARY PRAYER -
DRUMHELLER, CANADA

MY PENULTIMATE TRAVEL DESTINATION IS a small town, Drumheller, in the Alberta prairie country of west-central Canada. My penultimate prayer is actually a prayerful meditation from the philosopher, Pierre Teilhard de Chardin. Somewhere in the reflective recesses of my brain, both share time and space.

Passing at least twenty times through that peaceful nothingness of earth and sky, I always loved those distraction-free road trips. From the south, Highway 89 in Montana was the route taken before crossing over into a landscape of grain elevators and friendly Albertans on the other side of the border. From the east, the seemingly eternal straightness of the Trans-Canada Highway was a corridor of anticipation, and from the west the Rocky Mountain passage gradually diminished in elevation before flattening out completely near Drumheller. I never approached from the north.

A traveler's healthy solitude can be nurtured where colors, mountains, bodies of water, and throngs of people are not present, making the badlands of wind-eroded sediments and barren, fossil-rich hills suitable for meditation. That is Drumheller. In the town, of course, the solitude is interrupted by tourists, commerce, and the busy Royal Tyrrell Museum of Paleontology with its thousands of catalogued fossils and prehistoric skeletons. I last visited it with my daughter when she was small and, like most kids, enchanted by dinosaur lore. We were mutually intrigued by the sight of an intact borealopelta dinosaur on its stomach, bodily features perfectly preserved, and by numerous other specimens from a hundred-plus million years ago.

But the real attraction in Drumheller is the stratified outcropping known as the Horseshoe Canyon Formation. Like pages on top of pages containing the text of prehistory, its gray and white layers of shale and sandstone intermingle, revealing fossilized secrets of a past so distant, the limitations of human *presentism* keep them from seeming fully real. I, personally, have never been able to conceptualize time in such a way as to make the prehistoric past seem like it really happened. But that is what makes this place so meditative. You can wander for hours, or days, or longer, among the layers, lost in pure imagination capable of carrying your mind much farther away in time than you ever thought possible.

Time isn't of the essence here; it is the essence, the object of meditation. And as one meditates, one realizes that time is the most perfect thing, fluid and continuous, governed only by the order of what preceded what and what followed next. It contains the ancient past and the recent past, moves through the present and forward into the future, refusing to stop for anyone or anything. We can verify present time because we experience it. We watch in amazement as it happens. We know that it was transpiring before we were born, and it will continue after we die. Yet, those two reference points are what makes time so frustrating: we can't travel forward into the future, and we can't travel back into the past, and so we never actually see time, and what it holds, in those realms. Intellectually, we can adopt the physicist's concept of *eternalism*: the idea that the past, present, and future are equally real. But unless your intellect and imagination are stronger than my own, you'll feel as frustratingly trapped as I am.

I love it, though, when over the course of my life I have discovered those who have tried harder and gone farther than my capabilities have allowed. Concerning the distant, prehistoric past, for instance, I am quick to include Charles Darwin on my list of admired people.

Evolution has always given way to Darwin, the person, for me because a real person is central to any discourse or philosophy. I have to know the man or woman who formulated theories, more than the theories themselves, and trust in the person is essential. With Darwin, that has led to a personal quest of knowing more about the man who once studied theology and wanted to be a country vicar. Raised Unitarian, however, had given him such a broad worldview that he must have known early on that his true calling lay elsewhere. He didn't suddenly un-Christianize himself, though, and he was said to have maintained an orthodox faith even as he voyaged to the Galapagos to study active and fossilized life. Trouble, first with the variable portrayals of the Old Testament God, and later with an emerging agnosticism which didn't allow a reasonable balance between faith and science, had produced doubt: the involuntary response to objective criteria. So, he did his research, published his theory that nature, not God, does the selecting in our world, and in quiet retreat returned to England where he took long Sunday walks while his family worshiped in church.

I could not possibly fault anyone for following their inner voice. In fact, with Darwin, I used his 1873 book, *The Expression of the Emotions in Man and Animals*, religiously, in my final decade of teaching at a Christian university. It was such a valuable resource for providing backstory to suffering, attachment, catharsis, preference, enjoyment of stimuli, and other factors relevant to media consumption, that it became an irreplaceable text. I seldom mentioned evolution, other than to suggest that God works slowly and that things like design, order, and regulation, can be appreciated as divine processes as much as natural ones. Those were stimulating discussions which usually ended up with footnotes highlighting Darwin's life and how God calls each of us to purposes much different than we recognize at the moment.

The last time I experienced the Horseshoe Canyon Formation was with five old friends from Calgary, where I had been a frequent visitor since the early 1970s. We were fossil hunting, plucking bone fragments and prehistoric teeth cemented into rock, from layered sections of the formation. We knew each other well, and though I missed the solitude of previous visits, the guy-talk was fun. At one point, someone mentioned *Teilhard*, as in Pierre Teilhard de Chardin, whom we all loved with equal passion. A few of the guys were working on a computer start-up in Calgary and had named it after Teilhard, perhaps to emphasize that even computer technology can be appreciated philosophically and, indeed, spiritually.

Teilhard Technologies had some success until it went belly-up over patent-related issues. Not so, however, for the real Teilhard; his patent remains stable among legions of followers seeking hope and promise where evolutionary science often offers neither.

Raised by an amateur naturalist father and a spiritually inspired mother, Teilhard balanced his extensive learning in the hard sciences and stratigraphy with Catholic theology. He became a Jesuit priest, carried stretchers during World War I, traveled the world, and settled for two decades in China where he participated in the *Peking Man* excavations which unearthed Homo Erectus fossils dated to over seven hundred thousand years ago. Reading and experience had conditioned a worldview endorsing a creator God and an immortal human soul, beliefs which ultimately ascended to Teilhard's *Omega Point*: the idea that all things are moving toward a unified destination, from Alpha to Omega, first to last, as the *Book of Revelation* teaches. Some French Jesuits found Teilhard offensive to Catholic doctrinal teaching, and strict evolutionary scientists have criticized him as unserious, nonsensical, tedious, and filled with metaphysical conceit. "The quintessence of bad poetic science" is how Oxford evolutionary biologist, Richard Dawkins, has described his work.

Yet, Teilhard has always been a hero to writers, artists, spiritualizing nomadic travelers, and people like myself and my friends who were combing for fossils that day in Drumheller. We didn't find much in the prehistoric stratifications. But a long time ago we found hope in recognizing that a cosmic presence and its energies exists beyond the material, verifiable world of physical substance and function. We're like the two popes, Benedict and Francis, whom as Teilhard fans themselves are seekers of hope wherever it hides. Benedict once wrote that the cosmos is in movement: "it anticipates its goal and at the same time urges it on." Francis added that "the church does not presume to settle scientific questions . . . but to encourage an honest and open debate . . . ." What is not debated is how much our world craves hope.

Hope is the soul's energy.
Prayer is the poetry of hope.
Teilhard's prayer:

Above all, trust in the slow work of God.
We are quite naturally impatient in everything
to reach the end without delay.
We should like to skip the intermediate stages.
We are impatient of being on the way to something
unknown, something new.
And yet it is the law of all progress
that it is made by passing through
some stages of instability—

and that it may take a very long time.

And so, I think it is with you;
your ideas mature gradually—let them grow,
let them shape themselves, without undue haste.
Don't try to force them on,
as though you could be today what time . . . will make of you tomorrow.

Only God could say what this new spirit
gradually forming within you will be.
Give Our Lord the benefit of believing
that his hand is leading you,
and accept the anxiety of feeling yourself
in suspense and incomplete.

Chapter 49

Honor Thy

*"Then they cry unto the Lord in their trouble,
and he bringeth them out of their distresses."*

- A RENEWABLE BLESSING -
ESTERO BAY, UNITED STATES

THE YEAR 2020 IS COMING to a close, mercifully.

Here in Lisbon, the normally crowded and celebratory Avenida da Liberdade is almost empty, robbed of tourists and holiday revelers by the yearlong coronavirus pandemic. Never a big fan of the decorative explosion inspired by the holidays, this year I actually miss it and all it represents: tradition, commerce, goodwill, and at least the illusion of vibrant civic life.

As of today, the global statistical tally has the planet gasping for breath amid sixty million cases of Covid-19 with 1.4 million deaths. Lockdowns everywhere are accompanied by political instability, crippled industries, and at least a hundred million new sufferers of extreme poverty as defined by the World Bank.

Hope is on the proverbial horizon in the form of vaccines, though who gets them, when, where, and how they're going to be distributed among seven billion of us, is the current unsolved mystery. A greater hope is that we won't be having this same conversation a year from now.

At home I sit, anachronistically and archaically by techie standards, in front of a television screen watching Morgan Freeman's Netflix series, *The Story of God*. I can relate to a lot of it: the reflective man of travel to spiritual places, the desire to accommodate great varieties of religious texts and rituals, and the joy of spending one's retirement years talking to people about their faith and what it means to them. Another thing I can relate to is when Freeman goes back time and again to rural Mississippi and says, "This place defines me."

My own life has always felt too mobile to be defined by one place. Yet, if personal life-definition is based on returning over and over to a place of one's youth, for me it would have to be tiny Estero Bay, a body of water between Fort Myers Beach, Florida and the southwest Florida mainland. I still fly TAP from Lisbon to Miami most years and then drive up to that little barrier island north of Naples, where seven years of subtle adolescent changes amid a fair amount of family conflict occurred for me during the tumultuous 1960s. I don't celebrate it quite the way Freeman savors Mississippi, but perhaps it defined me more than I realize half a century later.

The story actually began in our tranquil suburb of Detroit, Michigan, where my family's stable and insulated 1950s world received a knockdown punch early one Sunday morning. Dad was on his way home after working the night shift as a police officer, stopping at a blind curve in the road to warn motorists away from a fallen light post. Sitting in his squad car, he was struck from behind so violently the car seats were flattened, and the lumbar portion of his back was crushed along with them. The intoxicated driver of the other car was taken away by ambulance, and Dad, too, was transported to a local hospital, where he underwent temporary surgery to repair some of the damage. The surgery was unsuccessful, though, and the years ahead were scarred by experimental spinal fusion operations which removed bone from his pelvis and transplanted it to his lumbar. After one operation, an attending nurse stole doses of his opioid, Demerol, leaving him in enough post-op pain to have him wishing to position himself next to his upper-floor window where he could more easily jump to his death, he told me years later.

During his multi-year recovery, marked by the loss of his career at thirty-five but given a disability pension, he lay in bed dreaming of Florida. He wanted palm trees, white sand instead of snow, a boat, and distance, both physical and psychological, between himself and that miserable chapter of his life. Mom was reluctant to leave her friends and family, however, and an experimental trip down there didn't help much. But she acquiesced to a point, and when for reasons understood only by women trapped within that era of helpless deference to their men, she said all right, she would go. Things happened very quickly at that point. Like an old family movie jumping from scene to scene, Dad was up and around with a cane, the house was sold, the pension money came through, a mobile home was purchased, loved ones were hugged, and we were ready to pull away. If that home movie had sound, we would all have heard the last thing said by my grandfather to my father that day: "Everything was okay until you broke up our family." He saw disillusionment in my mother's eyes.

Heat, uncertainty, and Mom's growing discontent marked the journey south. Cicadas provided the soundtrack while kudzu blankets and red clay painted scenic backdrops through Tennessee and Georgia.

When we arrived at Fort Myers Beach, which at that time still had quaint fishing village appeal, the long road trip was over. The Red Coconut Trailer Park became our new home. Cockroaches, flying palmetto bugs, lizards, and the unfamiliar faces of other human refugees from the north, became our new neighbors. The park itself was split into two parts by the island's main road, and Dad chose the Gulf of Mexico side to fulfill his fantasy of living by the beach. A few days after settling in, though, a tropical storm nearly blew us and our few belongings away, ripping the screened-in canopy from the trailer and imprinting a look on Mom's face none of us had ever seen before. Quickly, Dad scrambled to have us situated on the park's other side, by an insect-infested tropical forest. There for the next six months, we walked across pine-needled lanes to a bathroom facility that served the entire park, used the park office's lone telephone, and breathed the fumes of the mosquito fogger that came through once each day. At night, I was more than happy to sleep outside under mosquito netting for all six months, away from unhappy parents, adolescent sisters, and the misadventure that now characterized all of our lives.

But after that fall and winter of discontent, we moved into a house on the shores of Estero Bay, an attractive setting of mangrove islands and fishing boats. We acquired a small boat ourselves, which was mostly used by me in my effort to identify with other boys on the island, many of whom had boats. As preteens and older, we would meet up in deserted island alcoves, and on sandbars exposed at low tide, to live out our juvenile fantasies in which all boys indulge. One night, another storm blew through, tearing the boat away from its mooring and sending it across the bay where Dad and I located it through binoculars the following day. I wrote a story about it for school, recounting the incident set against a backdrop of family conflict, which angered Dad to the extreme. "You have quite the imagination," he said to me, annoyed.

On Sundays, we attended the local Baptist church, a nondescript structure built on short stilts in case of storm surges. Folksy and friendly but devoid of any youth appeal, the adolescent minds of my sisters and me tolerated this strange habitat of fundamentalist god-speak but craved reasons not to attend. Reality lay elsewhere: in school, in trashy relationships, and in the rebellious mood of the 1960s. We had moved to the island on the eve of the JFK assassination, left during the trial of the iconic Chicago-7 culture rebels, and with a few other national revolts and murders between, no one could help but be drawn into the chaos. That is when I first saw my mother on her knees praying beside her bed on late Sunday nights. I never knew, or asked, what she was praying about, though with her life as she had known it quite gone, inclusive of losing her children to the local delinquent youth scene, she may have been summoning the strength to leave, which she did for a summer, or the greater strength to accept things as they were and bloom where she had been planted. In her despair, she wouldn't have known Joni Mitchell's popular song, *Both Sides Now*, about "life's illusions" and not having a ghost of an idea of what life was about, but she was indeed living it.

That image of Mom praying has stayed with me my entire life. It was also the precise moment when I felt the need to launch out, which I did by taking my small aluminum boat out as often as possible; away into a private world of solitude unbroken by noise on the shore; out past the shipwrecks left by the yearly storms; past the sandbars and oyster bars, the old fisherman's shack by the wooden bridge, the dolphins and manatees playing at the water's surface, the leaping stingrays and flying fish, the mullet boats and shrimpers docked on San Carlos Island, and Mound Key with its history of Calusa Indian habitation and even some pirate lore. I always came back, though, as did Mom after her hiatus. Life is a process of going and coming, it seems, and perhaps prayer is in some ways simply the psychological record we make before God and ourselves of all the leaving and returning moments we experience across the course of living. I sometimes think of it that way.

I returned last year, 2019, to the island and the bay, renting a boat to navigate at leisure those waters I came to know as a kid. The island seemed overcrowded and overbuilt with little that would remind one of its past simplicity. The bay was brimming with fuller tides than the ones I remembered, and its open spaces were occupied by anchored yachts and sailboats. I couldn't find any of the old mid-engine mullet boats operated by the salty old souls who caught the vegetarian fish with nets because baited hooks wouldn't work. They were so symbolic of that old time for me, as were the antiquated shrimp boats, which are still there, modernized, and in smaller numbers. Locals say the sought-after pink shrimp have moved away from places where they once thrived, forcing the shrimpers who remain into longer runs clear across the Gulf of Mexico. Sometimes they return only with brown shrimp in their holds. At least they come back with something.

Sometime that afternoon, I returned my boat and joined the throngs at the annual Shrimp Festival, a ritual of music, beauty contests, tortoise races, and food, lots of food. Cuban sandwiches, key lime pies, barbecued grouper, conch fritters, oysters, and shrimp served in many variations, were displayed on picnic tables and romantic benches situated near the water, where diners seemed thankful for this festive tradition which has survived nearly seventy years. Even the blessing of the shrimp fleet was offered by a local minister. Abandoned for a generation, this ritual of saying a prayer while sprinkling holy water from a palm frond on the San Carlos shrimp boats was being revived, this first year by the rector of the Episcopalian church.

Accompanied by cross-bearing acolytes dressed in pure white, and a festival crowd of curious onlookers milling about under a partly cloudy sky, the rector stretched out his right arm, waved his hand over the fleet, and prayed:

> They that go down to the sea in ships, that do business in great waters;
> These see the works of the Lord, and his wonders in the deep.
> For he commandeth, and raised the stormy wind,
> which lifteth up the waves thereof.
> They mount up to the heaven, they go down again to the depths:
> their soul is melted because of trouble.
> They reel to and fro, and stagger like a drunken man, and are at their
>   wit's end.
> Then they cry unto the Lord in their trouble,
> and he bringeth them out of their distresses.
> He maketh the storm a calm, so that the waves thereof are still.
> Then are they glad because they be quiet;
> so he bringeth them unto their desired haven.
> Oh that men would praise the Lord for his goodness,
> and for his wonderful works to the children of men!
>   (Psalm 107: 23–31, KJV)

Epilogue

Dear Mom,

It is a rare wintery day here, where I sit looking over this manuscript, reliving yet again the travel experiences, educational episodes, and prayers which I hope have illuminated the narrative. Years ago, I remember hearing some extreme mystic say that, from heaven, prayers on earth can be seen as lights shining upward from wherever they are offered. I hope there is some physical truth to this, and that John 1:5 is more than purely symbolic: "The light shines in the darkness, and the darkness has not overcome it."

Surely the interplay of light and darkness is the basis for any piece of writing or art, and I certainly hope that light informs the textual character of this book. I also hope that my gratefulness for the survival of true things has left an imprint. Probably because of your example, I have always wanted a spiritual life inclusive of quietness, meditative cognition, reading and learning, the embrace of daily existence, fellowship with other seekers and believers, and ultimately a satisfied mind regardless of circumstances. Wherever I have traveled, or lived, those have been my goals. In this regard, I end with my own personal prayer:

> Mysterious God, maker of all that is made, and sustainer of all that is good,
> I thank you for a life lived within your eternal guiding presence.
> Wherever I have traveled, you have been there with me.
> Your presence is the column of light emanating from a slightly open door,
> and inside that door is the warmth of your dwelling place.
> The time will come when, like others before me, I will walk into that light,
> thankful and prayerful and maybe with new ways of expressing my gratefulness.

Mom will be there, and Dad too, and others I have known who now rest
 in you,
joyfully occupying their predestined places of peace and love.
Will all journeys cease in that dwelling place? I can't know.
Perhaps you grant safe passage throughout your multiverse of new
 places,
and if so, I will be in that line awaiting my ticket.
But my final hope is that wherever I go, I will always return to you.
 Always.
Amen.

The End

From the Author

Travel memoirs written for trade book audiences are not held to the rigors of documentation which exist in scholarship for academic audiences. However, I would like to emphasize my personal care in fact-checking the contents of this book. These efforts extended to the inclusion of relevant books, articles, movies, and songs; cultural and historical references; personal interviews with sources who were part of the narrative; personal memories, some going back fifty years or more; and, of course, the many prayers that form the basis of the text. Some minor corrections in spelling and punctuation were made, if only to enhance the presentation of some prayers, so that they might be fully appreciated by readers. Minor reordering of a few memories and events was also applied, again for the purposes of readability and understanding. All else is as accurate and faithful to the truth as was possible to achieve.

Selected Bibliography

Alexievich, Svetlana. *Chernobyl Prayer: Voices from Chernobyl*. London: Penguin, 2016.
Anonymous. "MacArthur's Son Shuns Military Life." *Associated Press* (April 9, 1964).
Anonymous. *The Way of a Pilgrim*. New York: Dover, 2008.
Aramago, Jose. *Journey to Portugal: A Pursuit of Portugal's History and Culture*. Translated by Amanda Hopkinson and Nick Caistor. London: Harvill, 2002.
Barclay, William. *The Lord's Prayer*. Edinburgh: Saint Andrew, 2008.
Baumol, Avi. *The Poetry of Prayer: Tehillim in Tefillah*. Jerusalem: Gefen, 2010.
Beach, Sylvia. *Shakespeare and Company*. Lincoln, NE: Bison, 1991.
Benedict, Ruth. *Patterns in Culture*. Boston: Houghton Mifflin, 2006.
Bickerdike, Jennifer Otter. *The Secular Religion of Fandom*. London: Sage, 2015.
Bouich, Abdenour. "The Translated Poems of the Berber Kabylian Poet Si Mohand ou-Mhand, 1845-1906." *Xanthos Journal* 1 (2019).
Bourdain, Anthony. *A Cook's Tour: In Search of the Perfect Meal*. London: Bloomsbury, 2002.
Boxer, C.R. *The Portuguese Seaborne Empire 1415-1825*. Manchester, UK: Carcanet, 1991.
Brodrick, James, S.J. *The Origin of the Jesuits*. Chicago: Loyola University Press, 1986.
Bunzel, Ruth. *Zuni Ritual Poetry*. Whitefish, MT: Literary Licensing, 1932/2007.
Butler, Anthea. *White Evangelical Racism: The Politics of Morality in America*. Chapel Hill, NC: The University of North Carolina Press, 2021.
Cameron, H.D. *Studies on The Seven Against Thebes of Aeschylus*. Berlin: De Gruyter Mouton, 1971.
Charles River Editors. *The Maori: The History and Legacy of New Zealand's Indigenous People*. Scotts Valley, CA: Createspace, 2018.
Cotner, June. *Graces: Prayers and Poems for Everyday Meals and Special Occasions*. Berkeley, CA: Conari, 2012.
Crispin, Jessa. *The Dead Ladies Project: Exiles, Expats, and Ex-Countries*. Chicago and London: The University of Chicago Press, 2015.
Cusack, Carole M., John W. Morehead, and Venetia Laura Delano Robertson, eds. *The Sacred in Fantastic Fandom: Essays on the Intersection of Religion and Pop Culture*. Jefferson, NC: McFarland & Co., 2019.
Darwin, Charles. *The Expression of the Emotions in Man and Animals*. 1872. Reprint. Las Vegas, NV: Filiquarian, 2007.
Davidson, Hilda Ellis. *Myths and Symbols in Pagan Europe: Early Scandinavian and Celtic Religions*. Syracuse, NY: Syracuse University Press, 1988.
Davis, Ellen F. *Getting Involved with God: Rediscovering the Old Testament*. Blue Ridge Summit, PA: Rowman & Littlefield, 2001.

SELECTED BIBLIOGRAPHY

Davis, Nancy Yaw. *The Zuni Enigma: A Native American People's Possible Japanese Connection.* New York and London: W.W. Norton, 2001.

Durrell, Lawrence. *Bitter Lemons of Cyprus.* London: Faber and Faber, 2000.

Earle, Mary C. *Celtic Christian Spirituality: Essential Writings Annotated & Explained.* Woodstock, VT: Skylight Paths, 2011.

Endo, Shusaku. *Silence.* Translated by William Johnston. New York: Taplinger, 1980.

Evangelisti, Silvia. *Nuns: A History of Convent Life.* Oxford, UK: Oxford University Press, 2008.

Finkelberg, Margalit and Guy Stroumsa, eds. *Homer, the Bible, and Beyond: Literary and Religious Canons in the Ancient World.* Leiden, NL: Brill, 2003.

Finkelstein, Norman G. *The Holocaust Industry: Reflections on the Exploitation of Jewish Suffering.* London: Verso, 2015.

Foerster, L. Annie. *For Praying Out Loud: Interfaith Prayers for Public Occasions.* Boston: Skinner House, 2003.

Franklin, Benjamin. *The Autobiography of Benjamin Franklin.* New York: Houghton Mifflin, 1923.

Furner, Jennifer. "I'm Not 'Blessed,' I'm an Atheist and I Don't Need God to Give Thanks or Show Gratitude." *Huffington Post* (Nov. 27, 2019).

Geiling, Natasha. "Prague's Famous John Lennon Wall: Is It Over or Reborn." *Smithsonian Magazine* (Nov. 21, 2014).

Gieryn, Thomas F. *Truth Spots: How Places Make People Believe.* Chicago: The University of Chicago Press, 2018.

Gilbert, Elizabeth. *Eat Pray Love: One Woman's Search for Everything Across Italy, India, and Indonesia.* New York: Penguin Putnam, 2010.

Guitton, Matthieu, ed. *Fan Phenomena: Mermaids.* Bristol, UK: Intellect, 2016.

Hall, Marcia, ed. *Raphael's School of Athens.* Cambridge, UK: Cambridge University Press, 1997.

Hardacre, Helen. *Shinto: A History.* Oxford, UK: Oxford University Press, 2017.

Hibbs, Thomas S. "Iris Murdoch, Spiritual Exercises, and Anselm's Proslogian and Prayers." *The Saint Anselm Journal* 3.1 (2005).

Hill, Jane H. *The Everyday Language of White Racism.* Chichester, UK: John Wiley and Sons, 2008.

Hillard, Harriet Low. *My Mother's Journal: A Young Lady's Diary of Five Years Spent in Manila, Macao, and The Cape of Good Hope, from 1829-1834.* Miami: Hard Press, 2020.

Hillesum, Etty. *An Interrupted Life: Diaries and Letters of Etty Hillesum (1941-43).* London: Persephone, 1999.

Hitch, Sarah. *King of Sacrifice: Ritual and Royal Authority in the Iliad.* Cambridge, MA: Harvard University, Center for Hellenic Studies, 2009.

Hitchcock, James. *History of the Catholic Church: From the Apostolic Age to the Third Millennium.* San Francisco: Ignatius, 2012.

Hjelmgaard, Kim. "Chernobyl: Timeline of a Disaster." *USA Today* (April 18, 2016).

Hoffman, Katherine E. and Susan Gilson Miller, eds. *Berbers and Others: Beyond Tribe and Nation in the Maghrib.* Bloomington, IN: Indiana University Press, 2010.

Hopkins, Keith and Mary Beard. *The Colosseum.* London: Profile, 2011.

Hughes, Bettany. *Venus and Aphrodite: History of a Goddess.* London: Weidenfeld & Nicolson, 2019.

Hurd, Michael. *The Templars: History & Myth.* London: Profile, 2008.

Ihimaera, Witi. *The Whale Rider*. Auckland, NZ: Penguin, 2008.
Ito, Mizuko, Daisuke Okabe, and Izumi Tsuji, eds. *Fandom Unbound: Otaku Culture in a Connected World*. New Haven, CT: Yale University Press, 2012.
Johnsen, Linda. *Lost Masters: Rediscovering the Mysticism of the Ancient Greek Philosophers*. Novato, CA: New World Library, 2016.
Karr, Mary. "Facing Altars: Poetry and Prayer." *Poetry Magazine* (Nov. 1, 2005).
Kidd, Thomas S. *Benjamin Franklin: The Religious Life of a Founding Father*. New Haven, CT: Yale University Press, 2017.
Kidder, Annemarie S. *Etty Hillesum: Essential Writings*. Maryknoll, NY: Orbis, 2009.
Koch, C.J. *The Year of Living Dangerously*. London: Penguin, 1983.
Lefkowitz, Mary and Maureen B. Fant. *Women's Life in Greece and Rome*. Baltimore: Johns Hopkins University Press, 2016.
Leonard, Brendan. "The List: The 9 Best Road Trip Books." *Adventure Journal* (Aug. 14, 2012).
Lipton, Judith Eve and David P. Barash. *Strength Through Peace: How Demilitarization Led to Peace & Happiness in Costa Rica, & What the Rest of the World Can Learn From a Tiny, Tropical Nation*. Oxford, UK: Oxford University Press, 2019.
Loving, Jerome. *Walt Whitman: The Song of Himself*. Berkeley, CA: University of California Press, 1999.
MacArthur, Douglas. *General MacArthur: Wisdom and Visions*. Nashville, TN: Turner, 2000.
Manco, Jean. *Ancestral Journeys: The Peopling of Europe From the First Venturers to the Vikings*. London: Thames & Hudson, 2018.
Matura, Thaddee. *15 Days of Prayer with Saint Francis of Assisi*. New York: New City, 2009.
McCarthy, David. *Seeing Afresh: Learning from Fresh Expressions of Church*. Edinburgh: Saint Andrew, 2019.
Merton, Thomas. *Thoughts in Solitude*. New York: Farrar, Straus and Giroux, 1999.
Moss, Sarah. *Names for the Sea: Strangers in Iceland*. London: Granta, 2013.
Muhammad, Maulana. *The Muslim Prayer Book*. Ohio, US: Ahmadiyya Anjuman Isha' at Islam Lahore, 1998.
Murdoch, Iris. *The Sovereignty of Good*. Routledge Classics. London and New York: Routledge, 2001.
Nouwen, Henri. *The Only Necessary Thing: Living a Prayerful Life*. New York: Crossroad, 2008.
O'Shea, Stephen. *Sea of Faith: Islam and Christianity in the Medieval Mediterranean World*. New York: Walker, 2006.
Paine, Lincoln. *The Sea & Civilization: A Maritime History of the World*. New York: Vintage, 2015.
Pantzar, Katja. *Finding Sisu: In Search of Courage, Strength, and Happiness the Finnish Way*. London: Hodder & Stoughton, 2019.
Pleins, J. David. *The Evolving God: Charles Darwin on the Naturalness of Religion*. New York: Bloomsbury, 2013.
Plokhy, Serhii. *Chernobyl: History of a Tragedy*. London: Penguin, 2019.
Pryke, D.R., ed. *The Legacy of John Lennon: In the Words of the Fans Who Love Him*. Haselmere, UK: Exposure, 2005.
Rees, Mary. *Being Prayer – Transforming Consciousness: Good News of Buddhist Practice*. Houston: Nutshell, 2006.

Ritivoi, Andreea Deciu. *Yesterday's Self: Nostalgia and the Immigrant Identity.* Oxford, UK: Rowman & Littlefield, 2002.
Roberts, Alice. *The Celts: Search for a Civilization.* London: Heron, 2015.
Rohr, Richard. *Falling Upward: A Spirituality for the Two Halves of Life.* Chichester, UK: John Wiley and Sons, 2011.
Rosenbaum, Steven. "The 5 Key Roles of a Killer Curator." *Forbes* (Nov. 6, 2014).
Ryan, Marah Ellis. *Pagan Prayers Collected.* Charleston, SC: Nabu, 2010.
Ryan, M.J. and Nicholas J. Higham. *The Anglo-Saxon World.* New Haven, CT: Yale University Press, 2015.
Salman, James and John Farina, eds. *The Legacy of Pierre Teilhard de Chardin.* Mahwah, NJ: Paulist, 2011.
Schlumpf, Heidi. "Time to Rehabilitate Teilhard de Chardin?" *National Catholic Reporter* (Jan. 27, 2018).
Shin, Sun Yung. "Poetry as Prayer and the Praxis of Emptiness: An Interview with Leah Silvieus about her Collection, *Arabilis*." *Hyphen Magazine* (Oct. 2, 2019).
Silva, Daniella. "Trapped in Tijuana: Migrants Face a Long, Dangerous Wait to Claim Asylum." *NBC News* (March 18, 2019).
Smelik, Klaas, Gerrit Van Ord, and Jurjen Wiersma, eds. *Reading Etty Hillesum in Context: Writings, Life, and Influences of a Visionary Author.* Amsterdam: Amsterdam University Press, 2018.
Stein, Gertrude. *Everybody's Autobiography.* Cambridge: Exact Change, 1993.
Taplan, Phoebe. *Outlander's Guide to Scotland.* London: Pavilion, 2018.
Taylor, Neil. *Estonia: A Modern History.* London: Hurst & Company, 2018.
Teilhard de Chardin, Pierre. *Letters from a Traveler.* Whitefish, MT: Kessinger, 2007.
Trickett, Peter. *Beyond Capricorn: How Portuguese Adventurers Secretly Discovered and Mapped Australia and New Zealand 250 Years Before Captain Cook.* Brompton, Aus.: East Street, 2007.
Urrea, Luis Alberto. *The Tijuana Book of the Dead.* New York: Soft Skull, 2015.
Ussishkin, David. *The Conquest of Lachish by Sennacherib.* Tel Aviv: Tel Aviv University Publications, 1982.
Van Geldermalsen, Marguerite. *Married to a Bedouin.* London: Virago, 2009.
Vetto, Vanya. *Bali Dreaming: ...into the Heart of the Hindu Gods.* Scotts Valley, CA: Createspace, 2016.
Waley, Arthur. *Three Ways of Thought in Ancient China.* Palo Alto, CA: Stanford University Press, 1939.
Walsh, Arlene Sanchez. *Pentecostals in America.* New York: Columbia University Press, 2018.
Whitman, Walt. *Specimen Days & Collect.* New York: Dover, 1995.
Wilson, Madeleine. *Prayers of Elvis.* Wolverhampton, UK: Shalom, 2002.
Wong, Eva. *Taoism: An Essential Guide.* Boston: Shambhala, 2011.
Yamakage, Motohisa. *The Essence of Shinto: Japan's Spiritual Heart.* New York: Kodansha USA, 2012.
Yee, Chiang. *The Silent Traveler in Edinburgh.* Edinburgh: Birlinn General, 2019.
Yen Mah, Adeline. *Falling Leaves: The True Story of an Unwanted Chinese Daughter.* London: Penguin, 2010.
Yourcenar, Marguerite. *Memoirs of Hadrian.* Translated by Grace Frick. London: Penguin, 2000.

Index

abbeys, England, 212–13
Absolution Online (website), 162
"Achilles Last Band" (Zeppelin), 115
Adjeksenila "Nila" (friend in Denmark), 107
Adventure Journal, 93
The Adventures of Huckleberry Finn (Twain), 162
Aeschylus, 89
Africa
    Berber ancestry, 41
    Cape Town, South Africa, 153
    "God's Ways in the Bantu Soul," 11
    Sao Tome, 107
Aidan of Lindisfarne, Saint, 217, 219
Akiko (Japanese friend), 58–61, 173
al-Aqsa Mosque, Jerusalem, 26
Alexievich, Svetlana, 170
Ali, Sherif, 179
Alice (Otaku fan), 103–4
All Along the Watchtower (song), 198
Allen, Woody, 85
Alpert, Herb, 173
"An Encounter with Silence" (O'Donovan), 175
Anderson, Hans Christian, 106, 107
Anglo-Saxon Chronicle, 218
Animal Farm (Orwell), 194
anime products, 103–4
Anselm, Saint, 8–9
Anselmian prayer, 9
Antonine Wall, England, 213
Antoninus Pius, Emperor, 213
Aramco World Magazine, 146, 180
Aristotle, 22, 43, 204, 205–6
"Arizona Lamentation" (Urrea), 173
Assassin's Creed (video game), 26

Ataturk, Mustafa Kemal, 47
atheism, 70–71, 74
Augustine of Hippo, Saint, 23, 147, 199, 205
Auschwitz (song), 198
Auschwitz-Berkenau Extermination Camp, Poland, 196–200
Avozinha (granny) Hilda, 118

bagpipes, history of, 209–10
Balfour Declaration, 183
Bali, Denpasar, 49–53
Barenblat, Rachel, 177, 180
baseball, 131–35
Bataan Death March, 15
Battle of Mons Graupius (83), 213
Beach, Sylvester, 120
Beach, Sylvia (formerly Nancy Beach), 120
Beatles
    (John Lennon) prayer, 101
    Sgt. Pepper's Lonely Hearts Club album cover, 204
    "Strawberry Fields Forever" song, 98, 99
Bedouin people, 178–79
Before Sunset (movie), 119
Begin, Menachem, 183
Being John Malkovich (movie), 91
Benedict, Ruth, 39
Benedict XVI, Pope, 206, 228
Berber people, 41–44
Bergoglio, Jorge Mario (later Pope Francis), 206
Bernadette, Sister (Ecce Homo Convent), 148
Beyond Capricorn (Trickett), 151

INDEX

Bilgi University, 46, 114
Blige, Mary J., 100
Bloom, Luka, 65
Blue Elephant Cooking School, (Bangkok, Thailand), 77–81
Border-Watcher's prayer, 175–76
Both Sides Now (song), 233
Boudicca, "warrior queen," 213
Bouich, Abdenour, 44
Bourdain, Anthony, 111
Brain, Behavior, and Mind conference (2010), 18
Bremond, Henri, 173
bucket-listing journey, 203
Buddhism, 60, 80–81
Buddhist prayers, 81
Buist, Anne, 92
Bunzel, Ruth, 39–40
Burroughs, William, 120
Butler-Ehle, Hester, 85

California, Solvang, 107–8
Camino de Santiago ("Way of Saint James"), 91–93
Canada, Drumheller, Alberta, 225–29
Candidius, Georgius, 55
candles, 138–39
Canticle of the Creatures, 75
Cardinal and Theological Virtues fresco, Raphael, 204
Carnation Revolution (1974), 118
Carter, Jimmy, 183
cathartic experiences, 43
"Cathedral" (Crosby, Stills, and Nash), 23
Cellini, Benvenuto, 143, 204
Celtic Christianity, 67
Celtic Christmas (song), 65
Celtic prayer, 66, 67–68
The Celts: Search for a Civilization (Roberts), 66
Center for the Preservation of Democracy, Los Angeles, 162
Chapman, Mark David, 98
Cheng, Patrick, 30
Chernobyl Nuclear Power Plant (1986), 168–170

Chernobyl Prayer: A Chronicle of the Future (Alexievich), 170
Cherry, Kittredge, 30
Chesterton, G. K., 23
Chiang Kai-shek, 54
China, Macau, 150–54
Christianshavn hippie commune, 106
Christ's prayer, 127
church, reflection on, 42
Church of the Holy Sepulchre, Jerusalem, 26
Ciara (Bloom), 65
Civil War, U. S., 29–30
Clement of Alexandria, 214–15
Clement of Rome, Pope, Saint, 23
Cobain, Curt, 100
Cobb, Ty, 132
cognitive narratology, 70
Collin, Edvard, 108
Colosseum, Rome, Italy, 141–44
Communism, Museum of, Prague, Czech Republic, 192–95
Confessions (Augustine), 199
Confucius, 55–56
Convento de Cristo, Tomar, Portugal, 26
Cook, James, 151
A Cook's Tour (Bourdain), 111
Costa Rica, Monteverde, 72–76
Covid-19 pandemic, 230
Crofter's Grace (Outlander prayer), 112
Crosby Stills and Nash, 23
Crowe, Russell, 141
Crusade (1096–1099), 26
Cunliffe, Barry, 66
Cushing, Frank Hamilton, 39
Cuthbert (hermit), 217–18
Cyprus, Paphos, 82–86
Czech Republic, Prague, 97–101, 192–95
Czechoslovakia, 193

da Gama, Vasco, 26
The Da Vinci Code, 26
Darwin, Charles, 226–27
Data Journalism in Thailand (Bangkok seminar), 77

INDEX

Davis, Mary, 29
Davis, Nancy Yaw, 38–39
Dawkins, Richard, 228
"A Day in the Life" song, 99
Dead Poets Society (movie), 28
Dead Sea Scrolls, 184
Deep River (Endo), 59
Deist's prayer, 158
Democracy Index, 46
Denmark, Copenhagen, 106–9
Der Judenstaat (Herzl), 183
Desperation prayer, 171
Detroit riots (1967), 160–61
Diakonia, Swedish Interfaith Development organization, 187
The Disputation of the Holy Sacrament fresco, Raphael, 204
Durrell, Lawrence, 120
Dylan, Bob, 198

East India Company, 151
Eastwood, Clint, 159–160
Eat Pray Love (Gilbert), 52
Ecce Homo Convent, Jerusalem, Israel, 145–49
Edward I, King of England, 209
Egypt, peace agreement with Israel, 183
Eliot, T. S., 120
Elizabeth I, Queen of England, 151, 217
Elvis American Cafe, 124
Elvis International Tribute week, 124
Endo, Shusaku, 27, 59
Enneads (Plotinus), 205
Eratosthenes, 115
Erdogan, Recep Tayyip, 47
Estonia, Tallin, Museum of Occupations, 187–191
Estonia: A Modern History (Taylor), 189
eternalism, 226
"An Evening Prayer" (Presley), 126
Evolutionary prayer, 229
The Expression of the Emotions in Man and Animals (Darwin), 227

"Facing Altars: Poetry and Prayer" (Karr), 172–73
Faisal, Arab Prince, 179
Falkirk tartan (230 CE), 209
Falling Leaves: The True Story of an Unwanted Chinese Daughter (Yen Mah), 17
A Fan Culture's Make-Believe World During a Time of Public Crisis, (Helsinki conference), 69–70
Fandom and the Brain (Pawley), 18
Fandom Unbound: Otaku Culture in a Connected World (Ito, Okabe, & Tsuji), 104
Father's prayer, 135
Faulkner, William, 28
Filipino Bishopric prayer, 15–16
Final Solution (Nazi Party policy), 197, 198
Finding Sisu: In Search of Courage, Strength and Happiness the Finnish Way (Pantzar), 70
Finish prayer, 71
Finkelstein, Norman, 196
Finland, Helsinki, 69–71
Fitzgerald, F. Scott, 119
Five Good Emperors of Rome, 214
Folkloric prayer, 109–10
Forbes Magazine, 188
Ford, Harrison, 178
France, Paris, 118–122
Francis, Pope, 47, 190–91, 206, 228
Francis of Assisi, Saint, 75
Francis Xavier, Saint, 27
Franciscan prayer, 75–76
Franklin, Benjamin, 155–58, 207
Frazer, Richard, 92
Freeman, Morgan, 230–31
Fugitive Offender's Ordinance (Hong Kong), 19
Furner, Jennifer, 70, 71

Gabaldon, Diane, 110, 111
Galician Carol (Nunez), 65
Geneva Bonnet, history of, 210
Gibson, Me., 50
Gieryn, Thomas F., 88–89, 91, 93
Gilbert, Elizabeth, 52

Ginsberg, Allen, 120
Gladiator (movie), 141
Global Initiatives Forum, Taiwan, 54
Global Peace Index, 43
"God's Ways in the Bantu Soul," 11
Goeth, Amon, 197
Gorbachev, Mikhail, 169
Graceland, Memphis, Tennessee, 122–27
Gran Torino (movie), 159–160
Greece, Delphi, 87–90
Greek prayer, 90
greencare, 70

Hadrian's Wall, Northumberland, England, 212–15
Hagia Sophia Grand Mosque, Istanbul, Turkey, 45–48
Haining, Jane, 199
Hans L'Orange Field, Honolulu, Hawaii, 131–35
Harry Potter (Rowling), 100, 108, 110–11
Hawthorne, Nathaniel, 28
He Touched Me (Elvis' album), 126
He Walks Beside Me (Elvis' album), 126
Hemingway, Ernest, 119, 121
Hendrix, Jimi, 198
Henry the Navigator, 26
Henry VIII, King of England, 217
Heraclitus, 204
Herod Agrippa, 92
Herodotus, 115
Herzl, Theodor, 183
Heughan, Sam, 111
A Higher Kind of Loyalty (Liu), 194
Hilda (Rissy's grandmother), 118
Hilda of Whitby, 217
Hillard, George S., 153
Hillard, Katherine, 153
Hillesum, Etty, 199–200
Himmler, Heinrich, 197, 198
Hindu prayer, 52–53
His Hand in Mine (Elvis album), 126
His Kingdom Prophecy (organization), 19
Hoegger, Martin, 11

The Holiness of Travel (Pawley), 42
The Holocaust Industry: Reflections on the Exploitation of Jewish Suffering (Finkelstein), 196
Holocaust Victim's prayer, 200
Holy Island of Lindisfarne, United Kingdom, 216–19
Homer, 90, 93, 115
Homeric prayer, 117
Hong Kong prayer, 17–21
Horseshoe Canyon Formation, 226–27
Hounsou, Djimon, 141
Huffington Post (newspaper), 30, 70
Hughes, Langston, 162
Hunt, Linda, 50
Husak, Gustav, 98
Hussein, Saddam, 115
Hyphen Magazine, 172

"I Am the Walrus" song, 99
Iceland, Keflavik, 136–140
Icelandic prayer, 139–140
Ignatius of Loyola, Saint, 26, 27
Ihimaera, Witi, 36
The Illiad (Homer), 90, 115, 116
I'm Off Then: Losing and Finding Myself on the Camino de Santiago (Kerkeling), 92
"Imagine" song, 98
Imagined Worlds - Worldmaking in Arts and Literature (Helsinki conference), 69
The Imitation of Christ (Kempis), 23, 199
IM/politeness in Japanese Twitter (Bangkok seminar), 77
"In My Life" (Lennon), 98
Indiana Jones and the Last Crusade (movie), 178
Indonesia, 14
The Innocents Abroad (Twain), 83, 150
Institute of Holy Land Studies, 146
International Conference on Language and Communication, 77
The International Review of Mission (journal), 11

INDEX

Introduction to Zuni Ceremonialism (Bunzel), 39, 40
Island Dynamics group, Shetland Islands, 106
Israel
   Egypt peace agreement, 183
   establishment of (1948), 183
   highway monuments, 124
   Jerusalem, 145–49
   Tel Lachish, 220–24
Italy, Rome, 141–44
Ito, Mizuko, 104

Jackson, Michael, 100, 125
Jackson, Peter, 36
Jacobi, Derek, 141
Jacobite rebellion, Scotland (1745), 209
Jagiellonian University, 196
James, William, 52, 121
James I, King of Scotland, 111–12
James III, King of Scotland, 209
James the Greater, Saint, 91–92, 93
Japan
   Akihabara, Tokyo, 102–9
   Himeji Castle, 58–62
   IM/politeness in Japanese Twitter (Bangkok seminar), 77
Jerusalem University College, 146
Jesuit prayer, 27
Jewish prayer for the Palestinian people, 184
Job's prayer, 223–24
Johansson, Scarlett, 59
John Lennon Wall, Prague, Czech Republic, 97–101
John of the Cross, Saint, 23
Johnsen, Linda, 22, 205, 207
Jordan, Petra, 177–181
Joyce, James, 119, 120–21
Jude, Saint of Lost Causes,, 144
Julie & Julia (movie), 119
Julius Caesar, 213
"Just Because You Are My God" prayer, 26

Kaplan, Jan, 193
Karr, Mary, 172
Kempis, Thomas a,' 23, 199
Kerkeling, Hape, 92
Kierkegaard, Soren, 106
Kingdom of Heaven (movie), 26
Knights of the Order of Christ, 26
Knights Templar, 26–27
Knox, John, 210
Koch, C. J., 14, 50
Krushchev, Nikita, 194

Langdon, Olivia, 83
Language Variation in Bangladesh Media (Bangkok seminar), 77
Lao Tzu, 55–56
Latin America Mission in Miami, 72
Lawrence, T.E., 179
Lawrence of Arabia (movie), 179
Lean, David, 179
League of Nations, 183
Leaves of Grass (Whitman), 29
Left Bank bookstore, Paris, France, 119–120
Lenin, Vladimir, 189, 193
Lennon (John) Wall, Prague, Czech Republic, 97–101
Leonard, Brendan, 93
LGBTQ+ community, 28–31
Lidia (Honduras migrant), 174
Lil Wayne, 173
Lincoln, Abraham, 29
The Little Mermaid (Anderson), 108
Liu Binyan, 194
Lochard, Metz, 162
Lodge, David, 92
Lonely Planet (travel bible), 75, 87, 160
Longshanks Siege, Scotland (1296), 209
The Lord of the Rings (Tolkien), 36, 108
Lost Generation writers, 120
Lost in Translation (movie), 59
Lost Masters: Rediscovering the Mysticism of the Ancient Greek Philosophers (Johnsen), 22, 205
Love in a World of Dreams, Doorways as Conduits to the Divine Realm (Helsinki conference), 69

Low, Harriet, 150, 151–53
Lucy, Sister (Ecce Homo Convent), 148
Luther, Martin, 147–48
Luther Seminary, Saint Paul, Minnesota, 46

MacArthur, Douglas, 13, 133, 134–35
MacArthur Arthur, IV, 134
Machiavelli, Niccolo, 55
Mao Tse Tung, 194
Maori community, 35–37
Maori Religion and Mythology (Shortland), 36
Maori Tattooing (Robley), 36
Marcus Aurelius, 142–43, 214
Married to a Bedouin (van Geldermalsen), 179
Marx, Karl, 193
Mary Queen of Scots, 111–12
Matisse, Henri, 121
Maximus Decimus Meridius, 141
Medieval Total War (video game), 26
meditation, 49–50, 226
Mediterranean prayer, 85–86
Mehmed II (Turkish conqueror), 47
Memoirs of Hadrian (Yourcenar), 214
mermaid myth, 107–8
Mermaids, Maritime Folklore, and Modernity conference, 106
Merton, Thomas, 23, 91, 94, 147
Mexico, Tijuana, 172–76
Midnight in Paris (movie), 119
Mighty Aphrodite (movie), 85
Miller, Henry, 120
The Mission (movie), 27
Mitchell, Joni, 233
Mitchener, James, 222
Monastic prayer, 219
Monnier, Adrienne, 121
Morocco, Marrakech, 41–44
Morrison, Jim, 100
Moss, Sarah, 137
Movie Mobile Branding in Malaysia (Bangkok seminar), 77
Murdoch, Iris, 8
Murray, Bill, 59

Museu da Escrita do Sudoeste (Museum of Southwest Writing), 66
Museum of Communism, Prague, Czech Republic, 192–95
Museum of Occupations, Tallinn, Estonia, 187–191
Museum of Southwest Writing (*Museu da Escrita do Sudoeste*), 66
Muslims and Christians (Luther Seminary committee), 46
My Mother's Journal: A Young Lady's Diary of Five Years Spent in Manila, Macao, and the Cape of Good Hope from 1829–1834 (Hillard), 153
The Mysterious Stranger (Twain), 82
Mystic's prayer, 94

Nabataeans, a Bedouin people, 178–79
Names for the Sea: Strangers in Iceland (Moss), 137
Nataly (on Chernobyl Disaster), 169–170
National Candle Association, 138
National University of Kyiv, 167, 169
National University of Taiwan, 54
Nazi Concentration Camps (movie), 197
NBC News, 174
New Zealand, Rotorua, 35–37
Nielsen, Connie, 142
Northern Illinois University, 161–62
Nouwen, Henri, 23, 113, 147
Nunez, Carlos, 65

Obama, Barack, 114
occupation, of nations, 187–191, 193
O'Conner, Flannery, 23
Odin's Gift, 139
O'Donovan, Leo J., 175
The Odyssey (Homer), 93, 115, 116
Okabe, Daisuke, 104
Old Nun's prayer, 149
Omega Point, 228
Oriental Studies Circle (National University of Kyiv), 169
Orwell, George, 121, 194

INDEX

O'Shea, Stephen, 47
Oswald, Anglo-Saxon King, 217
Otaku prayer, 104–5
Our Lady of Fatima, 92
Outlander fans, 110–13
Outlander Lists & Timelines (website), 112
Outlander prayer, 113
Oxford University, 97

Palestinian Territories, Jericho, 182–86
Pantzar, Katja, 70, 71
The Paris Review (magazine), 120
Parks, Rosa, 160
Parmenides, 204, 205
The Parnassus fresco, Raphael, 204
Parsimagi, Karl, 199
Patrick, Saint, 67
Pats, Konstantin, 189
Patterns in Culture (Benedict), 39
Paul and Ruth (missionaries, Costa Rica), 72–74
Pawley, Rissy, 83–84, 87, 118
Peace prayer, 15–16
Peking Man excavations, 228
Pentecostals in America (Walsh), 126
Personal Confession prayer, 163
Personal prayer, 235–36
Pew Research Center, 112
Philippines, Subic Bay, 15–16
Phoenix, Joaquin, 141
Picasso, Pablo, 121
"The Pilgrim Prayer" (Merton), 94
Plato, 22, 55, 204, 205–6, 207
Plimpton, George, 120
Plotinus, 204, 205
poems, prayers versus, 172–73
Poetry Magazine, 172
Poland, Auschwitz-Berkenau Extermination Camp, 196–200
Pope's ancient prayer, 24
popular culture, religion and, 35–36
Popular Privation: Suffering in Fan Cultures (Pawley), 104
Portugal
  Almodovar, 65–68
  historical empire, 151
  reflection on, 42–43, 194–95
  Tomar, 25–27
Powell, Roger, 111
Prague Spring (1988), 98
Pray with Me (website), 144
prayer
  breathing and, 40
  universality of, 2–3
"A Prayer for All Needs" (Clement of Rome), 24
"Prayer for Peace by Christian, Jewish, and Muslim Clergy," 48
Prayer to Aphrodite to Bring Love into One's Life, 85–86
Prayer to the Sower, 71
prayers
  Beatles, (John Lennon) prayer, 101
  Berber prayer, 44
  Border-Watcher's prayer, 175–76
  Buddhist prayers, 81
  Celtic prayer, 66, 67–68
  Christ's prayer, 127
  on compassion, 44
  Deist's prayer, 158
  of desperation, 171
  Evolutionary prayer, 229
  Father's prayer, 135
  Finish prayer, 71
  Folkloric prayer, 109
  Franciscan prayer, 75–76
  Greek prayer, 90
  Hindu prayer, 52–53
  Holocaust Victim's prayer, 200
  Homeric prayer, 117
  for Hong Kong, 19–21
  Icelandic prayer, 139–140
  Jesuit prayer, 27
  Jewish prayer for the Palestinian people, 184
  Job's prayer, 223–24
  LGBTQ+ community, 30–31
  Maori prayers, 37
  mealtime graces, 79–80
  Mediterranean prayer, 85–86
  Monastic prayer, 219
  monotheistic prayer, 48
  Mystic's prayer, 94
  Old Nun's prayer, 149

(prayers continued)
  Otaku prayer, 104–5
  Outlander prayer, 113
  for peace, 15–16
  pearl of great price, 11–12
  Personal Confession prayer, 163
  Personal prayer, 235–36
  poems verses, 172–73
  from Pope Francis, 190–91
  Pope's ancient prayer, 24
  Psalmist's Apocalyptic prayer, 195
  Qur'anic prayer, 185–86
  Rabbinical prayer, 180–81
  of regret, 144
  Second-Century prayer, 215
  for seeking God, 9
  Shinto prayer, 61–62
  Socratic prayer, 207
  Taoist prayer, 57
  Voyager's prayer, 154
  War prayer, 122
  Zuni prayers, 40
Prayers of Elvis (Wilson), 126
Presley, Elvis, 100, 123–27
Presley, Gladys and Vernon, 125
Psalmist's Apocalyptic prayer, 195
Pygmalian (play), 85
Pyotr S. (on Chernobyl Disaster), 170
Pythagorean theorem, 205
Pythagorus, 204, 205

Qur'anic prayer, 185–86

Rabbinical prayer, 180–81
Rand, Ayn, 55
Raphael (Renaissance artist), 22, 204, 206–7
Ratzinger, Joseph (later Pope Benedict XVI), 206
"Raving Fans Revisited" (Pawley), 54
Reagan, Ronald, 194, 220
Red Cross mission to Serbia (WWI), 121
Reformed minister's prayer, 11–12
Regret prayer, 144
Reiss, Steven, 100
Renewable blessing prayer, 234
Ricafrente, Angie, 14–15

The Rise of the Image the Fall of the Word (Stephens), 102
Rita, Sister (Ecce Homo Convent), 148
Ritualwell, Judaic organization, 184
Roberts, Alice, 66
Robley, H. G., 36
Rome, Vatican City, 22–24
Rosenbaum, Stephen, 188
Royal House of Chou Library., 55
Royal Sex: Mistresses & Lovers of the British Royal Family (Powell), 111
Royal Tyrrell Museum of Paleontology, 225–26
Rubber Soul album, 98
Russell, Bertrand, 170
Rutgers University, 28
Ruth and Paul (missionaries, Costa Rica), 72–74

Sadat, Anwar, 183
St. Anne's College, Oxford University, 7–9
The Saint Anselm Journal, 8
Salazar, Antonio de Olveira, 118, 194
The Samurai (Endo), 59
Saraswati, Sivananda, 52
Schindler's List (movie), 197
School of Athens fresco (Raphael), Apostolic Palace, Vatican City, 22, 203–7
Scotland
  ecumenical missionary conference (1910), 11
  Edinburgh, 208–11
  Linlithgow, 110–13
  reflection on, 42–43
Scott, Ridley, 141, 143
The Scottish Book of Common Prayer, 211
Scottish prayer, 211
Sea of Faith (O'Shea), 47
Second-Century prayer, 215
secularization, 47
Seljuk Turks, 26
Serra, Junipero, 173
Seven Against Thebes (play), 89

INDEX

Sgt. Pepper's Lonely Hearts Club album cover, 204
Shakespeare and Company bookstore, Paris, France, 120
Sharif, Omar, 179
Shaw, George Bernard, 85
Shinto prayer, 61–62
Shintoism, 59–60
Shortland, Edward, 36
Si Mohand ou-Mhand, 44
Silence (Endo), 27, 60
Silva, Daniella, 174
Silvieus, Leah, 172
Simonides of Ceos, 90
Simpson, Graeme, 92
16 Basic Desires theory, 100
Smithsonian Magazine, 99
Social Democratic Party, Czech, 193
The Society of Jesus, (Jesuits), 26
Socrates, 22, 161, 206–7
Socratic prayer, 207
Soul Leading (Outlander prayer), 113
Soul Peace (Outlander prayer), 112
The Source (Mitchener), 222
The Sovereignty of Good (Murdoch), 8
Spain, Santiago de Compostela, 91–94
Specimen Days (Whitman), 30
Spicker, Glenn, 192–93
Spielberg, Steven, 197
Spier, Julius, 199
Spirited Away (movie), 59
Spiritual Mermaid, 108
Springer, Mr. (high school teacher), 169
St. Peter's Square, Vatican City, 22–24, 203
Stalin, Joseph, 193
Star Trek episode ("Who Mourns for Adonis?"), 116
Starkey, James Leslie, 221
Stein, Edith, 199
Stein, Gertrude, 120, 121–22
Steinbeck, John, 93
Stephens, Mitchell, 102
The Story of God (Netflix series), 230–31
"Strawberry Fields Forever" song, 98, 99

Stuart, Mary (Mary Queen of Scots), 111–12
The Sun Also Rises (Hemingway), 121
Switzerland, World Council of Churches, Geneva, 10–12, 48

Taiwan, Sun Moon Lake, 54–57
Tanski, Tadeusz, 199
Taoist prayer, 57
Tartan fabric, 209
Taylor, Neil, 189
Teilhard de Chardin, Pierre, 225, 227–28
Teilhard Technologies, 227
Temple to Apollo, 89
Teresa of Avila, Saint, 23
Terry (friend from Santa Barbara), 146–47
Thailand, Bangkok, 77–81
theology, view on, 210–11
Therapy (Lodge), 92
"There is a Town in Mexico" (Urrea), 173
Thomas Aquinas, Saint, 23, 147
Thoreau, Henry David, 71
Three Ways of Thought in Ancient China (Waley), 55
The Tijuana Book of the Dead (Urrea), 172, 173
Toklas, Alice B., 121
"Tomorrow Never Knows" song, 99
travel
  bucket-listing and, 203
  insights into, 42–43
  prayer during, 49–52
Travels with a Stick (Frazer), 92
Travels with Charley (Steinbeck), 93
Triad Society (Hong Kong), 19
Trickett, Peter, 151
Trojan Horse replica, 115
Trojan War (Marvel Comics), 115
Troy I, II, III, IV, V, VI, and VII, 115
Trudy, Sister (Ecce Homo Convent), 148
Truman, Harry, 134
truth spots, 88, 91
Truth Spots: How Places Make People Believe (Gieryn), 88

Tsuji, Izumi, 104
Turkey
   Istanbul, 45–48
   Ruins of Ancient Troy, 114–17
Twain, Mark, 79, 82–83, 150
The Two Popes (movie), 206
Two Steps Forward (Simpson & Buist), 92

Udayana University, 51
Ukraine, Chernobyl, 167–171
Ulysses (Joyce), 120–21
UNESCO, World Heritage Site, 179
United Fruit Company, 74
United Kingdom
   Hadrian's Wall, England, 212–15
   Holy Island of Lindisfarne, 216–19
   St. Anne's College, Oxford University, 7–9
   Scotland (*See* Scotland)
United Nations High Commissioner for Refugees (UNHCR), 10
United States
   Estero Bay, Florida, 230–34
   Hawaii, Honolulu, 131–35
   immigration stories, 174–75
   Michigan, Detroit, 159–163
   Minnesota, Saint Paul, 46
   New Jersey, Camden, 28–31
   New Mexico, Zuni Pueblo, 38–40
   Pennsylvania, Philadelphia, 158
   Tennessee, 122–27
University for Peace, 72
University of Costa Rica, 72
University of Edinburgh, 35, 208, 210
University of Helsinki, 70
University of Otago, 37
University of South Florida, 161
Urban II, Pope, 26
Urrea, Luis Alberto, 172, 173
USA Today, 169
Uspenski Orthodox Cathedral, 70
Ussishkin, David, 221

Valentine, Jean, 172
Van Geldermalsen, Marguerite, 179–180

The Varieties of Religious Experience (James), 52
Vatican City
   School of Athens fresco, Apostolic Palace, 203–7
   St. Peter's Square, 22–24
Vikings (television miniseries), 218
Voices from Chernobyl: The Oral History of a Nuclear Disaster" (Alexievich), 170
Voyager's prayer, 154

Waley, Arthur, 55
Walker, Alice, 162
Walsh, Arlene Sanchez, 126
War prayer, 122
Wars I Have Seen (Stein), 121
The Way of a Pilgrim, 93
"Way of Saint James" (Camino de Santiago), 91–93
The Whale Rider (Ihimaera), 36
Wheaton College, 2
When Harry Met Sally (movie), 83
whiskey, history of, 209
Whitman, George, 120
Whitman, Sylvia Beach, 120
Whitman, Walt, 28
"Who Mourns for Adonis?" (*Star Trek* episode), 116
Wilson, Madeleine, 126
World Council of Churches, Geneva, Switzerland, 10–12, 48
World Heritage Site, UNESCO, 179
World War I, 121, 122, 167, 179, 228
World War II, 13–15, 60, 103, 121, 133–34, 217
Wright, Richard, 162

Xanthos: A Journal of Foreign Literatures and Languages, 44
Xavier University, 52, 77

Yad Vashem World Holocaust Remembrance Center, Jerusalem, 198
The Year of Living Dangerously (Koch), 14, 50
Yen Mah, Adeline, 17

Yost, Eddie, 132
"You Who Seek Grace from a Distracted God" (Urrea), 173
You'll Never Walk Alone (Elvis album), 126
Yourcenar, Marguerite, 214

Zelma (friend in Jerusalem), 145–46

Zenit.org, 15
Zeppelin, Led, 115
The Zuni Enigma (Davis), 38–39
Zuni Origin Myths (Bunzel), 39
Zuni Pueblo, New Mexico, 38–40
Zuni Ritual Poetry (Bunzel), 39, 40

www.ingramcontent.com/pod-product-compliance
Lightning Source LLC
Chambersburg PA
CBHW050344230426
43663CB00010B/1982